AN INCONVENIENT HERD

AN INCONVENIENT HERD

JOHN WILEY

Boyle
— & —
Dalton

Book Design & Production
Columbus Publishing Lab
www.ColumbusPublishingLab.com

Paperback: 978-1-63337-214-6
E-book: 978-1-63337-215-3

Printed in the United States of America

1 3 5 7 9 10 8 6 4 2

Pour Marie

ONE

TUESDAY

AS SOON AS IT WAS LIGHT ENOUGH TO SEE, Farmer bundled up against the autumn air and walked to the shed. He slid open its tall doors and went inside, started his Polaris Ranger, then drove to the back of the farm where his cattle were.

They had plenty to eat. He wouldn't move them to a fresh paddock until that afternoon. But it was his routine to check on them twice a day. If nothing needed to be done, he would park the Ranger alongside the cattle and sit there for half an hour or so before heading back to the house for breakfast. He would get his smartphone out and check the news; his email; the final scores of games that took place after his bedtime.

It would perhaps surprise even his wife, Sandy, to know that

Farmer talked to the herd at times like these, but to him it was a natural habit he had fallen into long ago.

"I canceled that appointment with the chiropractor," he might tell them. "My back feels better. I think it's OK."

Or, "Sandy's brother's coming to visit. Nathan. I like him, I just never know what to say to him. Now, since his divorce, it's even more awkward. Last time he was here he started crying one night at dinner."

He would talk about his plans for the day: "Going to hook onto the bush hog after this and get some mowing done. Maybe just those ten acres up by the road."

The cattle were like his personal support group. A therapy herd. They were good listeners, and they rarely if ever gave him bad advice. Lounging around contented, bellies full and chewing cud, they were a calming influence. Their well-being was deeply satisfying to Farmer. He was their steward, after all—a role he took seriously.

Farmer didn't travel. He settled down inside his home, chores done, before dark. He was in bed by eight thirty. He was outside every day regardless of the weather, and he didn't mind. The cattle were his anchor. In a number of ways he did not take for granted, they could be better company than people.

But this Tuesday morning, driving his Ranger across the farm, coming over that last rise, Farmer made a discovery that collided with his mild and measured status quo like a tractor trailer broadsiding an Amish buggy.

His cattle were gone.

Such a primal jolt. Before thoughts could form, Farmer's one cup of coffee—black, reheated from a leftover pot and bitter—started churning in his stomach.

He pulled up next to the half-acre paddock where he'd parked the herd the day before. The strand of white electric twine forming the perimeter was intact. Farmer saw no trampled forage outside the paddock.

What the hell?

He turned the Ranger off, got out, and stood staring at the partly full water tanks. The drag-along mineral feeder. Various cow patties scattered in the half-eaten orchard grass. He had just driven across the entire farm, so he knew the cattle were gone. Not just out of bounds, but no longer even connected to the landscape. All seven of them were abso-freaking-lutely gone.

It was like a bad dream.

He had his phone, but who could he call? Sandy, who was still asleep, warm in bed?

The Ranger could go forty-five miles an hour. All he had to do was press the accelerator and he would be racing along. But where?

The next discovery was more complicated. At first he'd overlooked it. A twelve-foot metal gate—the only gate in the high tensile fence between the back of his farm and woods that belonged to Karl and Betsy Rose. It was part of the paddock, but Farmer had paid it no mind. He could see it was closed. On top of that, he knew it was locked.

He'd locked the gate years earlier, when some hunters, trespassing to chase a wounded doe, left it open. Luckily the herd had been in another part of the farm. Farmer politely but forcefully escorted the hunters off his property. The next day he'd bought a padlock and chained the gate shut. Its only key was hanging on a nail in his tool room.

But after entering the paddock, searching in vain for clues, Farmer took a closer look at the gate. It was shut, yes, and the rusty chain still circled the wooden fence post. But the padlock was gone. Or rather, it was lying on the ground just outside the gate, its U-shaped bar cut.

TWO

"WHEN FENCES THAT HAVE HELD YOU IN all your life no longer surround you; when everything except the sky over your head is unfamiliar and you become the only constant in a whirlwind of situations; when you have left behind routines so well-established they seemed inevitable and face instead a relentless need to make choices, any one of which could be disastrous; that, my friends, is when you appreciate how lucky you are to be part of a herd."

"That's beautiful," 74 said. "How do you come up with stuff like that?"

"I don't know," 42 said.

27 said, "All I'm saying is, it doesn't do us any good to stick together if we all make the same mistake."

The cows were at the edge of the woods looking out. All morning, since leaving the farm, they'd kept under the high canopy of trees. They'd worked their way through scrub brush and fallen branches, on a carpet of rotting leaves, sometimes following deer trails through the dappled shade. It was nice and cool in there and they felt safe. Unobserved. But now the woods were all behind them. They could go out in the open. Ahead of them they could see a large area that was all green grass shining in the sun. There was little to eat in the woods other than low-hanging leaves, which, while exotic and fun to eat, were hard to fill up on. Or they could backtrack to the black asphalt path they had crossed not long ago. It ran through the woods in a straight line, which seemed to most of the cows to promise that it must lead somewhere.

"I've been following paths all my life," 27 said. "They never got me anywhere."

"Sure," 74 said. "But those were paths we made ourselves, back and forth. Between the water tank and the shed. Between the hay ring and the water tank. Between the shed and the mineral feeder. Those were ruts."

"There's grass here, it's true," 42 said. "And we're all hungry. But that path leads somewhere, otherwise why would it be there? And wherever it goes, there's bound to be grass there too. And maybe water. I don't see any water here."

74 said, "I say we go back and take the path. We follow it in the direction of the sun. Lernovski said Columbus is where the sun goes each day."

"Oh sure, quote Lernovski," 27 said. "As if that proves anything."

"Let's go," 74 said. She turned and started walking back into the woods.

Several other cows turned and fell in step behind her. Soon nearly all of them were walking away.

"Well?" 42 said to 27, who was still standing there.

"I just disagree."

"OK then," 42 said. She turned to catch up with the others.

"Oh for God's sake," 27 said. Suddenly feeling vulnerable, she bolted and managed to pass 42 so she would not be last.

THREE

THE USUAL NOCTURNAL SUSPECTS when it came to a farm gate left open—teenagers partying in the woods, coon hunters running hounds—would not have bolt cutters with them. Whoever cut the padlock on Farmer's gate had come along before dawn with that very thing in mind. This person knew the gate. Knew it was padlocked. Had someone watched for days, or weeks, till Farmer moved the cattle to this spot? In his steady orbit of the pasture, rotating the cattle daily, Farmer brought them around to this gate no more than three or four times a year—and only for a day or two each time. Was he paranoid to think of someone hiding in the woods behind his farm, watching as he did his chores? The whole thing felt kind of creepy.

If it had been rustlers stealing his herd, there would be tire tracks. They would have used a good-sized gooseneck trailer pulled by a full-ton pickup. They would have backed up to the gate and driven the cattle through it. But there was no such disturbance of the weeds behind the gate. And anyway—going back to the creepy part—this felt personal.

A few feet beyond where he found the padlock, Farmer saw a cow patty. He squatted down to get a closer look—like a scout in some old Western movie. *This patty's still fresh. They must have come through here three, four hours ago.*

Walking toward the woods, he came across another patty. Ahead of him a deer path, no thicker than a ribbon, entered the woods. He followed it, as cattle sometimes do. He had to work his way through thorny bushes at the edge of the woods, but once he was inside under the tall trees things opened up considerably. Here and there, fallen trees were in various states of decomposition. Poison ivy cloaked nearly everything.

He followed the deer path the best he could. Some places it would pass under a low-hanging branch and he had to detour. In the first quarter mile he came across two more cow patties. Then, coming along the edge of a ravine, he lost the path, or it fell apart, and he had to guess which way to go. He crossed the ravine and, coming up the other side, decided to keep heading south.

It was hard tracking cattle in woods. The dark mottled carpet of fallen leaves and twigs revealed almost nothing. Plus, Farmer knew, cattle could hide in woods the same as deer. They could be right there, perfectly still, watching as you went by.

Half an hour later, not at all sure he was on the right track, he came upon the bike path—a brand-new asphalt path that ran east-west between Granville and Columbus. It was part of the rails-to-trails network of bike paths in Ohio, which converted old unused railroad tracks into bike paths. He'd heard this one had been completed. You could take it from the center of Granville clear into New Albany, then join up to various neighborhood bike paths throughout the Columbus area.

It was in much better condition than the county roads Farmer used. It was smooth and shiny. To the west, in the distance, he could see a lone irregularity. He walked that way until he could see that it was, as he'd suspected, a fresh cow patty.

He was standing over the patty, looking down at it, when he heard a bell ringing behind him. Someone shouted, "On your left!" and Farmer, turning to look, felt a rush of air as one bicycle then a second and third and fourth flew by. He felt lucky he hadn't stepped in the wrong direction. They would have run him over for sure. They must have been going twenty miles an hour.

They were like creatures from the future, with their elongated plastic helmets and skintight bodysuits, all shiny and brightly colored—a high-tech blur as they whooshed past Farmer, their legs churning.

At other times Farmer had seen groups of bikers like these at rest, in the town square or outside a convenience store in Johnstown. Strangers in a rural setting. Even resting, they kept busy—

checking their pulses, doing stretches, making adjustments to their bikes. Their showy outfits made it seem like they were sponsored by various companies selling athletic and biking gear. But Farmer suspected they were paying fancy prices for everything they had.

Funny how everyone finds their own thing. Farmer would think that sometimes if he saw a private airplane flying over his farm. Here he was, in his pasture working on a stretch of fence, as always down on the farm, rooted in place (a way of life he found deeply satisfying) while above him, seeing Farmer in miniature below, passed a pilot who devoted most of his or her extra time and money to the joy of flying—to Chicago for lunch and a ball game, to coastal Carolina for a weekend with extended family. To Farmer, the pilot seemed adrift, missing some deeper point. But he could understand how, from the pilot's point of view, Farmer might look like a dumb animal in the mud, looking up stupidly, a splicing tool in his hand. As if he had never seen a plane before and couldn't understand how it stayed in the air.

Watching the cyclists recede as they pedaled toward Columbus, Farmer hoped his cattle had simply crossed the bike path instead of taking it. He guessed this was what they had done. But what if he was wrong? What if they were headed toward Columbus too, and these bikers, a mile or two farther west, caught up to them?

Farmer needed to get back home.

The truth was, he had no idea which way his cattle had gone.

He didn't see other patties on the asphalt path, to the east or to the west, but that didn't mean anything. The patties were not blazes marking a trail, each one intended to lead to the next. They were just cow patties.

He'd done what he could on foot. In fact, he'd come too far. He needed to get back to the house. He could talk things over with Sandy. She'd be up by now, having her first cup of coffee. Then he would go out looking in his truck.

He needed to call the sheriff. And, still thinking of those cyclists, it wouldn't hurt to touch base with his insurance agent.

FOUR

THE CATTLE BACKTRACKED to the path that went straight through the woods. They turned onto it, heading in the direction the sun would take later in the day. It was a good path—smooth and flat. It was easy walking. They went on: settled into a comfortable pace, heads bobbing lightly, making their way toward Columbus.

Two of the cows, 38 and 68, had calves with them. The calves weren't so young that they couldn't keep up. They were practically yearlings. But, however sturdy they'd grown to be (particularly the male calf, 106), they still exhibited, sometimes unexpectedly, silly-hearted play. Outbursts of nervous energy. In other words, they could be annoying (particularly the male calf, 106). Cows do not like being startled. They will allow for early youthful gamboling— tiny calves dashing and darting here and there, chasing each other, tails straight up. A certain amount of that sort of thing is inevitable. But, by six months, enough is enough.

After half an hour or so walking on the path, 106 left his

mother's side. He fell back until he was walking next to his half sister, 102.

Of the four calves he'd grown up with, 102 had always been his favorite. She didn't have 106's sense of humor, which was why he enjoyed teasing her.

She'd been born two hours after he was—pulled by Farmer after her mother, 68, couldn't give birth on her own.

"You should have been born first," 106 would tell her. "Your mom went into labor first. It was just her bad luck she had a calf with such a freakishly big head."

"My head is not freakish," 102 would say. "I was just taking my time. I knew when I came out I'd have to see you."

"Whatever you say, big head."

"Shut up."

"You shut up."

In frustration, she might start butting heads with 106. But after a few minutes of them pushing back and forth, forehead against forehead, he would say, "Ow! Stop hitting me with your giant head!"

102 would complain to an adult—whichever one was handy—and that, temporarily, would be the end of that.

Not long ago, Farmer had penned all five calves inside the board fence corral—their mothers nearby complaining loudly, the calves calling back to the mothers. It was upsetting for everyone, including Farmer. He loaded the other calves, all but 106 and 102, onto the trailer and drove the trailer to another farm. Later, with the empty trailer parked beside the barn and 106 and 102 back out on pasture with the herd, 106 had thought that, if only one other calf could remain, he was glad it was her.

Now, walking next to her on the path, he asked, "How is 102 doing?"

"OK," she said. "I'm getting tired of all this walking."

"It's exciting though, don't you think?"

"I guess."

"Come on. Cheer up, little sister. What would we be doing right now back home? Waiting for Farmer to realize we've eaten all the grass and move us into another patch he hopes will last a day or two?"

"Is that so bad?" 102 said. "I'm sorry, but I like things to be predictable."

"I knew you were going to say that," 106 said. He was kidding her but she didn't notice.

"My mom seems nervous," 102 said.

"Yeah, mine too. They all do."

"They're used to Farmer taking care of us. My mother wants to go back. She says we have no idea what we're doing."

"42 says this is how our ancestors lived."

"Until they settled down on farms. They must have had good reasons for doing that. Don't you think?"

"Jeez. I'm just happy we're doing something new and fun for a change and you're like all philosophical and gloomy."

102 said, "I am not gloomy."

"Doom and gloom! Doom and gloom!"

"Shut up," 102 said.

"Make me."

"Oh," she said, frustrated. She hurried a little until she was next to 74 and told her, "106 is bothering me."

"Well," 74 said. "Don't walk with him."

"Yeah," 106 said from behind. "Quit walking with me."

At this point 38, just ahead of 74, noticed the commotion and called to 106, "Boy, you get up here and walk with me."

"But I—" he started to say, but 68, behind him, lowered her head and rammed his thick rump, lifting him practically off his hooves— shoving him toward his mother.

"Get up there," she told him. "Do as you're told."

FIVE

IN THE KITCHEN, having coffee with Sandy, Farmer told her everything.

"But who would do this?" she asked.

"Heck if I know."

"It's hardly an innocent prank."

"I know, right? I can't figure it out. And I have no idea where the cows have gone. I guess I'll drive around."

"You need to go see Brett."

"You're right, I should."

Brett Sanders ran the Johnstown Feed Mill. He knew everyone. Talking to Brett was as close as Farmer could come to putting out an Amber Alert.

"I can drive around the neighborhood," Sandy said.

"You don't mind?"

"I just need to feed the dogs first."

"OK, thanks," Farmer said. "I've got to make a couple phone calls, then I'll go to the mill."

"You should eat something."

"I'm really not hungry."

"Well then, don't drink any more coffee. Come on, dogs," she said. Max and Chloe leapt up from under the table and followed her into the mudroom.

Farmer looked up the number for the Licking County Sheriff's Office. He called the number for filing a report or having a deputy dispatched.

"Sheriff's Office," a woman's voice said.

"Hello, I'm calling to report that my cattle are out."

"Sir?"

"My cattle got out this morning, and I don't know where they are."

"You don't know where they are?"

"I'm calling to see if someone has reported seeing cattle loose. Have you received any calls like that?"

"What is your name, sir?"

"Farmer."

"And your address, Mr. Farmer?"

"13062 Cooper Road. In Johnstown."

"And is this where the cattle are located?"

"Well normally, yes, but they're not here now."

"We cannot dispatch a deputy, sir. Unless someone has been

injured. Has someone been injured?"

"Not that I know of."

"You really need to get them back in, Mr. Farmer. You under-stand you're liable for any damages your animals might cause. You would be at fault if someone hits them with a vehicle."

"I understand. That's why I'm calling. Has anyone reported see-ing cattle loose in my area?"

"Sir, we are not a lost and found. Won't they just come back when they need to be milked?"

"These are beef cattle," Farmer said, irritated.

"Oh. Well, good luck with it. Have a nice day." She hung up.

Farmer called Jim Miller's office.

"National Insurance, no one faster in times of disaster, all we do is care for you, Angela speaking, how may I direct your call?"

"Jim Miller, please."

"Your name?"

"Farmer."

"Hold, please."

A recorded voice said, "Did you know fraud is the number one reason why insurance costs keep rising? Reporting fraud pays! Ask your agent for details… Hey, your dog is your best friend. Shouldn't he have the same comprehensive health insurance you do? Our new pet policies make sure *all* members of your family are protected. Ask your agent for details…"

"Farmer," Jim Miller said abruptly. "Long time no hear, buddy. What's up?"

"My herd is out. They've been gone all morning."

"Now hold up. What are we talking, Farmer? Sheep? Pigs?"

"Cattle."

"Got it. So… Moo moos gone missing. They're eating greener grasses, you're getting an ulcer. Is that it?"

"Yes."

"Has anyone been injured?"

"Not that I know of."

"Well, that's good."

"I just wanted to let you know what's happening."

"Greatly appreciated. And don't you worry. We've got you covered. Just get them back in when you can. If anyone wants to make a claim, give them my information."

"OK."

"How are you liking that pickup?"

Farmer recognized this as the point in the conversation when Jim had Farmer's file opened up.

"It's fine," Farmer said.

"And the Subaru. Candy still liking that?"

"Sandy," Farmer said.

"That's right. Sandy. I notice we're only carrying liability on the Subaru. No collision."

"Well, it's eight years old… Jim, I really need to go."

"Sure. The big roundup. I get it. Good luck with that. And don't worry. All we do is care for you."

"Thanks, Jim."

Farmer hung up. Outside, he could see the dogs chasing each other in the backyard. Prelude to their morning dump.

Sandy came back in the kitchen.

"What did the sheriff say?"

"Not much."

Pouring some coffee in a travel mug, Sandy said, "I'm thinking of going up and down Cooper and Van Fossen, then Drury Lane."

"Sounds good. I just hope they're still in the area. As weird as it seems, I'm worried they got on that bike path. They could be headed to Columbus."

"Let's hope not," Sandy said. "But if they are, then we'll just go get them, that's all. They're coming back to the farm."

She walked over and put a hand on his shoulder. "Everything's going to work out," she said.

"OK."

She kissed the top of his head.

"Go see Brett."

SIX

JUST BECAUSE they were off-farm having an adventure didn't mean 38 and 68 were going to neglect their calves' education. 106 and 102 had a lot to learn. When the herd took a break—walking off the path into the woods, lying down to rest—the two young mothers called for 106 and 102 to come settle down beside them.

"We'll do a lesson," 38 said.

106 said, "Do we have to? Can't we just learn as we go? I mean now that we're out in the world having real experiences?"

"Are you saying you'd rather learn things the hard way?"

"Instead of the boring way. Yes. Anything is better than school."

"I'm ready," 102 said. "I don't mind."

"I don't mind," 106 said, mocking her.

"You, 106!" 74 said. She'd started chewing cud and didn't need anything disturbing her digestion. This young bull of 38's had the persistence of a horsefly. "You want to learn things the hard way, we can start right now. Is that what you want?"

"No, ma'am," 106 said. He settled down.

68 had no experience teaching—102 was her first calf—so she let 38 take the lead.

"OK, let's go back and review about predators," 38 said. "Remember?"

"Predatorology," 102 said. "The science of anticipating predator behavior based on what we know about them."

"Yes! Very good. Predators can be studied and understood. And it's important that we do this. It's part of being properly vigilant."

"Curiosity is part of caution," 74 said. She was the most experienced mother, and easily the wisest.

"We're not flight animals," 102 said.

38 said, "Right. It's not good enough to just be skittish all the time. We're not built for lots of running. Plus, if you always run you become predictable. Predators can use that against you."

"We're not deer," 68 said. "Sometimes we *decide* to run."

"OK," 38 said. "So…starting with people. What do we know about them? 106?"

"They only notice what they want?"

"Good. Yes. People have a narrow, straight-on way of seeing things. They are always focused so closely on whatever they are after, they see only a thin sliver of the great big world at a time. They have no peripheral vision. Their eyes are close together, set deep in the flat front of their faces."

102 said, "They have to turn their heads to look at things."

"Yes. They need both eyes, so whenever something is even just a little to one side or the other, they have to face the front of their heads in that direction in order to see it."

"Aw," 106 said. "Poor head turners."

"The point is, 106—you can always tell what a human is looking at by which way the person's face is pointing. If you look at a person and you see no eyes or only one eye, probably you're not being targeted. But if you see two eyes at the same time, that's when you need to be careful. This is true for all predators. Two eyes means a predator is looking right at you."

"And that's never good," 68 added.

"It's bad to be noticed," 102 said.

38 said, "That's right. Safety is when you can see everything and nothing can see you."

"It would be awesome if we were invisible," 106 said.

"Never you mind about being invisible," 38 told him. "Just stick with the herd. There is safety in not being alone. Remember that. Now I need to tell you about human hearing."

"What?" 106 said.

"Human hearing," she said, realizing as she did so that she had fallen for his stupid joke again, for like the tenth time.

"What?" 106 said.

"All right," 38 said. "Humans stopped listening long ago. As a result, over time, they've lost most of their hearing."

"They have fixed ears," 102 said.

"That's right, they can't move their ears," 106 said. He swiveled *his* ears—the left one facing forward, the right one facing back, then reversed each ear, and then reversed them again.

"Stop that," 38 said. "Yes. Human ears are fixed. That means if they want to listen closely to something they have to turn and aim the side of their heads toward the sound."

"Their necks sure do get a workout," 106 said.

"Do they have a strong sense of smell?" 102 asked. "Like coyotes and dogs?"

"No, they've lost that too. That's why, sometimes, they buddy up with dogs. In case they need to track a scent."

"But how can they be so weak and survive?" 102 said.

"They don't have to worry about predators—they're the top creature—so they don't have to be careful. They learn from their mistakes! But we're getting away from the lesson… Let's say we're hanging out, grazing, and you notice a predator in the distance. You see two eyes. What do you do? 106?"

"Turn and face the predator. Make sure the herd is aware of it."

"And 102, what does the herd do?"

"Come in closer. Watch in all directions in case there's more than one. Some predators work in packs."

"And who is the predator going to single out?"

"The weakest," 106 said.

"So what do you do?"

"Show no weakness."

"What if your leg is injured?"

"No limping."

"Never show pain," 102 said.

"Good, good. See, 74? They're learning."

"They're good students," 74 agreed.

102 said, "What about Farmer? Is Farmer a predator?"

"Well, yes and no," 38 said.

"He takes care of us. You guys let him scratch your necks."

"He's a good scratcher," 68 said.

"It's complicated…" 38 said.

74 said, "Farmer is a domesticated predator. He's become so familiar, he's almost part of the herd. He makes sure we have plenty to eat and drink. He protects us from other predators…" She lost the thread of what she was saying. "42?" she said. 42 was more clever than she was, and had a knack for explaining things.

42 said, "Farmer keeps other predators away because, in his mind, we belong to him. He thinks of us as being his, like the fields and the barn and the tractor are his."

"For real?" 106 said.

"That's how *he* sees things," 38 said. "I prefer to think of him as our servant. If we bellow and he comes running and sees we're out of water, he drops everything and gets us water right away. Or hay if that's what's needed. If I'm having a difficult birth, he brings in the vet and they doctor me. Even though the vet costs Farmer an arm and a leg."

"An arm and a leg?!" 106 said.

"That's predator talk," 74 said. "It just means the vet is expensive."

"See?" 38 said. "Farmer does everything he can to make sure we're OK. In my mind that makes him our helper."

"But ultimately he does with us as he wishes," 42 said. "There are so many of us who, once we're loaded in the trailer, go away and never come back. Most of our children…"

74 said, "Farmer is a polite predator. We live with him on his farm, where we can relax and become calm prey."

"Why did we leave the farm?" 102 said.

"It's a compromise," 42 said. "And when a gate is left open, or there's a hole in the fence, we go through it. That's what we do. We're roamers. We believe the best lies ahead. We don't hurry or have schemes the way predators do. We meander, with curiosity and hope. In our dreams we're always on the move, moseying here and there, enjoying things but never getting attached. It's because of the way we are that people had to invent fences in the first place."

"The herd is the constant," 74 said. "Being together is the only thing that matters."

SEVEN

HEADING INTO JOHNSTOWN, Farmer tried hard to think of anyone he might be at odds with.

Nobody came to mind.

Farmer never quarreled or gossiped. He gave everyone a friendly wave and smile. He was respectful toward young children, hoping they might take it easy on him later, when they became teenagers. He would spend all afternoon in the thick of a February blizzard on his tractor, using his blade to clear everyone's driveway. In the spring, when he had the six-foot rototiller hooked onto the tractor, he would go around offering to till neighbors' gardens.

Farmer was a nice man. But his being agreeable was also part of his farming method. He aimed to establish an extended zone of calm around his farm, an additional buffer against unwanted drama.

If you were going to have cattle, you needed to build up all the goodwill you could. The day was always coming when you could find your herd in someone's yard, possibly when the ground was soggy with rain, each step the half-ton animals took gashing the manicured grass, leaving pockmarks inches deep.

Even when you took good care of them, living with cattle was like living with the sea. You did the best you could, but sooner or later, hopefully not often, something would happen that you could not control. It was a lie to say they would never get out.

For the life of him, the only unpleasantness Farmer could recall, and it seemed petty and a long time past, was when he met that college student at Glory Haven, Lucy Kellerman's organic vegetable farm, earlier that summer. Paul something. From Cleveland.

"He's a good worker," Lucy had told Farmer. "But man is he intense." He had an edge to him—even when working in the fields, wearing cutoffs and sneakers and one of the floppy straw hats Lucy gave her interns. Lucy told Farmer, "At first I just thought, 'Oh, he's from Cleveland.' You know. But it was more than that."

Farmer met the kid at a cookout Lucy had to celebrate summer solstice. Her farm was just a mile from Farmer's place, so he and Sandy went over in the Ranger. Farmer was standing in the line creeping toward the grill, holding a paper plate with a scoop of potato salad and an empty hot dog bun on it, looking forward to a nice juicy brat, when this kid Paul, just ahead of Farmer in line, turned and said, "So you're the cattle farmer." Something about the way he said it seemed accusatory. Farmer had learned to be somewhat guarded around vegetable people.

"Yes," he said. "Our place is just up the road. We've known Lucy for like twenty years."

"You're on the wrong side of history, man," the kid told Farmer. "You're doomed. Humanity keeps progressing—bettering itself. Pretty soon, keeping animals prisoner and killing them for food will be declared a crime once and for all."

"That is a possibility," Farmer said. "It's hard to know for sure."

"No it's not. It's inevitable. People used to think it was OK to own slaves, but not now. It's the same thing. You're a disgrace."

Nick Jensen, Lucy's next-door neighbor who was working the grill, called out to the kid, "You're up, Paul."

The kid, holding out his plate, said, "The carrot burger is mine." With the orange-and-green patty sitting on his gluten-free bun, he walked off without turning to say anything more to Farmer.

★ ★ ★

When Farmer got into Johnstown, he pulled his truck into the parking lot of the Stop-N-Go and parked. He called Lucy.

"Hey, Lucy," he said when she answered. "It's Farmer. I hate to bother you."

"No, you're fine," she said.

"The reason I'm calling—who was that kid from Cleveland who worked for you this summer? The one who was so intense."

"Paul Lernovski. From Case Western."

"Lernovski. He was a good worker, isn't that what you said?"

"He was great in the fields, but I couldn't take him with me to the farmers' market. He kept getting into it with customers. God help them if they asked for a plastic bag. He would start lecturing them. I tried telling him, 'Hey, these people get out of bed early Saturday morning, even if it's raining, to go to a farmers' market. They're supporting local food. Maybe you can cut them some slack.' But that didn't make any sense to him. 'Slack?!' he would say. 'Cut them some slack?! How is that going to change anything?' So I just left him working on the farm Saturday mornings. I took the other intern in."

"Did he go back to college?"

"No, he's taking a year off. Why are you asking about him?"

"Last night, someone cut a padlock on one of my gates and let my herd out. I couldn't think of anyone who would do something like that. But then that kid came to mind. He just seemed so radical."

Lucy said, "Oh my God, Farmer. Paul is renting that old travel trailer from Karl Rose."

"What?!"

The trailer was in the woods behind his property. He'd passed within a hundred yards of it that morning tracking the cattle. Karl had pulled it back there with his tractor and left it three years ago, thinking to use it as a hunting camp. But each fall, when it was cold and damp, it seemed a better idea to sleep in his own bed, then head out to the woods in his heated pickup truck. Leave it to Karl to figure out how to make a little money off it.

"Karl told me," Lucy said. "I ran into him at Kroger last week. Why, what's wrong? Aren't your cattle back?"

"No, we're still looking for them."

"Do you need help?"

"When we find them. Maybe then."

"OK. Just call me. Man, if it turns out it was Lernovski, I'm going to feel like the whole thing is my fault."

"It's nothing to do with you," Farmer said. "You're all right."

EIGHT

PURPLE-BLOSSOMED ALFALFA. Soft young tufts of orchard grass. Heavy-headed rye, stout and starchy. Tall-stemmed timothy gone to seed. Wild clover, low to the ground, with tight white flowers. The red clover Farmer frost seeds in spring: taller, with plush velvet blossoms more pink than red. In among these: the flat white tops of Queen Anne's Lace; yellow-petaled black-eyed Susans; clusters of little bluets—four pale lavender petals with a bright yellow center. All swaying gently, animated by breezes.

A warm sunny afternoon, bright and calm. The coming and going of bees and butterflies and other insects buzzing and chirping. Praying mantises. Dragonflies. Red-winged blackbirds vigilant atop fence posts, worried we might tromp nests they have hidden in the grass. The screech of a red-tailed hawk, perched in a nearby tree watching us, knowing we are disturbing little creatures: field mice and garter snakes. High in the hazy sky, turkey buzzards gliding around in circles.

Later in such an afternoon could come a sudden drop in temperature; a darker bluing of the sky; wind gusting as a storm approaches. Swallows darting and swooping close to the ground. Then rain, cooling and steady. Afterward, the air not humid. Refreshing. Fragrant with clover blossoms and the smell of dirt.

These, some thoughts of 27, in no way political. Just a reverie. A bit of nostalgia indulged in while walking on a paved path toward an uncertain future.

NINE

SANDY, IN HER EIGHT-YEAR-OLD SUBARU, was driving slowly, cruising the neighborhood.

She went up Cooper Road, past the Green place. Old Linda Green who never left home, wouldn't come to the door, and watched out her living room window like a hawk. Then the Humphry place. Ben Senior was out yard-mowing on his Dixie Chopper, his walker strapped on behind the engine. He didn't see Sandy go by. After that, the dozen new houses where the Miller farm used to be.

Turning left on Van Fossen, she drove by Lucy Kellerman's vegetable farm—Glory Haven. Near the end of Van Fossen she turned around in the driveway of a ranch house in good condition that had a FOR SALE sign in its yard. She got out to grab an info sheet. Sandy kept a close eye on real estate values in the area, maintaining a kind of rolling appraisal of what their home and farm were worth.

She drove south on Van Fossen, through the stop sign at Cooper and down the hill to the little bridge over Otter Creek. A doe and twin fawns leapt out of the woods along the creek and crossed Van Fossen ahead of her.

She turned right onto Drury Lane. It was unpaved. There were hardly any houses on Drury—just crops. A cloud of dust followed her as she drove between huge fields of yellowing soy beans and corn.

Drury curved around and brought her back to Cooper. More new houses, then Frank and Shelly Smith's place, their little house and barnyard up the dirt lane, hidden by rows of pine trees.

She passed Frank and Shelly's fields, all planted in corn, then some new houses on both sides of the road and, beyond these, the entrance to her and Farmer's place. She drove past her own mailbox, starting a second lap.

It was frustrating driving around like this. It felt random and futile. Sandy wondered if she should turn back. There was no sign of the cattle. If she went home she could at least get some things done. She was in the middle of backing a quilt; she could work on that. There was laundry to do. Bills to pay. She could go out once an hour or so and drive around some more.

It wouldn't have been like this ten years ago, she thought.

Cattle, when they got out, tended to go to cattle. The way to find them was to stop by nearby cattle farms. Even if your cattle had not turned up, you could leave word they were out. Other farmers would watch—would know, if cattle did turn up, to call you. And would help you round them up if it came to that, just as you would help them.

When Frank Smith had his herd—back when Sandy and Farmer were starting out and until Frank quit farming a few years ago—his cattle and theirs were within calling distance. If Frank's ran out of hay some winter afternoon, they would bawl about being hungry; Farmer's, hearing them, would answer. Or Farmer—weaning calves, penning them up in the corral—would set the mothers and calves to calling back and forth; Frank's herd would get upset and add to the racket.

The few times her and Farmer's cattle did get out, they always went to Frank and Shelly's. When Sandy and Farmer drove up the lane, Frank might already have their animals penned in, calmly eating hay. Frank would walk up to Farmer's side of the pickup smiling. "Missing something?" he'd say.

But Frank's cattle were long gone now.

They'd been the last remaining herd in the area other than theirs. One by one, farmers had sold their livestock. They'd rolled up the fences. They rented the ground to croppers who, with huge equipment and vats full of chemicals, raised corn and soy beans. Land owners could make more money doing this than by fooling with cattle (or sheep or hogs or, well, anything). Plus, they could travel. Could spend winters in Florida or South Texas. They hadn't a worry in the world. On the other hand, they could no longer call themselves farmers.

Some places fell abruptly into the hands of grown children who'd moved away and were back for a funeral, driving rental cars and staying in motel rooms, impatient to settle things and get back to their lives in San Diego or Tucson. Cattle and any other live-stock were rounded up and hauled to auction. The farm would be cut into eight-acre parcels, each sprouting a cheaply built home, a new driveway and roadside mailbox, and, where cattle or sheep had grazed, acres of grass kept trim by riding lawn mowers.

Soon after she passed the Green place again, Sandy's cell phone rang. It was Mrs. Green.

"Mrs. Farmer, it's Linda Green. I see you going by again. Is everything all right?"

"The cows are out," Sandy told her.

"I haven't seen them."

"No, they got out in back."

"I wondered what happened. I saw you going by again and I knew something was wrong. How long have they been out?"

"A few hours, Farmer thinks."

"I hope they don't get hit by a car. The way some of these folks drive, it's downright reckless. I don't know why they're in such a hurry. I called the sheriff last week about that boy who drives that little red truck. Do you know who I mean?"

"I think so."

"I tell you, I see some funny traffic through here. Cars stopping at some of these houses at all hours."

Sandy was passing by the Humphry place. Ben Senior had finished mowing and was gone.

"I heard coyotes again last night," Mrs. Green said. "Maybe they scared the cows."

"I don't think so."

"Well, I'll keep an eye out. I've got the police scanner on. If anything comes across there, I'll let you know."

"Thanks," Sandy said.

"Unfortunately, I do have to leave at noon. Sonny's taking me to Licking Memorial. I need to see a doctor about my elbow."

"Oh," Sandy said.

"They want to make sure the pin hasn't slipped. The doctor they gave me is Indian. They can't seem to find American doctors anymore. I mean we have medical schools, but Sonny says half the students there are from other countries. I'm not saying they make bad doctors. It's just hard to understand what they're saying."

"Mrs. Green, I really need to go now."

"I should be home by three. I just hate the idea of those cattle being out. I remember one time, back when we were milking, it must have been seventy-four or seventy-five. Well, it had to be seventy-five because Sonny had just got his driver's license and he would have been fifteen."

"I've got another call coming in, Mrs. Green. It's Farmer. Thank you." Sandy hung up and put the phone down. The last thing she needed this morning was a full dose of Mrs. Green.

Her mood was not improved by other drivers passing her on

Cooper Road not returning her wave. When they had moved onto the farm twenty years ago, one of the things she and Farmer liked best was how folks waved. Everyone had their own style. Some folks lifted just one finger from the steering wheel as they went by. Even children in back seats or looking down from school bus windows would wave. Everyone would.

These days, you were more likely to get a blank stare. Or nothing. For the third time since she'd been out looking for the cattle, here came another big SUV in a hurry, its driver a woman staring dead ahead. Sandy waved in vain. In her rearview mirror, she saw the SUV turn into the driveway of one of the new houses less than half a mile from her farm. *Oh, a neighbor*, she thought sarcastically.

People moving out into rural areas to get away from town mistake the countryside for a setting in which each individual is self-reliant—in rugged isolation. They don't notice that the only way rural life (and particularly farming) works is through a web of reciprocities and common understandings that form a safety net. The idea of being disconnected from others is actually a city thing. When they move out into the country, these people bring it with them like a virus. They have no idea how unfriendly they seem.

If the cows had gotten on the bike path and were headed toward Columbus, Sandy thought, they needn't have bothered. In another five years or so Columbus would come to them.

TEN

WHEN FARMER GOT TO THE FEED MILL, he went inside the little building that served as office and salesroom. Brett wasn't there.

"He's out in the shed helping a customer," Karen said from behind the counter. "One of those fancy horse people," she added, snorting a little.

Karen manned the register and answered the phone at the mill. Out one window she could keep an eye on the boys working the dock in case they tried sneaking away for a cigarette. Out the other window she could see the scales, where farmers came to weigh livestock trailers or loads of corn and soy beans. She kept track of Brett's comings and goings. And she held court, speaking her opinions, many of them critical, to customers appearing before her.

"Some of these folks have more money than sense. You know that?" she said to Farmer. "They move out here and build a house, and the first thing they do is put in a pole barn and get a couple

41

horses. Now I ask you—where are they going to ride them? Huh? They haven't thought about that."

Farmer didn't comment. He and Sandy had moved out from Columbus themselves, twenty years ago. They'd fit in OK, mainly because they took up farming.

The countryside was changing. With city folks moving out and country folks needing to take jobs in Columbus—everybody commuting back and forth for money—the old ways were unraveling fast.

"They say they want to live in the country," Karen said. "But, you know, the first time the power goes out, if a transformer blows, you know what they do?"

Farmer shook his head no. He looked down to the end of the cluttered room, past the dusty shelves and displays of animal medicines and work gloves, halters and manure forks, rubber boots in boxes and fence chargers and garden trowels and mousetraps. There, splayed out in wooden chairs between the antique pop machine and the glow of the weather radar monitor, were two old men, well into their eighties. Farmer recognized them though he didn't know them by name. They were familiar fixtures at the mill, in rotation with others just as old, sitting around drinking the bad coffee Karen made, watching the weather radar, and gossiping.

"They pack the kids into the car and hightail it right back to town. They get a motel room. Don't they, Henry?" she added, addressing the old man closest to the pop machine.

"Sure. Gives them a chance to do some shopping."

Farmer looked out the front window. The brand-new Land Rover he'd parked next to was still there. The customer Brett was with.

"They're just over in the big shed if you want to go see him," Karen said. "They're after pasture seed."

"I can wait."

Henry said to Farmer, "You're over on Cooper Road, aren't you? You must know Frank Smith."

"Sure," Farmer said. "I've made a lot of hay with Frank."

"How is that old son of a bitch?"

"He's good."

"You tell him Henry Poole said hey. Frank used to date my sister."

"Livonia?" the other old man asked.

"Yep."

"Listen to you old farts," Karen said. "What's that been? Sixty years?"

"She passed five years ago this August," Henry said.

"In Chicago, wasn't she?" Karen said.

"She and Frank used to go dancing." Henry told Farmer, "There used to be a dancehall behind where the fire station is."

"The Greens are on Cooper Road," the other old man said abruptly.

"They're right across the street from me," Farmer said. "They're good neighbors."

"They're a good family. Sonny's father was a good man."

"Bill Green?" Karen said.

"No, his kid brother Tommy. Bill lived up in Martinsburg. He married one of them Boone girls from over by Utica."

"They was a wild bunch," Henry said.

"They come in here from West Virginia. Right out of the mountains."

The bell on the front door tinkled and Brett and the woman he was helping came in.

Brett was in his forties, tanned and fit. He was wearing a plaid button-down shirt and jeans, and had a brand-new red Purina hat on his head.

"Hey, Farmer," Brett said. "I thought that was your truck out there."

"Hey."

"I'll be with you in a minute." He walked past Farmer to go behind the counter next to Karen.

"Well, let's see," Brett said to the woman. She was young, in her early thirties, and quite beautiful, but serious. There was an elegance to her, a sophistication. And, on her slender hand, the biggest diamond ring Farmer had ever seen. "Twenty pounds of pasture mix at two dollars a pound. That's forty dollars…" He was writing on a small receipt pad.

"And I can spread that any time this month," the woman said.

"Well, the sooner the better. This week would be good. August is really the better month but we're still having some nice warm days."

"I appreciate your help," the woman said. "What do I owe?"

"Let's see. Forty dollars for the seed. With tax…" He punched buttons on the calculator. "Looks like forty-three-thirty."

She handed him a Visa card.

"Karen," Brett said. "You'd better do it." He handed her the card. Brett sometimes needed to swipe a card a dozen times in the plastic terminal before it would take. Karen had the magic touch.

"Thanks for coming by," he told the woman as Karen moved around behind him to the terminal. "I hope everything works out."

Brett went to the back of the counter where Farmer was. "Want to walk with me, Farmer?" he said. "I need to go to the shed."

They left the sales room and stepped out onto the dusty gravel of the parking area. It was a warm day.

"How are things with you, Farmer?" Brett asked as they walked toward the big open entrance of the shed.

"My cattle got out last night."

Brett stopped walking. "Oh my. Are they back in?"

"We still haven't found them. Sandy's out driving around the neighborhood."

"Are there any cattle around you?"

"No, they're all gone. They wouldn't go to horses, would they?"

"They don't care anything about horses. They might take an interest in an alfalfa field. If there were a good stand of alfalfa near some water like a pond or creek, I'd bet money that's where they'd be."

"There's nothing but corn and beans around us."

"Hmm." Brett took off his hat and scratched his head. "I don't know, Farmer."

"They went in the woods, but I couldn't track them in there… I called the sheriff. They're no help… I don't know what to do."

Brett said, "Poor cows. They're probably starting to wish they were back home about now. You say they got out at night? That's unusual. Did something spook them, you think?"

"Well, that's another story. Someone let them out. Cut a padlock on one of my gates."

"Oh my."

"I have an idea who it could be. But all I really care about is getting my cattle home."

"Well sure."

Brett started walking again. He and Farmer went in the shed. It was high-ceilinged and dusty, its rafters in shadows, its concrete floor lined with aisle after aisle of skidded farm supplies: bags of feed and seed, quarter-mile rolls of barbed wire, baling twine and salt blocks, Havahart animal traps and plastic buckets full of fencing staples, bales of straw, water softener salt, pelletized lime and dog food and fertilizers. At the far end of the room a forklift was plugged in and recharging.

Neither Brett nor Farmer knew that in less than two years that room would be empty, its big sliding doors padlocked shut, the mill out of business. Brett would get a job at Kroger. Farmer would have to drive clear up to Knox County to get supplies.

"I'll tell you the crazy part," Farmer said. "In the woods about a mile or so from my farm is that new bike path between Granville and Columbus. I'm worried they got on that bike path."

"Well, what if they did? It goes into Columbus, you say?"

"I think that's the direction they would take."

"Those cows are not far off, whichever way they went. Don't worry, Farmer. I'll ask around and let you know what I hear. They're going to turn up directly. It'll all work out."

"I hope so."

"Go on home. Keep looking. And say hey to Sandy."

ELEVEN

THE CATTLE were getting hungry.

However long they'd followed the path, it never came out of the woods. It was a nice path, wide and flat and cool in the shade. It was easy walking. But it needed to bring them to a place where there was something to eat.

Coming around a bend, the cattle could see a big patch of sunlight ahead, spilling onto the asphalt from the left, through what looked to be a big interruption of tree cover. Sunlight meant grass. Even the youngest calf knew that. So, kicking up their hooves, leaping and twirling, they set off running toward the light.

And sure enough, when they got there, coming abruptly to a stop, they looked to the left and saw a wonderful sight—a long expanse of thick overgrown grass, mostly Kentucky fescue, with some rye and wild white clover. The lush lawn rolled gently downhill a long distance from the path, toward the back of a small white building all by itself. Hedges bordered the grass on both sides. It was calm and private.

One of the cows started eating where she stood, then a couple others did. Soon they all fell to grazing, heading slowly out into the open, leaving the path behind. The only sounds were the tearing of grass as they pulled thick mouthfuls of it free, swallowing quickly and taking more, gulping it down. There would be plenty of time later for regurgitating and chewing. The objective at this time was simply to get food into their stomachs.

As they worked their way downhill, they came closer to the white building. It was old and a bit tilted, having settled unevenly on its cracked foundation. But it was freshly painted and bordered with trim flower beds. It had colored glass windows along its sides and a little tower on one end.

38 had the idea of seeing how the building would work as something to rub on. She stepped into the mulch of a flower bed, got her thick haunch up against a corner of the building, and started moving back and forth. It was very satisfying.

"Oh my," she said to nobody in particular. "This is delightful."

27 rushed to another corner of the building before anyone else could get to it. She lowered her head, got her neck up against the whitewashed shingles, and started rubbing up and down vigorously.

This was the first time the cattle had been to church.

Around in front of the building, near its entrance, a car was parked in the thinly graveled parking lot—a dark blue sedan with license plates that read 4H1M. It belonged to Pastor Rod Shiflet, who had come in this morning to catch up on some paperwork. "Gettin' down to business," he called it.

He was inside the church, in his study. Before him, spread out on his desk, were files and documents relating to the finances of the Holy Jesus Buckeye Tabernacle, including some items he had received via registered mail. Pastor Rod was an optimist at heart, even though he was living in end times. But he had to admit things were bad.

"I'm trying, Lord," he said. "I'm doing the best I can. But I need a little help. Otherwise I'll lose the church. It's on you, God—you and Jesus."

As was his habit when praying, Pastor Rod paused, in case God came through immediately, making further supplication redundant and even disrespectful.

"Thy will be done," he added when nothing happened.

Then, "Just your humble servant…"

Irritated, he decided to review. "Here's the quote I got for a new roof," he said, picking up the estimate and waving it over his head. "Five thousand dollars. And this here—" picking up another piece of paper. "A letter from the bank saying I've got ninety days to get caught up on the mortgage. There's a hole in the bucket, God, and it's not up high near the handle. Come on now."

At that moment, he felt something. The church was moving. He'd never been in an earthquake, but at first he wondered if that was what was happening. Would God destroy the church for the insurance?!

Then he noticed there was a kind of rhythm to the movement.

He went over to the window and pulled the curtain aside. Looking down, he saw 38's big butt rubbing against the corner of the church just below him. He looked up and saw several other cows grazing nearby.

It was a miracle! Talk about abundance! Counting quickly, he made out the herd to be five cows and two calves. Unless some others were around in front of the church.

It was doubly lucky because Pastor Rod had grown up on a farm and was familiar with cattle. He knew how to deal with them. You had to be patient and steady. More than anything, you had to figure out their point of view and take it into account. You had to engage them in a genuine dialogue.

He called Deacon Jones's cell phone.

"Yello," Deacon said.

"Brother Jones," Pastor Rod said, still watching the cows out his window. "What were you telling me the other day about the price of cattle?"

"Higher than it's ever been."

"Praise Jesus. Does that cousin of yours still haul?"

"Yep." Dave Monroe. Made a living hauling cattle, mainly to and from the auction barns, with an aluminum trailer that could carry up to twenty head.

"Well, Brother, I've got some cattle showed up over here to the church. If we can get on it in the next hour or two, I think we can get them loaded and off to auction."

"They must belong to someone, Pastor."

"There's no cattle farms anywhere near here," Pastor Rod said. "They are a lost tribe. God brought them here. He delivered them. And let me tell you, Brother, they are some fine lookin' creatures too. Just as plump and sleek as you could hope for. If we could get even two or three of them loaded, the church could be spared a great many indignities."

"I'll call Dave," Deacon Jones said. "We should be over to the church in less than an hour."

"Bring you some buckets with corn in them," Pastor Rod said. "We might need to bait them."

He hung up. He put his jacket on and left the study, went through the little kitchen area toward the back door of the church to go outside. He needed to get the cattle comfortable with him before Deacon and his cousin showed up.

He stepped outside. Looking down and moving slowly, he walked the few wooden steps down to the grass. He could tell, out the corner of his eye, that the cattle started a bit when they saw him. 38 and 27 stepped out of the flower beds and moved away from the church. 106 and 102 hurried to be with their mothers. All the cows stopped grazing, lifting their heads to see him. But they didn't flee. They didn't want to leave behind this grass unless they had to. Every one of them was watching Pastor Rod closely.

He acted like he hadn't seen them. He walked, eyes down, over to a picnic table and sat. Leaning forward, he untied then retied one of his shoelaces while sneaking a peek at the nearest cow. Her ear tag said 74. She put her head down and resumed eating, but kept an eye on him.

Pastor Rod sat upright then, seeming to notice the cattle for the first time.

"My goodness. I didn't know I had visitors."

Then he said, "I'm so happy you all stopped by. I wondered how I would get this grass trimmed. Pretty good, is it? I see the clover is still in bloom."

"It's delicious," 68 said.

Pastor Rod breathed a sigh of relief. He had not lost his touch with cows.

"Yes, I expect it is delicious," he said. "But there's no water. You must be thirsty."

"We need water," 74 said.

"Water," 27 said.

38 said, bellowing loudly, "Water! Water! Water! Water! Water!"

"Well, I think I can help you there," Pastor Rod said. "I've got this big plastic tub we use for baptisms. Hold on."

He went back inside the church, into the kitchen area, and emerged again carrying a big blue plastic tub. He placed it on the grass near the flower beds, where a garden hose was coiled up beside an outside faucet. He turned the water on and put the end of the hose in the tub.

When water started filling the tub, Pastor Rod backed away from it. He returned to the picnic table and went around behind it, so as not to present a reason for them to hang back.

"Go ahead," he told the cattle. "It's city water, so it might taste funny, but it's nice and cold and there's plenty of it."

74 and 27 went to the tub first. 27 let 74 drink, then regretted that and tried to push 74 aside so she could get some. 74 dug in and kept her head down inside the tub. The other cattle fell in behind these two and, with a lot of pushing and shoving, each of them in turn got some water. 106 and 102 went last.

As each cow got enough to drink, they went back to grazing.

"You all certainly were thirsty," Pastor Rod said, turning the water off and coiling the hose up again.

"I know it's hard, always needing to look for food and water. It never ends. You can satisfy your needs momentarily but, before you know it, before you can relax, your stomachs are empty again and you've got to keep searching. A restless wanderer never home."

"We settle down at night," 74 said.

"But laying there hungry in the dark, knowing there's no respite before the dawn… What a tribulation that long night can be."

"It's true," 38 said.

"Yes, I know your struggle and feel your pain," Pastor Rod said.

"And in the winter, when the farmer brings you hay and you hope it might be second cut, soft to the mouth, with some real protein in it to help you ward off the cold. But it turns out to be one of those old bales that's been languishing on the fencerow. Moss growing through the net wrap. And when he drops it down in the ring you can see the dust of the mold spores fly. How your heart sinks then and you bellow and bellow but it does no good."

"Yes!" 27 said. "It's happened to me!"

"Or in the summer. You've 'et everything you can get to—nibbled it down so close to the dirt only a goat could get another bite. You look through the fence and there you see the juiciest, best looking grass you've ever seen, right there in front of you, so thick and bushy. But can you get to it?"

"No!" 68 said.

"No, that's right, you cannot," Pastor Rod said.

"Because of the fence," 68 said.

"Yes, they put the fence around you and turn that which should be yours into a temptation."

"Yes!" 68 and 38 and 42 cried in unison. The herd was coming together in front of Pastor Rod, fascinated by what he was saying.

"We're outside the fence now!" 42 said.

"Yes, but where will you go?" Pastor Rod said. "Where can you hope to find enough to eat and still be safe from Mr. Predator?"

A ripple of alarm went through the cattle, like a shiver from a chill wind.

"You know about Mr. Predator. How he does. Where there's food and drink to draw you in, that's where he waits. Like a spider on the web. Low in the grass, uphill from the water. His yellow eyes watching your every move."

"Keep back, Predator!" one of the cows cried out.

"You're all he thinks about," Pastor Rod said. "If he's a sleepin', you're in his dreams. Old Mr. Predator don't never take a day off. No sir. He don't go on no vacations. He's got too much to do. Can I get an Oh No?"

"Oh No!" all the cows cried.

"What's that you said?"

"Oh No!"

"Friends. Dear friends. Again I ask you. Where can you go? Where can there be shelter?"

74 said, "We're going to Columbus."

Pastor Rod was not expecting this answer. It threw him a little. "Columbus?" he said.

"City people are civilized," 42 said. "They will respect our rights."

"Who told you about Columbus?"

"Lernovski," 74 said. "He said follow the sun until we get to Columbus."

"Lernovski? That sounds like a communist name."

"Just because someone is a community organizer doesn't make them a communist," 42 said.

Pastor Rod was confused but he didn't have time to sort things out. He needed to get back on track. Deacon and his cousin Dave would be pulling in any minute.

"What if I told you there's a place much better than Columbus?"

"Oh, you mean Cleveland," 38 said.

"Go Calves," one of the other cows said.

"No," Pastor Rod said. "I'm talking about a place much better than Columbus or Cleveland. Better than any city. I'm talking about a place that has the thickest most delicious grass you could ever dream of. Better than any you've ever tasted, more than you could ever eat. Slow-moving rivers that never get muddy. Salt licks everywhere you turn. There's never any winter there, no need for hay.

"And friends, this place I'm talking about has no predators. Not a one. You can relax, really relax—roaming wherever you want, never knowing hunger or fear."

"It sounds wonderful," 68 said.

"Yes, it is wonderful, 68," Pastor Rod said. "The most wonderful place of all. It's my special gift to you."

"What place is this?" 74 said. "It sounds too good to be true."

"It's called heaven, 74."

"But how can there be room for us?" 42 said. "Everyone must want to go there."

"Oh yes there's room in heaven. There's room for you and me," Pastor Rod sang, invoking an old spiritual. "Room enough for all."

"Where is it?" 68 said.

"Not far."

"I don't know," 74 said. "We're supposed to go to Columbus."

"Are there flies in heaven?" 106 said.

"No, young fellah, you'll be glad to know, there's no flies in heaven. No horseflies. No deer flies. None of them little ones. Glory to God and thank sweet Jesus, there's no flies in heaven!"

"I want to go there," 68 said.

"Me too," a couple other cows said.

"OK," 74 told Pastor Rod. "We'll go to heaven."

"I am so happy to hear that," Pastor Rod said. "I'm gratified to know what joy you'll find. And look," he said, turning to point out the red truck hauling an aluminum stock trailer that was just pulling into the church parking lot behind him. "Here comes your ride."

"We can go now?" 68 said. "All right! The sooner the better!"

"Yes, my friend Dave will deliver you right up to those pearly gates, where Saint Peter is waiting. Oh how welcome you'll be."

"Pearly gates?" 42 said.

"Yes, those gates where all who enter pass."

"Why are there gates?" 74 said. "I don't understand."

"It's fenced!" 42 said. "Heaven is fenced!"

"No," Pastor Rod said, trying to calm them.

The truck had come to a stop in the church parking lot and sat there, its diesel engine rumbling.

"It's a trick!" 74 said. "Let's get out of here!"

And the cows whirled and took off running, back up the hill, 106 and 102 keeping up the best they could.

"No!" Pastor Rod called after them in vain. "Come back!"

When they got to the path, they turned left, toward the west. They ran fifty yards or so before slowing to a walk.

"That was a close call," 42 said.

74 said, "We need to be more careful."

TWELVE

WHEN FARMER GOT HOME, Sandy's Subaru was parked in front of the garage.

He found her in the kitchen making a ham and cheese sandwich.

"How'd it go?" she asked.

"Brett's on it. He says not to worry. How about you?"

"I just got back. I didn't see a thing." She finished making her sandwich, cut it in half and put it on a plate. "You want me to leave everything out?"

"Yes, please."

She carried her sandwich to the little table and set it down. Farmer got a plate and went to the sandwich-making spot, started fumbling in the bread bag.

"Do you want some water?" Sandy said.

"Yes."

"After lunch, I'm going to Utica for gas. Then I'll drive around some more. It's like they vanished into thin air." She put two glasses of water on the table, then sat in front of her sandwich. "Oh, and Mrs. Green is on board. She'll let us know if anything comes across the police scanner."

"Well, we got that going for us." Farmer brought his sandwich to the table and sat across from Sandy. "Also, we have a suspect."

"We do? Who?"

"That kid who was an intern for Lucy this summer. The one from Cleveland."

"The one who told you we're doomed?"

"Paul Lernovski. He's still around. Lucy thinks he's living in that old trailer of Karl's."

"You're kidding."

"She seemed pretty sure about it. I'm going to go check it out."

"You be careful."

"I doubt he's dangerous."

"You don't know that. I mean he's got to have a screw loose, right?"

"OK," Farmer said. He started eating his sandwich. The more he ate, the more he realized how hungry he was. He never skipped breakfast.

Sandy said, "I'll wait here till you get back before I drive around again." Then she said, "You know, Farmer, I was thinking…" She waited to be invited rather than blurting out her suggestion like some newlywed.

Farmer bristled. "What, Sandy? What were you thinking?"

"I don't know if it would help…"

"What?"

"What if we made signs? Like people do when they lose a dog? I could put them up on telephone poles, on stop sign posts. I still have plenty of poster board from when we had the garage sale."

"No," Farmer said.

"We could put *my* cell number on them. That way people would call *me*."

"No," Farmer said. "What would you do? Give a description?"

"Just how many. Beef type. Real simple. I'd just put them up around here, where I'm looking."

"No. If they turn up around here, we'll see them as soon as anyone else. It's embarrassing enough already."

"Oh, Farmer. There's nothing to be embarrassed about."

THIRTEEN

THE HERD KEPT TO THE PATH, moving on from their experience at the Holy Jesus Buckeye Tabernacle. Like many who feel out of place at church, it was hard to know whether the cows were not suited for churchgoing or whether they had simply, through bad luck, tried the wrong denomination. Sometimes even just a change of pastor can make the difference.

Through the narrowing border of trees they could see more and more houses—so many of them!—on both sides of the path, crowded close together. Each had hardly any ground.

"I think we're in the city," 42 said to 74.

They were walking together, just ahead of the others.

"I think you're right."

"Lernovski said there would be lots of people."

"I don't see even one person," 74 said. "Just all these houses."

"They must be inside."

They came to a small grassy area beside the path. The grass was short, mainly rye and fescue. It did not look particularly healthy.

There was a wooden sign that said:

Lawnview Park

New Albany Department of Parks and Recreation

Closed after Dark

Not that the cows could read it. They understood the sign to say, if anything, Rub Butt Here. On either side of the little park were homes and backyards bordering the bike path. The cows stood still, looking around. They saw no people anywhere.

"I want to eat," 38 said.

"Eat!" 68 said. "Eat! Eat! Eat!"

"Eating time!" 27 said.

"OK, all right. Settle down," 74 said. "We'll eat. But stay close."

They walked out into the grassy area and started grazing. The grass was almost too short to eat. It was delicate and soft, but had an odd taste—a kind of bitterness.

"Something's wrong with the grass," 102 told her mother.

"Yuck," 106 said, letting some blades fall from his mouth.

"City grass," 38 muttered.

"There's no use complaining," 42 said. "Just eat what you can and we'll move on. If we find better grass, that'd be a good thing. But we don't know what we'll find. This might be as good as it gets."

"It better not be," 27 said.

They grazed without enthusiasm, taking no pleasure in it. 68, losing interest, went over to the park sign and started rubbing on it. She was disappointed almost immediately when part of it broke off and fell to the ground.

"Hey, there's a human," 38 said. "Look." The others raised their heads and looked where 38 was facing. Sure enough, there was a man. He'd just come out of a nearby house. The herd watched him. He zipped up a jacket he was wearing, then walked through the grass behind the house to a miniature red barn.

"That's like the cutest barn ever," 102 said. "It's just like a real one but tiny."

"Hush," her mother said.

The man opened the little barn's double doors and went inside. He had to stoop a little. A moment later the cows heard an engine start. To their amazement, the man emerged from the barn riding the tiniest tractor they'd ever seen. It was a John Deere.

He engaged a mower deck underneath the tractor and started mowing.

"I don't understand," 68 said. "City folks have miniature farms? They have tiny barns and tractors?"

"Apparently," 27 said.

"I bet they have miniature cows," 106 said. "That's so cool. We're like giants."

The man was mowing around in little circles behind the house.

Already he was half finished. He seemed very serious, so focused on doing a good job that he didn't notice the cows.

They kept an eye on him and resumed their half-hearted grazing of the funny-tasting grass.

Then the man on the tractor finished mowing. He disengaged the mower deck and drove the tractor around behind the barn. The cows lost sight of him.

"Where is he?" 38 said.

They could still hear the tractor's engine.

The man drove out from behind the barn, now pulling the world's smallest wagon. It bounced along behind him. He turned the tractor off and stood, got a rake from the wagon, and started raking the cut grass into small piles. He picked the piles up, pressing each of them against the head of the rake and dumping them in the wagon.

The cows watched him, fascinated.

"Danger," a voice said behind them.

They whirled to see a young boy. He was smaller than Thomas, the boy who lived in the yellow house next to the farm. The young boy was standing in the grass not far away. "Danger," he said again.

"What danger?" 74 said.

"I'm not supposed to talk to strangers," the boy said.

"We're not strangers."

"You're not?"

"We're cows," 74 said.

"Cows go moo."

"Sometimes, yes."

"I'm four-and-a-half," the boy said.

"Pleased to meet you. I'm 74."

"I'm 38," 38 said.

One by one, the cows all introduced themselves, even the calves.

"Where's your mother, 4½?" 42 said.

"She's asleep. She fell asleep on the sofa."

"Maybe you should go home. She'll be worried."

"I can go outside. I live right there." He turned and pointed to the house behind him. "I can't leave the yard and no talking to strangers. You want to see my truck?"

"You have a truck?" 106 said.

"I got it for my birthday. It makes real noises and it can carry stuff. It has really big tires. You want to see it?"

"I want to see it," 106 said.

"It's in my room. Come on."

"Can I, Mom?" 106 said.

"You most certainly cannot. Did you learn nothing in class today?"

"Always stick with the herd," 102 said.

4½ said, "You guys get to go to school?"

"Yeah, get to. Like every day," 106 said.

"I'm not old enough yet."

The whole time they were talking with 4½, the cows kept an ear swiveled around and one eye turned, maintaining awareness of the mowing man. He'd finished raking. He'd put the little wagon away behind the barn. Then, twisting around in the yellow plastic seat to see behind him, he'd carefully backed the little tractor into the barn. He came out of the barn, shut its double doors, and walked toward the house. This is when he saw the cows and the boy.

"What the..." they heard him say. He came walking toward them.

"Hey now," he said. "Mason," he said to the boy. "You go on now. Go on back inside."

"I can go outside," 4½ told him.

"Go on, Mason." The man's voice was calm but firm. He turned to the herd and said, "Shoo, cows. You go on too. You got no business here."

"We stopped to eat some grass," 42 said.

The man stared at 42. His mouth was open.

"What?" 42 said.

"You talk."

"You're not the boss of me," 4½ said.

"No, he's right," 74 told 4½. "You should go back to your mother."

"I don't want to."

"Talking cows," the man said. Then he said, "Mason, I told you to go home. Now go!"

"Oh, all right," 4½ said. "Goodbye, cows. Bye, 106." He waved to them, then hung his head and walked back to his house.

"He's lonely," 74 told the man.

"Yeah, I know. But his mother doesn't watch him. Maybe she should fence her yard."

The cows didn't say anything.

"You guys really shouldn't be here. Somebody is going to call the police. You're lucky the neighborhood watch dudes haven't come by. Are you lost?"

74 said, "I don't think so."

"We saw you with your tiny tractor," 68 said.

"What?"

"The one you were riding."

"Tiny?!"

"It's cute," 27 said. "It looks just like a real one."

"A real one? That's the John Deere X-304. It's the second biggest one they sell at Lowe's." He shook his head, then said, "Listen, you need to mosey on now, or whatever it is you do."

"We're going," 74 said.

"The grass here is no good anyway," 68 said.

The cows walked toward the bike path. They got on it, heading west.

"Cute," they could hear the man saying to himself as he walked back to his house. "Cute, for God's sake."

FOURTEEN

AFTER LUNCH, Farmer returned to ground zero—the paddock where, that morning, he'd expected to find his cattle. He drove the Ranger over that same last rise with some hope. He'd left the back gate propped open with a small branch he stuck in the ground—in case the cows came back. It would be awesome if they had. They would be lounging, some sleeping, tired from their escapade, acting like nothing had happened.

But, for the second time that day, he found the paddock empty.

He'd thought, driving home from Johnstown, at least they'd gone through a gate. If not—the padlock unmolested—then what? An alien abduction? His cattle swept up inside some UFO, now hurtling through space? You could bet that their abductors, for all their interstellar know-how, would be ill-prepared for dealing with cattle. They would be shocked and appalled when those cows started shitting and pissing all over everything, rubbing up against control panels, kicking at whatever made them nervous.

Farmer would have felt awkward going to see Brett about his cattle being abducted. He would have done it, though. And Brett would have helped somehow: "Well now, let's see. I heard about a fellow up in Knox County who had some hogs go missing. He ended up getting some money from NASA. They've got a program for that. Lonnie Kaurich was his name. I can get you Lonnie's phone number. He might be able to help. Or you could check with Bob Reynolds over at the extension office."

Farmer parked the Ranger and got out. He was going back into the woods, this time to get a look at that trailer. He'd tried calling Karl Rose to ask permission but he couldn't get through. Like a lot of older farmers, Karl had a cell phone. His family had insisted he get one, in case something happened to him while he was alone out on the farm. He could call for help. But that didn't mean he was going to answer the damn thing.

Once in the woods, Farmer headed west, away from the back of his property. He knew where he was going. Less than ten minutes later he stepped into the rough clearing. Karl's hunting camp. Across from Farmer was the worn out little travel trailer. It wasn't going anywhere. Splotched with mildew, partly obscured by poison ivy, it was resting on cinderblocks and railroad ties. Someone had tried skirting it with pieces of wooden lattice. In front of the trailer, in its yard of packed dirt and tree stumps, was a sagging picnic table; a laundry line stretched between two trees; a circle of stones around a bed of ashes.

Was this Lernovski's lair?

"Hello," Farmer called as he walked across the clearing. "Hello?" No one answered.

He went to the trailer. He could see on one of its windows some stickers from its heyday: *Discover Holland, Michigan! Hershey, PA— the Sweetest Place on Earth.* There were KOA and Jellystone Campground logos. And a bumper sticker Karl Rose had probably added himself, a local joke: *Where in the Hell is Croton, Ohio?*

"Hello," Farmer said again, knocking on the trailer's little door. "Anyone there?"

He found the door unlocked, opened it, and stepped up inside the trailer. It was a funky mess. The air was heavy with patchouli oil. There was an army cot at the far end of the room with a shiny orange sleeping bag on it. Around the cot were piles of dirty clothes. The kitchen counter was a confusion of empty beer cans, torn energy bar wrappers, empty humus tubs, tins and boxes for many kinds of tea. Hanging over the sink was a red flag with a single yellow star.

On the booth-like table at the front of the trailer Farmer saw a half-burnt candle stuck in a wine bottle; a box of wooden matches; a hardback he recognized because he had it too and knew it well, Temple Grandin's *Animals Make us Human*; a coffee mug full of ballpoint pens; a red spiral-bound notebook. Someone had written the word JOURNAL in thick black letters on the notebook's cover.

Farmer went to sit at the table—he meant to have a look inside that journal—but there was something on the bench. Bolt cutters! He picked them up, noting how heavy they were. And how new—they still had a price tag on them.

What the hell? Farmer thought. Each confirmation that he was on the right track, rather than settling his thinking, managed to disorient him further. How could any of this be happening?

He sat at the table. *OK*, he thought, pulling the notebook closer and opening it. The lined pages were full of careful tiny printing. Near the back, he found the most recent entry, dated that same day at 7:00 a.m.:

The (Moo)vement begins! They are free! I opened the gate but they were the ones who had the courage to go through it. Oh, my beautiful Bovinae! With their natural genius for horizontal collectivism, they hardly needed any organiz-ing. They know how to stick together. Good luck, cowpa-dres! You are making history! YEE-HAW! When this is written of by others—when it is laid down—I am confident my role as facilitator will be appreciated. How my coming here this summer to learn about organic farming turned out to be like the landing of a comet in this redneck county. A comet of truth and justice! Initially, it is critical I remain in the background. The cows need to be perceived as acting on their own. People would be all too ready to use the role

I've played to undermine the importance and dignity of their quest. I am the spark that lit this bonfire of liberty—a spark that was needed, true. But the inexhaustible fuel for that bonfire is the wretched injustice of animal farming. And the oxygen fanning the flames is the spirit of these noble creatures.

Farmer had a hard time reading such jibber jabber. But he understood one thing. This freak had let his cattle out. *He wishes them luck?* he thought. *What a jerk.* He flipped to the start of the journal and looked at the first entry, dated nearly two months earlier:

Sarah broke up with me. She blurted it out while peeling turnips for dinner. She's going back to college and needs to focus on getting into grad school. Her father is threatening to cut her off. He's been totally bumming since he caught us in the beach house that time. Oh well, she's not your little girl anymore, sir. Sorry about that. Now he's pulling on the purse strings. She's his little marionette and I'm the odd man out… What I should do is take up golf. Get really good at it and then challenge her old man. Kick his butt— at *his* game. BAM!

Farmer flipped through the journal, moving on without reading if he saw the name Sarah. In this way, he progressed quickly through many pages. He caught snippets such as, "Good riddance, siren! Better I should find out now!" and, much later, "Sarah! Sweet Sarah! The smell of your hair. Your vegan tattoo. Oh, forever gone."

Then he came across this entry:

Tonight, I told them about New York City—the intellectual and cultural intensity there. I explained about the month I spent in Brooklyn. I'm trying to get them to see that they need to leave the rural area they're in. Their best shot at overcoming speciesism is in a city. They could be viewed as contributing to diversity—adding something special. I keep telling them, "Go to Columbus." Not that Columbus is so great. But it's what is close. I tell them, "Follow the sun. Columbus is where the sun goes each day."

I wonder if that's what they've done? Farmer thought. He backed up some, to see if he could find an earlier reference to the cattle. A dozen or so pages back he came across this:

I am determined to make a difference. I am going to liberate these cows and hope they can be a catalyst. Sooner or later, someone is going to be the Rosa Parks of animal rights. Why not them? Society is ready!

And several pages later:

I tried explaining the Cuban Revolution, but they were a

poor audience tonight. I can't help but think that the timing of when they shit or urinate sometimes seems suspect—editorial rather than random. I know I have a tendency to take things too personally so I could be wrong…

And then, in an entry dated only a couple days ago:

These evenings hopping the fence and heading across the pasture, settling down with these noble creatures, embedding myself, delivering the night's lesson—these have been some of the most exhilarating times of my life. This is why I'm taking a year off from college. To do something real. "Revolution is not an apple that falls when it is ripe. You have to make it fall." (Che Guevara)

Farmer had read enough. The intensity of the language; the freakishly careful tiny printing, all in capitals; the heady smell of patchouli—were conspiring to give him a headache. He shut the journal. What more did he need to know? Lernovski had let his cattle out, then left them to fend for themselves. Farmer needed to find them and get them home. Meanwhile, they were in harm's way and he couldn't protect them.

His cell phone rang. Someone was calling from the mill.

"Hello?" he said.

"Farmer, it's Brett."

"Hey, Brett."

"I sure hate to bother you. I wanted to let you know, I think I've heard something about your cows."

"You have?!" Farmer's heart leapt.

"Well, Dave Monroe came by the mill here a while ago. You know Dave."

"Sure. He used to haul for me before I got my own trailer."

"He does a good job. Anyway, he was driving his rig when he stopped in. I was kidding him about what it must cost to drive around empty, the price of diesel being what it is. And he said something about almost having a load."

Farmer listened patiently.

"He said his cousin Charlie Jones—I don't think you know him."

"No."

"He's a plumber. Seems like a nice fellah. Anyway, he's a deacon at this church over on 305. The Holy Jesus Buckeye Tabernacle. It's about halfway to New Albany, on the north side of the road. Just across from the Mahindra dealer."

"OK."

"Well, Charlie called Dave today and asked him to pick him up at his house and carry him to the church. Some cattle had shown up there and the pastor wanted someone to haul them. Dave said they were beef type, different colors, some white-faced. He thought there were seven or eight head, a couple calves… So I thought that sounds like your herd."

"Yes, it does. Did he get them loaded?"

"He never even got to try. When he pulled in at the church, his truck must have spooked them. They took off. He said he didn't know how they were going to get them in the trailer anyway. There were no panels there, nothing to work with."

"Where was he going to haul them?"

"I don't know, Farmer. I didn't ask. But I'll tell you something else I think is interesting. That bike path you were talking about, it runs along near 305 through there. It passes right behind that church."

"I guess that makes sense."

"I thought I should call and let you know."

"I appreciate it."

"Sure. Now, when you get caught up to them, you call me if you need help. Dave could be handy too. You'd have to hire him, but I'm sure he'd take it easy on you."

"OK. Thanks, Brett." Farmer hung up.

Well, that was that. They'd taken the bike path toward Columbus. They were doing just what Lernovski wanted them to.

He called Sandy.

"Brett just called," he told her. "The cows were spotted halfway to New Albany, near 305."

"You're sure they're ours?"

"They're ours all right. They're on that bike path—just what I was worried about."

"I don't understand. How can that be?"

"You don't know the half of it," Farmer said. "It was that kid Lernovski who let them out. He's been coaching them—telling them to go to Columbus."

"What?! What do you mean?!"

"I'll tell you at home," Farmer said. "I'm still in Karl's trailer. I'm leaving now. I need to take the truck and go check out where they were seen."

"OK. If I don't need to drive around, then when you get back, I might go see Frank and Shelly—see how they're doing."

"Good. I keep meaning to get over there."

"I'm worried about Frank. Seems to me he's lost more weight."

"See you in a few minutes."

They both hung up.

Farmer was taking the journal with him. Sandy could see it for herself. That would be easier than him trying to explain it.

Extricating himself from the tight-fitting booth, Farmer stood. He took one last look around, grabbed the journal, and stepped to the door. He opened the door and—in a moment of furious astonishment—saw and recognized Lernovski. The actual real Lernovski, pale and scruffy, in the flesh.

He was coming home if that's what the trailer was to him, wearing army surplus green and a black beret. He was carrying a messenger bag.

Lernovski, in that same moment, looked up and recognized Farmer. There was a flash of intimacy—both men seeing in the other's face the shock they felt themselves. Then, as quickly, they diverged. Farmer becoming angry, shouting, "Hey you!" And Lernovski, panicked, turning to run, never making a sound.

Farmer came flying out of the trailer. He chased Lernovski on a narrow path through the woods for about fifty yards, until his lungs were burning and he could hardly breathe. He stopped running, leaned against a tree, and tried to catch his breath. When he could, he shouted after Lernovski, "You jerk."

Realizing Farmer had given up, Lernovski stopped running too. He turned and called to Farmer through the woods, "I did it for you too! Slavery mars the master!" Then he turned and went on, trotting along a path that led to the old milking barn out by Drury Lane, where Karl kept his tractors and Lernovski parked his van.

Farmer walked back to the trailer's clearing. Still breathing heavily, he picked up the journal where he'd dropped it and walked into the woods in the other direction, back toward the propped-open gate where he'd left the Ranger.

FIFTEEN

THE COWS KEPT ON, tired and hungry.

They were deep inside the city. No matter how many houses they passed there were more ahead, so much alike they all seemed familiar. The path was straight, but it felt like they were going in circles.

Everywhere, the grass was so short there was no use stopping to eat.

They liked how calm it was—they still weren't seeing any people—but that was starting to bother them too. It was such a pleasant day, sunny and warm, with nice little breezes. How could people not be outside?

106 and 102 were walking together, ahead of 42, who was bringing up the rear.

"I don't think I've ever been this hungry," 102 said.

"74 says not to worry, we'll find plenty to eat."

"I'm not *worried* about being hungry. I *am* hungry."

They walked some more.

"I liked 4½," 106 said.

"Me too."

"He's smaller than Thomas."

Thomas sometimes came out of the yellow house, crawled under the fence, and spent hours at a time with the herd. He would act out the adventures of superheroes, or bring comic books and sit and read them, sometimes aloud.

102, slowing her pace, fell back so she could talk to 42. 106 fell back too.

"42?" 102 said. "Are we going to stop and rest soon?"

"We need to find food."

"Maybe the city isn't a good place for us."

"The best always lies ahead, 102. You know that."

"But how far ahead?"

"Wandering around hungry, hoping to find something to eat—this must be how predators feel," 106 said.

"That's an interesting point of view," 42 said. She would have expected something like that from 102.

74 and the other cows ahead of them stopped walking. They'd come to a crossroads. There was the path they were on, broad and smooth, curving gently up ahead to the right, about to enter mature woods. And there was a narrow dirt path, hard-packed and dusty, that came from the left and dead-ended into the path they were on. It was impromptu and rustic, like paths they knew back

home. It made its humble way across an open area of worn out grass more dead than alive, toward several large buildings. The path went alongside one of the buildings.

"I like this little path," 74 said. "I somehow trust it."

42, who had walked ahead to join the deliberation, said, "It's made by many feet." The path they'd been on since morning had been made *for* many feet. It was not the same thing.

"OK, let's decide," 74 said. "42?"

"I say we take this new path."

"I agree," 27 said.

All the cows agreed—even the calves, though nobody asked them.

74 went first, stepping down off the black asphalt. The others followed. They walked single file—on high alert, ears swiveling—following the dirt path toward one of the big buildings, then around behind it.

SIXTEEN

IT WAS ONE THIRTY when Sandy turned onto Frank and Shelly's lane. She followed it back through the pine trees, up to the little white house. The Buick was in the carport.

They'd lived in that house almost seventy years. Frank told Sandy and Farmer once, "When we got married—after the ceremony—we drove straight here. I got a shovel from the trunk of the car and started digging the foundation."

Shelly added, "That's how it was back then. You did one thing and then you went ahead and started in on something else. You didn't have time to worry the way folks do now. You were just always busy."

"And tired," Frank added.

They'd done everything small farmers in Ohio had needed to do to get by. For years they'd milked a small herd of cattle. When that stopped paying, they switched to hogs. When grain got too high, they got rid of the hogs and started raising grain. All the while they gardened and canned, baked their own bread, and kept chickens for eggs. They'd built their house and both the barns; dug the well by hand; did their own car and tractor repairs. Like most farmers, they had side businesses. Shelly ran a little hardware store in Homer for years. Frank was a dealer of fencing supplies. Frank also drove a school bus, for the insurance as much as for the salary.

When Frank got older and was letting younger farmers with modern equipment crop his land, he'd kept a small herd of beef cattle around, on hilly ground up near the house and barns, mainly for something to do. And for the company.

Frank and Shelly were in their seventies when Farmer and Sandy bought the Martin place and became their neighbors. Farmer gravitated toward Frank. Started working with him some afternoons and weekends—making hay; patching rundown fence; caring for cattle. Not quite forty, he'd been the "kid," scrambling up into the mow to stack hay bales as they came off the elevator, going back to the barn for some tool Frank forgot. He'd learned a lot. He kept track of his hours and Frank would settle with him every other month or so, handing him a check Shelly had written.

At some point, Sandy had started going over with Farmer and would visit with Shelly while Farmer and Frank were outside working.

Farmer would never forget Frank telling him once, when they were up in Frank's big hay mow, resting after they'd knocked some bales down to feed, "I've spent sixty years in this barn. Good years, most of them. I'd gladly spend another sixty in here if I could."

Five years back, Frank got rid of his cattle—one of a series of simplifications he and Shelly carried out over time, working to stay in their house as long as possible. They were trying to be smart about it.

When Sandy knocked on the glass door to the back porch, Shelly appeared wiping her hands on a kitchen towel.

She was nearly blind. She cocked her head a little, peering with her cloudy green eyes to see who'd come to visit. She was wearing khaki shorts, a blouse, and brand-new sneakers.

"Shelly, it's Sandy."

"Come on in," Shelly said, holding the door. "You hungry?"

"No." Sandy followed Shelly into the kitchen.

"Well, you might as well sit down," Shelly said. "I've got some cereal. Betty bought it at Kroger. It's a new kind, I never heard of it. I can't remember how it's called."

She pushed a cereal box across the kitchen island to where Sandy was sitting.

"Oh, it's Raisin Bran," Sandy said.

"Raisin Bran," Shelly said. "That's it. Raisin Bran. You want a bowl?"

"No, I'm not hungry."

"Frank won't even try it. He hardly eats breakfast anymore.

Sometimes he'll eat some oats, but he's not interested in food. He'll eat some oats or maybe half a banana. But by God open up a gallon of ice cream, it doesn't matter what time of day it is, you better get the hell out of his way."

"Where is Frank?"

"He's around here somewhere. He was reading the paper."

"How is he?"

"I don't know. He gets tired. His doctor told him, 'There's no cure for being eighty-five, Frank, but I hope when I'm that old I'll be in as good a shape as you are.'"

"You're both tough old birds," Sandy said.

"My eyes are bad. I can't go out in the sun. I'll be doing OK, but I'll get distracted while I'm doing something and I'll fall. See?" she said, pulling up her left shorts leg to show Sandy a big purple bruise on her thigh.

"Shelly! When did you do that?"

"A week ago. I was down in the basement getting some potatoes. I started up the stairs and missed the step."

"Shelly!"

"I'm doing one thing and I start thinking about something else," Shelly said.

"You need to pay attention!"

"Yes, I suppose that's true. You want something to drink? I've got some ginger ale."

"No thanks."

Shelly opened the fridge and started rummaging around inside. "I've got some tomato juice…apple juice…there's a bottle of root beer in here somewhere."

"I'll take some water," Sandy said.

"I don't know where Frank is." Shelly filled a glass with water and slid it across to Sandy. "Maybe he decided to take a nap."

"I'm going to go find him," Sandy said.

She got up and crossed the living room, heading for the dining room around the corner.

"Frank?" she called.

He was on the sunporch in one of the glider chairs, still wearing pajamas. He had rag socks on. Sandy stepped out onto the porch.

"Hello there," Frank said. He put his hands on the arms of his chair and leaned forward, preparing to stand.

"Don't get up," Sandy said. She leaned down and kissed him on the cheek.

"Thank you!" he said, smiling brightly.

Sandy sat in the chair next to his.

"Reading the newspaper, Frank?" she said, indicating the various sections, including one called Lifestyle, spread out on the coffee table in front of him.

"That's right," he told her. "Now and then I like to check the obituaries. Make sure I'm still alive."

Her eyes were drawn to his hands—thickened and calloused permanently by so much hard work, so many decades out in the weather, and stiffened by arthritis. He couldn't button his own shirts.

"How's Farmer getting along?" Frank asked.

"We're having a tough time," Sandy said. "The cows are out."

"They're having an adventure."

"Yes. And so are we."

"Has he found them?"

"He thinks he knows where they are. But when he does catch up to them, we still have to figure out how to get them back. They've gone quite a ways."

"They'll be ready," Frank said. "They like an adventure but then they get tired of it."

"Do they get homesick, Frank?"

"Well, you could say that. They're a lot like people but even more so. They like what they know."

"But they always go through an open gate… Why do they do that?"

Her visit was social, but suddenly she was appreciating the opportunity to consult someone who had lived with cattle for seventy years.

"Greener grasses!" Frank said. He smiled and somehow there was that twinkle in his eye that Sandy loved. "They're wanderers. But they're after the same things they have at home: Grass to eat; water;

a little salt if they can find it. Shade when it's hot. Windbreak. And as much calm as they can get. It's the calm that usually runs out first."

"That makes sense…" Sandy said.

"If the grass is always greener on the other side of the fence, then sooner or later, when they're outside the fence, the grass inside starts looking good. Does Farmer need help? I'd have to put some clothes on…"

"No, he'll probably hire Dave Monroe. Brett Sanders has offered to help."

"Jack Sanders's boy."

Shelly appeared in the doorway.

"What's that?" she said. "Whose boy?"

"Brett Sanders," Frank said. "Down to the feed mill."

"Brett," she said. "He went to school with Linda. He was a nice boy. Played football."

"I'll say," Frank said. "He was quite a player. He was the fastest boy on the team. And the biggest. They say Woody Hayes came out one night to see him play."

"Brett Sanders," Shelly said. "Yep."

"Farmer called the sheriff too," Sandy said.

"Called the sheriff?" Shelly said. "Why? What's happened?"

"Farmer's herd is out," Frank said.

"Well the sheriff won't be any help. They don't care about the farmer."

"They've got bigger fish to fry," Frank said.

Shelly said, "Hey, Frank, remember Tommy Osborne's cattle, how they used to get out?"

"Sure. His fence wasn't any good."

"You'd be outside doing something and there they'd be, coming up the road again. Seemed like it must have happened once a month or so."

"They were an ornery bunch," Frank said.

"Somebody would go get Tommy, and we'd help him put them back in," Shelly said. "Neighbors looked out for each other back then."

"We probably should have helped him with the fence," Frank said.

"This one deputy got so irritated with those cows always being in the road, he finally told Tommy the next time he saw them out he was going to fine him. A hundred dollars, wasn't it, Frank?"

"Something like that."

"Not a week later, here they were coming down the road and that deputy happened along and sat watching them from his cruiser. Frank went out into the road and the deputy said to him, 'Aren't these Tom Osborne's cattle?' And Frank said, 'No sir, they belong to me.' So the deputy helped Frank herd them through a gate we had there, into our pasture. He'd never had any trouble with us, so he was nice about it. Then the next day we got some neighbors together and moved them back up the road to Tommy's."

"Frank!" Sandy said.

"Just being neighborly."

SEVENTEEN

IT WAS NEARLY TWO O'CLOCK when Farmer, heading west on 305, found the Holy Jesus Buckeye Tabernacle.

By the dusty shoulder of the road was a glassed-in message board bearing the church's name and address. It read: "Down in the mouth? Time for a faith lift!" Behind the sign was an empty gravel parking lot and the church—a small white building with a tall steeple on one end. It was set in a deep piece of property that rolled uphill in back to woods. There were no cows.

Farmer parked near the church's entrance and got out. It felt like he was the only person there. He decided to walk around the outside of the building, to look for evidence of the cattle having been there. It would make sense if they had. The church's lawn was overgrown, thick and lush, with lots of blooming clover. It looked delicious.

The first thing Farmer noticed was the plastic tub half full of water. The water had pieces of grass floating in it, just like in the water tanks back home. Cattle *had* been here! They had been drinking this water!

Behind the church he saw places where the lawn had been grazed. They were scattered. The cattle had not been there long. He discovered a cow patty, still fairly fresh, then several others, including a smaller one that could have come from a calf.

At the top of the hill he saw where the bike path came close to the edge of the woods. Near there, more concentrated and sustained grazing had taken place. An entire area had been eaten down. Oddly, the shorn grass was striped with lines of thin, watery cow shit—the kind that came squirting out of cattle when they were afraid. It was in stripes because they had been running. The stripes led in a northwestern direction, and Farmer, following them, found himself on the bike path, where the thin shit persisted, splattered on the asphalt to the west.

Farmer assessed what he'd learned, based on his observations.

The cattle, coming from the east on the bike path, were attracted by the lush lawn. They grazed heavily at the top of the hill, getting a feel for their surroundings before venturing farther into the open. As they relaxed, they spread out. They started to wander, eating selectively, working their way down toward the church. Then someone offered them water in the blue tub. Someone kept filling that tub as they drank. It was so small, they would have drained it otherwise, then knocked it over and chewed on it in frustration. Not long after they drank, something spooked the cattle. Maybe the arrival of Dave Monroe. They took off, running back up the hill—across the area they'd first grazed. They got back on the bike path headed west.

Well, Farmer thought, *whatever frightened them, I'm glad to know they got some decent grass and some water. I don't know how they'll find enough to eat and drink in town.*

He called Sandy. She was home.

He told her, "I'm at that church just outside New Albany. They were definitely here, and they headed west when they left. It's right on that bike path. That's what they did—they took the bike path."

"Do you want me to come there?"

"No, I don't know where they are yet. I'm going to keep looking. I'll check in again."

"I've been reading that journal. It's so sad."

"What, are you feeling sorry for him?"

"No, it's just depressing. I had to put it down. It's such a nice afternoon, I'd rather be outside. I'm going to work in the garden. I feel like I haven't done anything all day."

Looking down the hill, Farmer saw a man standing in the grass behind the church looking at him. He told Sandy, "Hey, I need to go."

"All right. If they're headed for Columbus, call my sister. She knows the city better than we do."

"OK." He hung up and started down the hill.

The man was waiting for Farmer. He was heavyset and balding, wearing jeans and a white dress shirt. When Farmer got close, the man said cheerfully, "Hello, friend. Is there some way I can help you?"

Farmer said, "Hi. I heard you had some cattle come through here."

"Well now," the man said, smiling. "That's the God's honest truth. I'm the pastor here. Rod Shiflet. Everyone calls me Pastor Rod."

He reached out and shook Farmer's hand.

"I'm Farmer."

"Let me guess—first name Cattle?"

"I hope you don't mind my looking around. I've been tracking those cows all day. I got a call from someone who said you were trying to get them loaded with Dave Monroe."

"Yes. I found them to be quite skittish. I nearly had them convinced to get in the trailer, so they could go home, but they seemed bound and determined to get to Columbus. They didn't welcome any new thinking."

"I know," Farmer said. "That's what's so weird."

"They mentioned a fellow by the name of… I can't remember… Lemonski, Lablonski… I remember thinking it sounded like a communist name."

"Lernovski."

"Lernovski! Yes! He seems to have filled their heads with some funny ideas."

"Yes, I'm aware of him."

"Well, I'm sorry it didn't work out. We could have had them back to your place by now. Just like nothing ever happened."

"I'm glad they got something to eat while they were here. And some water." Farmer gestured to the tub. "That was nice of you."

"I could see they were thirsty."

"Seems like you understand cattle."

"Well, I grew up around them. Plus, like you, I also am a shepherd. Caring for a flock or herd, or a congregation—you develop a knack."

"How would you have found me?" Farmer said.

"What's that?"

"How would you have found me? If you'd gotten them in the trailer?"

Pastor Rod laughed. "I wasn't worried about that. It's not hard to find a man who is missing cattle."

"I'm grateful for the hospitality you showed them."

"Friend, there are so many ways to serve the Lord, I just try to pay attention and keep up the best I can."

The two men started walking toward the front of the church.

"How long ago were they here?" Farmer asked.

"About three hours ago. They skedaddled back onto that bike path."

They got to the parking lot. Farmer saw the dark blue sedan with the license plate 4H1M parked next to his truck.

"Well, I need to keep after them," Farmer said. "Thank you for your time."

He and Pastor Rod shook hands again.

"You know, Farmer," Pastor Rod said. "Over the years I have learned to notice the little ways that God takes a hand. He brought those cows of yours here. And they led you here. It could be that all this is happening for a reason. I want you to think about that. I don't know if you are a churchgoing man."

Farmer didn't say anything.

"I can't shake this feeling that there's some reason why you're here. I don't know what it is. Maybe you're meant to join us. Or maybe you're supposed to help the church some way. I just feel like God has drawn us together in this special moment—this moment of opportunity—and it would be a real shame if we let it get away. Will you pray with me, Farmer?"

"I wish I had time," Farmer said, shrugging. "I really need to get going. I want to find them before dark."

"Well then, that's what we'll pray for. Oh Lord," Pastor Rod said, raising his arms as if to embrace the sky, "let this man find them poor dumb critters before anything bad happens to them. Help him get them back home where they belong. He's a good man, Lord. Look after him! It's in the name of Jesus that I ask it."

"OK," Farmer said. He opened the door of his truck and got in. He started the engine.

"Farmer!" Pastor Rod shouted.

Farmer rolled down the window of his truck.

"I don't have your phone number. If they come back through here, how would I reach you?"

"You're right. Do you have something to write with?"

Pastor Rod got out his cell phone and tapped on it a few times. "Shoot," he said.

Farmer told him the number. "That's my cell."

"And your email?"

"You don't need that," Farmer said.

"It's for the monthly newsletter."

"That's OK," Farmer said, shifting into reverse. He backed up slowly, turning the truck around. He shifted into forward and pulled ahead to the edge of 305. He could see Pastor Rod in his rearview mirror gesturing for him to stop and hurrying toward him. Farmer hit the gas and spun out of the gravel. He turned right onto 305, headed west.

EIGHTEEN

THE DIRT PATH came around the big building, leading the cows to a kind of dead end. They found themselves in a sad patch of grass bordered by several big buildings, all alike. Next to the buildings were many cars parked close together. There were concrete paths and other patches of grass. It was calm, no people in view, but the cows remained on high alert, collectively watching in all directions.

Gradually, it seemed to them they could relax.

They lowered their heads to check out the grass. It was rye, not as short as some they'd seen, but thin and sickly. It had the same bitter taste as the grass where 4½ lived.

Unwittingly, as if washed ashore, the cows had entered the Royal Crest Apartment Complex. Usually visitors arrived by way of the main entrance on Cherry Bottom Road, crossing the little bridge above what was meant to resemble a moat, passing the billboard-like coat of arms sign sporting a yellow banner that read, "13th month free! If you lived here, you'd already be home! Fun pool and clubhouse!"

Not far from where the cows were standing, behind the full-length drapes of his ground floor one-bedroom in Building D, Royal Crest resident Danny Young was hungry too. There was nothing to eat—not even, it turned out, in any of the pizza boxes in the kitchen.

He was rushing around, getting ready for work. He was going to be late. He'd fallen back asleep on the sofa listening to Pink Floyd. Then he couldn't find one of his sneakers. It turned out it was behind the bathroom door, under a towel.

Danny had been late so often that Max, the manager of the bookstore, had put him on a tardiness action plan. Danny signed the form and brought his copy of it home. He hadn't read it, but it wasn't good.

He decided he should call the bookstore and tell them he was running late. Ginger answered. He asked for Max.

"Max went to the bank," she said.

"Oh. Is Doug there?" The assistant manager. "I'm calling because I might be late."

"You don't work today," Ginger said. "You're not on the schedule till tomorrow."

"Really?!" Danny felt an enormous wave of relief. "Man, that's awesome! What time tomorrow?"

"Ten o'clock."

"Thanks, Ginger! Take it easy!"

Danny hung up. He danced around in the living room, wearing one sneaker and holding the other. The universe didn't intend for him to get fired just yet. Meanwhile, he had this day entirely to himself. He could do whatever he pleased. The world was his can of Pringles.

Danny put on his other sneaker. He put on his Ohio State ball cap, grabbed his wallet and car keys, and opened the door to start his day.

It was three thirty in the afternoon.

Stepping outside, Danny saw the cows. They looked up in unison from their listless grazing and stared at him, some with bits of grass hanging from their mouths.

"Whoa," he said. "Cows!"

The herd stared at him.

"You're so big!" Danny said. "Wow! You are totally blowing my mind!"

"We're blowing your mind?" 74 said.

"*Talking* cows! Whoa! I'm like Doctor Dolittle. How's it going, cows? What's up?"

"We're hungry," 74 said.

"Me too. I'm heading over to the Speedway to get a bean burrito."

"Speedway?" 38 said.

"Yeah. Gonna get my burrito on."

"Why do you have such a big house?" 38 said.

"What?" Danny turned around and looked at Building D. "Oh," he said. "No, I just have a little place. There's like thirty apartments in each of these buildings."

"Apartments?" 42 said.

"Yeah. See all the doors? Each door is like a different house."

"People are crowded together, living on top of each other? They don't have any ground at all? That doesn't seem right," 42 said.

"I'm talking with cows!" Danny said. "Far out! I'm Danny, by the way."

"We're hungry, Danny," 74 said.

"Hungry!" 68 said.

"Hungry!" 106 and 102 chimed in.

Soon all the cows were saying it, bellowing at him.

"Whoa, hold up," Danny said. "Chill. There's no need for you to be like *yelling* cows."

"We can't find good grass," 38 said.

"Hey, I feel you," Danny said. "Believe me. The main thing is, don't let it get you down. Sometimes you just have a run of bad luck is all."

Danny saw Angel coming up the sidewalk. She was carrying one of her big purses and a Kroger bag. She lived in the apartment next to his and was his favorite neighbor. She was gorgeous, for one thing. Really gorgeous. Angel was the name she used down at Sirens, the club where she danced. Her real name was Mary.

"Danny," she said, smiling as she walked up to him. "Are these your cows?"

"Hey, Angel. No, they were here when I came outside. I'm just hanging out with them. Aren't they cool? Guys, this is Angel. She lives there." He pointed to her door.

"Where did they come from?" Angel asked.

"I don't know. Where did you guys come from?"

"The farm," 74 said.

"Oh my God," Angel said. "They talk?"

"Yeah. Isn't it awesome? Talking cows!" Danny said.

"Are you guys lost?" Angel asked the herd.

"Not that we know of," 42 said.

74 said, "Why does everyone ask us that?"

"I love it. They're so cute. Look at you, you little baby cow," she said to 102. She stepped closer, hoping to pet her. 102 backed up and hid behind her mother. "Don't be shy, I love animals. Here, Danny," she said. "Take a picture of me with them." She tapped and swiped her smart phone's screen until it was a camera and handed it to him.

She stood in front of the cows. "OK, now don't be nervous," she said. She posed and Danny took the photo.

"Terrific!" She looked at the photo. "I'm a cowgirl!"

She turned to face the cows again. "So, are you guys in town for long?"

"Just one day so far," 74 said.

"Well, I hope you enjoy your visit."

"We can't find good grass," 68 said.

"We're hungry!" 38 said.

"Hungry!" 27 and 42 said.

"Settle down, you guys," Danny said. "Yelling isn't going to change anything."

The cows stopped bellowing.

"Cows!" someone said. It was the old man from D21. He was coming out of the stairwell near Danny's door wearing plaid pajamas and slippers, probably on his way to check his mailbox in the foyer of the clubhouse. He was a total grouch. He called management about Danny's music being too loud on a regular basis.

"I can't believe it," he said. He was smiling—the first time Danny had ever seen him do that. He shuffled toward the cows. "Miss; young Daniel," he said as he passed Angel and Danny.

"You're the first cows I've seen in like twenty years," he told the cows. "What a wonderful treat."

"Aren't they adorable?" Angel said.

"They are splendid," the old man said. "Absolutely splendid. Angus, with some Hereford and Limousin mixed in and…Simmental?"

74 said, "The bull Farmer borrows is half Simmental. He's from Knox County."

"Wow, I'm impressed," Angel said.

"I grew up on a farm," the old man said. "Here you go, sweetheart," he told 68, walking toward her slowly with one hand held out. When his hand was near her nose, 68 sniffed it. She remained still while he stepped closer and scratched her forehead. Then he scratched below her ear. She lifted her head, stretching it, and he made long sweeping scratches along the underside of her powerful neck, up almost to her jaw.

"Oh yes," 68 said.

"Oh my God! You're like a cow whisperer!" Danny said.

"I want some," 38 said. "Let me have a turn."

"I call next," 27 said.

"No, I already said something," 38 said.

"Everybody can get some," the old man told the cows, although Danny could see he was slowing down, already getting exhausted. The cows were too eager to wait politely. They started pushing forward, jostling. Only the two calves, who were more timid, hung back.

"Hey. Come on now," the old man said. "Take it easy."

"You better be careful, mister," Angel said. "Danny, they're going to knock him over."

"No, they're fine," the old man said. By then he was scratching 38.

Angel and Danny watched.

"OK, OK, that's enough," the old man said finally. "I'm stopping. My arm hurts." He started rubbing one of his shoulders. "For a minute there I forgot how old I am."

"How old are you?" 68 said.

"Too old."

"You've lived with cows?" 74 said.

"A long time ago, when I was a kid. We always had one around for milk and then we would raise the calves. When he had the money, Dad would buy a club calf for one of us to show at fair. Her senior year, my sister Mary Lou went to State with hers. She had that steer so tame, when the judges were finished, she jumped up on him and rode him out of the ring. Folks talked about that for years. They just couldn't get over that."

Danny's mind was getting blown all over again. This old man, who would just grunt at Danny if they passed on the sidewalk—who could have known he had actual conversation bottled up inside. Stories and shit. It was as unexpected as talking cows.

"We used to have pigs and chickens too," the old man said. "And the garden! My mother would can so much stuff. We had a stove in the mudroom she would use so the house wouldn't get hot. We had shelves in the basement and she would fill them all. Beans and tomatoes, pickles…her bread and butter pickles! I can still taste them! Nothing like what they sell in stores. Potatoes we kept in bushel baskets on the basement floor. Apples too. Good keepers like Red Delicious or Gala could last clear through till spring. Mother'd be in the kitchen, she'd say, 'Joe, go get me some apples, I'm going to make a pie.' Man!"

"Why did you leave?" 42 said.

"Aw hell, that's the question, isn't it? I wish I could say. I was young and so full of myself. I couldn't wait to get away. Now look where I've ended up."

He started crying.

Danny walked up to him.

"Yo, don't be sad, Joe."

"Huh?" the old man said, surprised. He immediately stopped crying. He got a handkerchief out and dabbed his tears, then blew his nose.

Danny put a hand on the old man's shoulder and gave it a slight squeeze.

"I never knew your name. I just thought of you as the guy in D-twenty-one who hates music."

"My name is Joe Martin."

"I'm Danny Young."

They shook hands.

"I'm Mary Carmenovski," Angel said. "I'm in D-fourteen."

She and Joe Martin shook hands, then she leaned in and gave him a little kiss on the cheek.

"Ms. Carmenovski," he said.

"Angel's what I go by."

"Danny," Joe Martin said. "I can honestly say these cows are the only friends of yours I've ever liked."

"They are the coolest," Danny said.

"Yes, but I'm worried management will disapprove of them."

"Yeah? Well, I disapprove of management," Danny said. "When are they going to fix that pool?"

"I was thinking; maybe you could take them to the park. They might like it there."

"That's a good idea."

Sutter Park. One of the bigger parks in the metro parks system. Its entrance was almost directly across the street. It was one of the reasons Danny had moved into the apartment complex. The cows would certainly dig it.

"There's better grass. Plus, there's a pond they can drink from."

"Better grass!" 38 said.

"Better grass!" 27 said.

"Better grass!" 106 and 102 said.

There was a whirring sound—the noise of an electric motor—and Angel said, "Oh hell, Monroe is coming."

A golf cart came out from behind Building C, hesitated, then came straight toward them. It *was* Monroe. A mountain of a man, moody and bitter. Technically he was the complex's maintenance man, but none of the residents had ever seen him fix anything. It was in his other role, as rent collector, that Monroe excelled.

Monroe drove the golf cart up close to them, turning it sideways so he could talk without having to stand. The golf cart sagged heavily under him.

"What in the world?" he said. "You know you can't have no cows up in here."

"Hey, Monroe," Danny said.

"Been a while since I read that pet clause, but I know it still says dogs under thirty pounds. Which one of you fools these cows with? You, old man?"

Joe Martin said, "These cattle are here of their own accord. I suppose it is no crime to be friendly to visitors."

"Visitors supposed to sign in," Monroe said.

"Aw, be nice," Angel said. "They're not bothering anyone."

"You know how big their shit is?"

"Monroe. Chill, dude," Danny said.

"You know I have to report this to Ms. Duncan. If I don't, I get in trouble. She gonna freak, too."

"What's wrong?" 74 said. "What's the problem?"

"Problem is you," Monroe said. "Hold up. Why I'm talking to a cow?" He pointed a finger at the residents, telling them, "You all playing a trick on Monroe, you better stop. Don't be playing tricks on Monroe."

"They talk," Danny said. "For real."

"Who's Monroe?" 42 said. "I'm confused."

"*You* confused," Monroe said. "I got talking cows on the premises."

"We're just passing through," 74 said.

"Well, pass on through then," Monroe said. "Don't make me get all agricultural on you."

"I'm about to take them to the park," Danny said.

"All right, then," Monroe said. "I come back through here they better be gone." He hit the accelerator and the golf cart clicked to life, whirring as it carried him back toward Building C.

"Well, I'm going to the clubhouse," Joe Martin said. "I'm expecting my check." To the cows he said, "It was a pleasure meeting you."

"Pleasure meeting you," 74 said.

"Later, Joe," Danny said.

"Bye," Angel said.

"Ms. Angel."

Joe Martin shuffled on down the sidewalk.

"I'm going too," Angel said. "I need to try to sleep a little before going to work. Goodbye, cows! Take care of yourselves!"

"Goodbye, Angel Carmenovski," 74 said.

"See ya, Angel," Danny said. "Come on, cows. Follow me."

Danny started walking and the cows fell in behind him. He got on the dirt path they came in on and led them back around the corner of Building D, toward the bike path. "Yeah, you guys will like the park," he said.

When they got to the bike path, Danny stopped walking. He told the cows, "OK. You see this path? You need to take it that way." He pointed to the west, where the woods were.

The path not taken.

"You'll cross Cherry Bottom Road. After that, follow the path into the woods. They're part of the park. But then, you'll see, you'll come out in an area that's like a big field. There's a pond there. That's what Joe was talking about."

"Thanks, Danny," 74 said.

"Thanks, Danny," 38 said.

All the cows, even the calves, thanked him.

"Aw. You guys. You're the best. I'll try to catch up to you later."

He turned and headed toward Building D.

The cows got back on the bike path.

NINETEEN

FARMER FOLLOWED 305 till it dead-ended, then drove west on 161 toward New Albany.

He called Sandy's sister Nancy—the busiest person he knew. She ran a big organic vegetable farm in Union County, near Marysville, with delivery trucks coming in to various farmers' markets in Columbus, as well as making drop-offs at restaurants. Frustrated with the way farmers' markets were being run, she'd taken on management of them, one after another, including, finally, the premier central Ohio market: the Worthington Farmers' Market, which paid a salary. In her spare time she was on the board of half a dozen sustainable ag and local foodshed groups.

In an article about her in the *Columbus Dispatch*, she'd been dubbed "the queen of local foods in central Ohio."

Now, heading into Columbus, he expected to get her voice-mail. *God knows how many phone calls she gets in a typical day*, he thought. She was a blur, doing three things at once, somehow coming up with new ideas and launching fresh initiatives while already juggling too many things. She'd been that way as long as Farmer had known her. Sandy said she was like that even as a little girl—her kid sister. Nancy could be brusque, but there was no arrogance in her. She was just passionate about what she was doing.

It was a happy surprise when she answered the phone.

"Farmer," she said. "What's up?"

"Sandy said I should call you. We need your help."

"Why? What's going on? Is Sandy OK? What's wrong?"

"Sandy's fine. My cattle are out and I can't find them."

"What do you mean you can't find them? Where are they?"

"Actually, they're somewhere in Columbus."

"OK. Ha ha. Good one."

"I'm serious. I've been tracking them all day. I just talked to a guy who saw them outside New Albany three hours ago. They're heading west on that new bike path from Granville."

"Farmer, come on!"

"I swear, Nancy! I know it sounds crazy. It is crazy! But I could really use your help."

"You *are* serious, aren't you? This is really happening? Where are you?"

"On 161, near Hamilton Road."

"OK, I've got an idea. Take the Hamilton Road exit and go south. You know where the Home Depot is?"

"Yes."

"Go park in the parking lot. I'll be there in ten minutes. I'm not far. I'm on a stakeout in Gahanna."

"If you're busy…"

"No, I'm coming. We're going to find your cows, Farmer."

She hung up.

When Farmer got to the Home Depot he parked in the middle of its parking lot, a long way from the dozens of cars clustered near its imposing orange storefront. He got out of his truck and waited.

Before long, Nancy's truck turned into the parking lot. Nancy saw Farmer waving to her, came toward him, and parked.

She really needed to get a new truck. This one was old when she bought it and she'd had it for a long time. It wasn't vintage old. It was more like *runs OK but gets bad mileage, has no air conditioning, burns a quart of oil every other week* old. Its outdated cap, patched here and there with duct tape, was full to the top of its windows with a jumbled mess of stuff she'd been hauling around for years.

Nancy got out and came over to Farmer. They hugged briefly.

Farmer said, "I really appreciate this. What did you say—you were on a stakeout?"

"Yep. Diane Lindsey, a vendor of mine at Worthington. Misty Meadows Poultry. I got an anonymous tip that Misty Meadows is actually apartment thirteen-D in the Kensington Grove Apartments."

"You're kidding."

"Oh, she is so busted. I just wish I knew where she's been getting all those eggs."

"I guess there's more to managing a farmers' market than I realized."

"It never ends. Now what about these cows of yours? What the heck is going on?"

"This guy let them out this morning. A kid who interned for Lucy Kellerman. He's vegan and thinks eating meat is immoral. So he let them out but then he abandoned them. They got on this bike path that's like a mile from our farm and they followed it into Columbus."

"That's wild, Farmer. Where do you think they are?"

"Right around here someplace. New Albany, or maybe Westerville."

"OK," she said. "Here's the thing. I haven't told anyone yet, but a couple months back one of the grant proposals I wrote got approved. So now, thanks to a Farmers' Market Support Fund established by Chipotle, the Worthington Farmers' Market has a drone."

"A drone?" Farmer said, bewildered.

"For farm inspections. It's too time consuming for me to drive around from farm to farm. Look at Misty Meadows. It took me a two-hour round trip, all the way up to Sunbury last week, to find out the address she gave me for her farm was actually her mother's hair salon. That's just one vendor out of a hundred. With this drone, I just punch in their location coordinates and off it goes. When it comes back, I download the images it took."

Farmer went with Nancy around to the back of her truck. She lowered the tailgate and reached inside the truck bed, which was full of many things—big sandwich board signs; boxes full of brochures; folding tables and chairs; plastic statues of pink pigs; umbrellas and towels and rolls of duct tape. She pulled a big cardboard box out onto the tailgate, then lifted it and put it on the ground behind her truck.

She opened the box, revealing the drone. It had four sets of helicopter-like blades.

"This is going to be perfect," she told Farmer. She pulled the drone out of the box and set it on the asphalt of the parking lot.

"It has multi-species recognition software. I just set it to cattle…" She was tapping a touch screen controller that had been in the box with the drone. "I mean it's not like there's going to be multiple herds of cattle roaming around New Albany. It'll keep circling in a search pattern till it finds your cows, then it will tell us where they are."

"This is amazing," Farmer said as the drone's blades started whirring. It lifted off the ground and hovered in front of them, about four feet in the air.

"It's freaking awesome," Nancy said. "Here goes." She tapped the touch screen again and the drone leapt straight up to a height of at least a hundred feet, then raced off in a southeasterly direction.

"Thank you, Chipotle!" she shouted as the drone disappeared from view.

TWENTY

AT THREE THIRTY, Sandy was in the vegetable garden. She had her cell phone with her in case Farmer called.

For half an hour she'd been on her knees, working the tomatoes. The season was nearly over. All August she and Farmer had gorged on tomatoes till they were sick of them and started to neglect the pruning and picking. Sandy had to prune now just to be able to get her hands in through the cages. She picked dozens of ripe fruit hidden inside. As many were on the ground, some half rotten. These she tossed in a five-gallon bucket. They'd go into the compost pile.

When she finished, she got the hose out to give the tomato plants a good soaking. Everything else was done for the year—the cucumbers, zucchinis and yellow squash, green beans—all exhausted, half buried in a riot of weeds.

In a week or so they would give up on the tomatoes too, picking all the remaining fruit, even the green ones—laying them out in the mudroom to ripen if they could. She and Farmer would pull out the trellises and cages, storing them in the shed.

Sandy was watering the tomatoes when she heard a vehicle turn onto the gravel of their lane. It kept coming. The dogs, lying in the front yard, jumped up and started barking as Sandy turned to face the crest of the hill, where the lane came into view. She had no idea who was coming. It didn't sound like the UPS truck. The dogs kept barking. They had their front paws up on the fence and were wagging their tails.

An old orange-and-white VW van came up out of the ravine. It showed a lot of rust, was missing its back bumper, and had tires that looked too small. A young man was driving.

The van pulled up beside Sandy's Subaru and stopped, sputtering and coughing for nearly a minute before it died. The young man got out. He was thin, wearing green army surplus pants and a blue T-shirt that said KALE. He was not smiling. Behind him, leaping at the fence, the dogs were going nuts, but he ignored them—didn't even turn to look at them. He came walking toward Sandy.

"Can I help you?" she said.

"I'm looking for Farmer."

"He's not here right now. I'm his wife. Maybe I can help you?"

"Well…I believe he has something that belongs to me."

All of a sudden she realized who he was.

"You're Lernovski!" she said.

"Paul Lernovski. I'm kind of a neighbor."

"You've got some nerve coming here."

"Yeah, well…"

"You better hope none of those cows get hurt."

"Hey, they chose freedom," he said. "Don't hold that against *me*. They had enough of life here at Auschwitz Acres."

"You idiot. You don't know anything about cows."

"I know they yearn."

"Like you do for Sarah? Sweet beautiful Sarah, oh, forever gone?"

"You've been reading my journal!"

"Good for her," Sandy said.

"Shows what you know. She called me today. She wants to get back together. We're going to live in her dorm room."

"She'll be sorry."

"Just give me my journal."

"I don't think so."

"It's mine. I need to get it before I leave town. I'm going back to Cleveland."

Sandy looked down at the hose's spray head she was holding. It was set to "gentle shower." She changed it, turning the dial to "jet spray."

"Your husband stole it. He had no right to—"

Sandy aimed the spray head at Lernovski. She squeezed the plastic trigger and a high-pressure stream of water flew toward him.

The water hit him with such force, in his face and chest, that he staggered back. Sandy released the trigger and the water stopped. Lernovski was sopping wet.

"Why did you do that?" he asked. "What's wrong with you?"

"Oh, I'm sorry," she said. "Did I interrupt you? I didn't mean to do that. Please, continue. You were saying something about how wrong it is to mess with other people's property?"

"I—" he started to say, but then she really let him have it, holding the trigger down, blasting him nonstop. He hopped around frantically, holding his hands up to protect his face. Then he turned and ran to the van. The stream of water hit him in the back as he hurried around the front of the van to the driver's side and jumped inside.

Sandy was about thirty feet from the front of the van. She couldn't get the right angle to spray Lernovski through the driver's side window, which she could see was open.

She heard him starting the van. *Well*, she thought, *I got him pretty good*. She dropped the hose. The dogs, who'd had that same hose turned on them numerous times (and for similar reasons) were silent now, sitting quietly on the porch trying to look like good dogs.

The van's engine kept struggling but did not turn over. Lernovski couldn't get it started!

Sandy quickly ran back to the garden and grabbed the five-gallon bucket. There were at least twenty half rotten tomatoes in there. Hurrying toward the van, she pulled one out and let it fly. It hit the van's windshield right in front of Lernovski's face, exploding with a splat. Lernovski stared at Sandy in disbelief through the juicy red pulp and little seeds. He kept trying to start the van as she advanced, throwing more tomatoes.

When she got closer, Lernovski frantically rolled up the driver's side window. He got it done just in time. A tomato burst against it.

Then the van started and Lernovski, desperate, backed up, away from Sandy and her bucket, turning till he could shift into forward and drive out the way he came. One last tomato hit the back of the van as it disappeared down into the ravine.

Sandy laughed. Here she'd thought she wasn't going to get much accomplished that day.

TWENTY-ONE

BART JENKINS, the mayor of Columbus, was in New Albany most of Tuesday attending a meeting of the Central Ohio Regional Planning Commission.

All morning, representatives of various outlying communities took turns airing grievances and asking for money. At noon a catered lunch was brought into the room—deli sandwiches, potato salad, chocolate chip cookies. While eating, attendees saw a short video depicting Columbus as an exciting tourist destination. Then the lights came up and they slogged through more agenda.

Jenkins made many promises. He was up for reelection in just two weeks.

He drove himself to the meeting, a rare pleasure. He'd just bought a 700 series BMW and had hardly had it out of the garage. He was always in the back seat of some Lincoln or Cadillac, on the phone or being prepped en route by staff.

Campaigning was such a grind.

"You know what? I can drive myself to New Albany this morning," he'd told his chief of staff on the phone, expecting her to argue.

But she'd said OK. "No problem. I'll have a couple aides meet you there. They'll have the notes from last night."

"Thanks, Sally."

"Don't forget. The Teachers Union is coming to meet with you at four thirty. You know how they feel about tardiness."

"Got it."

"Enjoy the beamer, sir."

It had given him some solace during the planning meeting to know that his car was outside in the parking lot waiting for him.

Now, at last, he was behind the wheel—alone, Ray-Ban sunglasses on, the sunroof open.

He was heading down Cherry Bottom, an older back road that rolled and curved through wooded hills—a green belt niched inside the city alongside Big Walnut Creek. It was a fun road to drive. The woods were beautiful and there were hardly any stop signs. The car was terrific, hugging curves easily as he flew along doing fifty, sixty miles an hour.

So what if he was a few minutes late for his meeting with the teachers.

Nearing the entrance of Sutter Park, he slowed in anticipation of a well-marked bike path crossing just ahead. As he rolled to a stop at the crossing, he saw cows approaching from his right. Six or seven of them. They were walking along by themselves, headed to the park, apparently.

He stopped the car and sat stupefied, watching them. Without any interruption of their steady pace, they started crossing the street in front of him.

Halfway across, one of the cows stopped, arched her back, and let fly a gushing stream of urine that splashed everywhere when it hit the pavement. Jenkins was certain it was splashing up onto his car. The cow, while urinating, looked over and made eye contact with the mayor. She did not look away.

This was adding insult to injury, he decided, and he tapped the accelerator just a little, jerking the car forward toward the cow. Her reaction was so quick he had to work it out later, replaying it in his mind. She seemed to leap straight up and twist in midair, letting go a kind of sidewinder kick with one of her back legs. She was already running when she landed and then all the cows were—faster than Jenkins would have thought possible. Tails up, bucking and galloping, they rushed into the woods.

Had the cow kicked his car? If so, it was his own fault. He had advanced into the crossing while pedestrians were in the roadway. Even being cows, they had the right of way. Didn't they?

Driving through the crossing slowly, he looked to his left, peering into the woods. The cows were gone. He couldn't see anything but trees.

A bit farther, where the shoulder of the road was wide enough, he pulled over and stopped. He got out to look at the front of his car. Spots from the cow's urine were all over the front grill and bumper. Even the little Bavarian Motor Works hood emblem, admired the world over, had been sullied. But there was no evidence of damage from the cow's kick. It had not landed, apparently. That was good.

Back inside his car, he called Sally.

"Sally, there are cows over here. Cows in the city!"

"What's that, sir?"

"Here a moo! There a moo! Everywhere a moo moo!"

"Sir, are you OK? Where are you? What's happening?"

He calmed himself. "I'm on Cherry Bottom Road, near Sutter Park. I just saw a herd of cows."

"Are you sure?"

"It's hard to be confused about seeing cows. They're cows!"

"But what are they doing there?"

"I don't know. Going to the park, I think."

"Sir, the teachers will be here in fifteen minutes."

"We cannot have cows in the city, Sally."

"I understand, but—"

"What's our campaign slogan?"

"Making Columbus a Now Town?"

"Yes, yes, a Now Town. As opposed to…"

"A Cow Town. Ah. I see your point."

Columbus had long been called a cow town—something probably started by Clevelanders.

"Those cows need rounded up and hauled away. They're a wandering photo op we don't need. Egg on our face. If I didn't know better, I'd suspect Parnell's people of releasing them just to mess with me."

Parnell. The opposition. In a dead heat with Jenkins two weeks before the election and surging. Their only debate was Wednesday night.

"Call Chief Williams and light a fire. The last thing we need is for the *Dispatch* or the TV channels to get hold of this."

"OK, I'll call him now."

Jenkins shifted his car into gear and pulled back onto Cherry Bottom. He told Sally, "I'm on my way. I'll be there in twenty minutes."

"What should I tell the chief if he asks for a description?"

"There were six or seven of them. Mainly black, some with white faces. I got a partial tag from one of them: sixty-something."

"Got it. OK, I'll let you know what he says."

"Thanks, Sally."

He hung up.

He couldn't help wondering if the appearance of these cows was somehow connected to the urban farming scene that had taken root in Columbus—a cultural development he'd resisted. Sally and others had counseled it was trending and to just accept it, but it really bothered him.

If folks want to farm they should move out into the country, he thought. *What good is zoning if you can't stop someone from having a milk goat? How can you uphold noise ordinances with roosters crowing at dawn? The whole business of managing a city is to keep it from spinning into chaos, and this urban farming thing has chaos written all over it. Homeowners tilling up their front yards, putting in pumpkin patches and rows of corn. Beekeepers setting up hives and the police getting emergency calls about swarms. Chickens turning up at animal shelters. Now there are cows?*

He drove down to where the glade of Cherry Bottom ended rudely, at its intersection with Morse Road. He turned into the tempo of heavy traffic in the afternoon glare, surrounded by power lines, curb cuts, and parking lots.

Why, he wondered, *can't folks be satisfied with the city as it is?*

TWENTY-TWO

IN THE HOME DEPOT PARKING LOT, waiting for the drone to come back, Farmer and Nancy sat on the lowered tailgate of her truck.

"So, when are you going to tell your vendors you'll be spying on them with a drone?" Farmer said.

"At the spring meeting, I guess. Think they'll be excited?"

"Some more than others."

"The thing is, the honest vendors, like your neighbor Lucy, who really are farming instead of loading up at Amish produce auctions, those guys should be happy. They're the ones I'm trying to protect."

"People are funny, though, about their privacy."

"Tell me about it."

Farmer and Nancy had been watching the sky while talking and now, hearing a high-pitched whine, they turned their heads and saw the drone. It was about fifty feet up, above the festive façade of the New Open Chinese Buffet. It was coming toward them.

Nancy picked up the controller and guided the drone in to a soft landing on the parking lot behind her truck. Its blades slowed, then stopped. She and Farmer walked over to it.

"Well, let's see," she said, squinting at a roadmap on the controller's screen.

"Looks like they're in Sutter Park," she said finally. "Just west of here, maybe a mile."

"On Cherry Bottom Road."

"Yep. It's huge. I can't get an exact fix on them, but they're in there somewhere. See?"

Squinting and cupping his hands above the screen to block the sun, Farmer looked at the image.

"Yeah, they're in a big open area way in back. I know where it is."

"Well, let's go!"

"No, it's better if I go alone."

"Are you sure?"

"I just want to lay eyes on them. If they seem OK, I'd rather let them be and come back first thing in the morning, when I'm rested. Pretty soon now, they'll start settling down for the night."

"I'm in an all-day conference tomorrow," Nancy said. "How early would you come in? I don't have to be there till nine."

"No, you're fine," Farmer said. "I've got people I can call to come help tomorrow. People who know cattle."

"Hey!"

"I'm kidding. You've done plenty."

"Uh-huh. I see how you are."

"No, really. I appreciate your help."

"How Sandy puts up with it, I don't know. Here, help me put this away."

Farmer held the cardboard box open while Nancy carefully put the drone inside. She shut the box's flaps and Farmer picked it up. He put it on her truck's tailgate.

"This thing is great," he said.

He lifted the box and wedged it inside the cap, between its fiberglass roof and the piles of stuff already inside. Nancy swung the tailgate up and shut the cap.

"All right then, Farmer," she said. "Good luck getting your cows home. Let me know if you need anything."

"I will."

"Hi to Sandy."

By the time Farmer was settled inside his truck—his keys wrangled up out of his pants pocket, his seatbelt secured, his phone connected to its charger—Nancy was long gone.

TWENTY-THREE

RON JACKSON, chief superintendent of Sutter Park, emerged from the park's maintenance building at exactly four thirty. He stepped briskly to the landscaped base of the big flagpole, and prepared to lower the American flag. Jackson was in his early forties, fit and trim, his shoes polished to a shine, his khakis creased. The raising and lowering of the flag was something he enjoyed attending to personally. The greatness of America and the freedoms and privileges its civilians enjoyed thanks to the sacrifices made by military heroes—this was what gave purpose and meaning to his days on duty at the park.

He lowered the flag and unclipped it, then started carefully folding it. As per normal, when he was done he would secure Old Glory inside the maintenance building; conduct a brief end-of-shift touch-base with the park's staff; lock up; then accompany the workers to the parking lot where, saying their goodbyes and each getting into their own vehicle, they would scatter.

Routine was the backbone of Jackson's equilibrium.

Today, however, just as he finished folding the flag, he saw the cows coming out of the woods at the top of the hill. Five adults and two calves. They had no escort that he could see. Where they had come from he had no idea. Not that he cared. Their presence in the park was simply unacceptable.

It was like in his vegetable garden at home. He would sometimes get volunteer tomato plants, in the compost pile or in among the lettuce or peas. His wife would think that was fun—serendipity!— and want to bring them along. But Jackson knew better. A weed was any plant out of place. Even if he relocated them—to where tomato plants should be; and if they prospered—he would never know what variety they were. Besides, he had already decided how many tomato plants to have. Better to destroy such volunteers, if possible prior to Mrs. Jackson learning of their existence.

Carrying the perfectly folded flag, Jackson approached the cows.

"Hey!" he shouted. "Hey! Go on! Go!" He made gestures intended to get them to leave. "Get out!"

"We just got here," 74 said.

Jackson stared at her. "Did you say something?" he said.

"We just got here."

"Oh good. I thought I was hearing voices." He breathed a sigh of relief, then said to the cows, "What exactly do you think you're doing here?"

"I think I'm eating grass," 38 said.

"Me too," 68 said.

"Eating grass," a couple other cows said.

"No."

"We're not?" 74 said. "Oh, I know. Talking with you?"

"No!"

"Give us a hint," 38 said.

"Is it a trick question?" 74 said.

"Stop talking!" Jackson had been told any number of times that he had communication issues, but this was the limit. He couldn't communicate effectively with cows?

He said, "Cows are not allowed in the park. You have entered a bovine-free area. Absolutely bovine-free. So now you will leave. You will turn around, go back the way you came, and once you are gone you will not come back."

"But we just got here," 42 said.

"We haven't even been to the pond yet," 38 said.

"That pond is strictly off-limits. I forbid you to go near it."

"We're thirsty," 74 said.

"You're not hearing me."

"We hear you," 42 said. "We just don't agree with what you're saying."

"There's nothing to agree about." Jackson could feel the anger rising up in him. "These are statements of policy."

"In your opinion," 42 said.

"Everybody has one. That's what Farmer says," 38 said.

"Please," Jackson said. "I don't want trouble."

"We're hungry," 74 said. "We're having a hard time finding enough to eat. Friends of ours recommended this place and we're glad they did. From the look of things, the grass here can hold out for two or three days. Then we'll be on our way. We don't mean to be any trouble."

"Please," Jackson said, but without much hope.

He knew nothing about cattle. But he could tell that once they decided they were not going to do something, they were not going to do it, period. They seemed to him the most intractable creatures he'd ever met.

"Please," he said again.

The cows did not reply. Some of them had resumed grazing.

Jackson took several deep breaths. If he could not control himself, how could he expect to control the park and everything in it?

Getting angry was a choice. It was a decision.

"It's OK, Ron," he told himself. "Just start over at the beginning." He made the high-pitched beeping sounds of a forklift backing up—a technique he'd learned in court-mandated sessions with Dr. Bernie Kohl, author of *Keeping the Rage Inside the Cage*.

When he was ready to "shift into forward," he said to the cows, "I'm sorry. I failed to properly introduce myself. My name is Ron

Jackson. I am chief superintendent of this park. I would like to speak with you about your unexpected appearance here. Can you please tell me which one of you is the head cow?"

The cows, still wondering about the beeping sounds, stared at him without saying anything.

Jackson pointed to 74, who was closest to him. "What about you, number 74? Are you in charge?"

"We sort of decide everything together."

"We're like a collective," 42 said. "We have a flat, non-hierarchal structure."

"Listen," Jackson said. "You seem like nice cows. But you cannot stay here. I don't mean to be rude, but I don't have time for this."

"Apparently you do have time," 27 said.

"What's that?" Jackson turned to face her. He could feel the composure he'd cobbled together already unraveling. "Are you giving me an attitude? Is that what you're doing?"

Thus confronted, 27 lifted her tail and let fall a piteous trail of thin manure that splattered on the grass.

"He's singling me out," she said, moving to get behind the others. They resisted, but she lowered her head and pushed between them, still trailing manure in fear.

"See, this is exactly what I'm talking about," Jackson said, pointing to the splattered shit. "This is totally inappropriate. Young children come here to play for God's sake."

"You're the one who made her nervous," 74 said.

"You singled her out," 42 said.

"Yeah, you blew her mind," 38 said.

"Just so we're clear. You're refusing to leave?"

74 said, "We are staying."

"OK," Jackson said. "That's fine. Just perfect. You guys stay right here. I'll be back."

He turned and walked away from the cows. When he got to the bottom of the hill he headed across the parking lot toward his Jeep Commander. He reached in his pocket for his key fob. He happened to have his golf clubs in the back of the Jeep—luckily, they were just what he needed. But which one? The stoutness of the wedge seemed like a good idea, but it was short-handled. One of the woods, perhaps.

"Mr. Jackson?"

It was Betty Marsh, one of his employees. She was older than Jackson, tall and athletic. She was wearing shorts and running shoes. She said, "We didn't know what to do when you didn't come back from taking down the flag, sir. We've been waiting for you. I came out to see if you're all right."

"Ah, yes, of course," Jackson said. Her voice saying his name was like a beacon calling him to shore. Just like that he could feel his rage subsiding. "I appreciate your concern, Betty," he said. "I'm fine. I got distracted by our bovine visitors."

She'd saved him from making a spectacle of himself. It might take a little longer than he would like, but he would remove those cows from the park. In a dispassionate and professional manner. With his dignity intact. He would study on it that evening.

"What are they doing here?" Betty said. "Why wasn't I notified?"

"They just showed up."

"Where did they come from?"

"I have no idea. But don't worry. They'll soon be gone."

Checking his watch, he saw it was five-of-five. "Come, Betty. Let's go inside. We can do without closing remarks today. I'll just lock up and we can all still leave on time."

They walked toward the maintenance building.

"What's that on the flag?" Betty said.

Jackson looked down at the flag and saw several brown spots on it. *Cow shit! Jesus Mary and Joseph! They desecrated the flag!*

TWENTY-FOUR

AT 4:45 P.M. OFFICER CHRIS MCCARTHY was at the Columbus Police Department gun range. He'd been there since two thirty, starting inside the main building shooting at paper targets, then progressing to a series of action scenarios outside—the so-called "obstacle course." All part of an annual review of his fitness to protect and serve.

For his fourth scenario, McCarthy was sitting in his parked cruiser waiting for the signal. A red light would blink.

When the light blinked, he unholstered his pistol, swung it out the car window, and waited. The front door of the mock convenience store opened and a target came out. McCarthy emptied all the rounds from his pistol as quickly as he could. At a distance of one hundred feet, he figured the more shots the better.

Reviewing with his instructor, he learned he'd killed the convenience store clerk, who was coming out of the store to talk to him, as well as a customer just inside the store and a dog left tied to a bike rack on the sidewalk. The perp, in this scenario, had gone out the back door.

The instructor stood beside McCarthy's cruiser holding a clipboard. He was not happy. "What's with you, McCarthy?" he said. "This makes you a perfect oh-for-four. I think this is even worse than Scenario Two."

Scenario Two: a domestic disturbance call. McCarthy had shot the couple's two young children.

"You're putting me in a tough spot here," the instructor said. "Honestly, you shouldn't be on the streets."

"You guys come up with the weirdest scenarios," McCarthy said.

"All based on true events. FYI, in this scenario we were hoping you would get out of the cruiser. Did that even occur to you?"

McCarthy didn't say anything.

"I'm failing you. We'll call your precinct to arrange a re-test next week. If you fail that one, you'll be reassigned to a job where you don't need a gun. You got one more chance." The instructor signed the form on his clipboard, tore off a copy, and handed it to McCarthy.

"All right. Thanks, Jim," McCarthy said.

The instructor, shaking his head, walked off.

McCarthy got a call from his sergeant. "Are you finished over there?"

"Just finishing now, Sarge."

"I need you to get over to Sutter Park, see if there are any cows there."

"Please?"

"Cows, McCarthy. This is coming from the chief, so don't mess around. Get over there."

"What's the story?"

"No story, just confirm if there are any cows in the park. Let me know. The chief is waiting to hear back."

McCarthy hung up. He drove to the automatic gate at the entrance to the training complex and waited for it to open.

He was just a few miles from Sutter Park. The training complex was on Morse Road between Karl and Cleveland, part of the re-purposing of the old Northland Mall site.

He merged into eastbound rush hour traffic.

It was five fifteen before he reached Sutter Park. He slowed down. Rolling by its main entrance, he didn't see any cows.

Continuing north on Cherry Bottom, he called in.

"Sarge, I'm over at that park. I don't see any cows."

"OK. Thanks."

"I see a zebra. I don't know if—hey, wait, there's a giraffe."

"All right."

"We got nothing better to do? What, are we animal control now?"

"Word came down, that's all. From high up, too. I'll pass it along."

"OK, Sarge."

McCarthy turned onto Old 161 and headed east. Since he was up this way, he would stop by the White Castle on Hamilton Road, grab a sack of sliders and some coffee. He could park behind the Walmart and eat, maybe catch a little shut-eye. His shift would be over at seven.

TWENTY-FIVE

IT BOTHERED 74 that the park—the only place they'd felt comfortable since coming to town—bore such an uncanny resemblance to the farm. The open grassy field surrounded by trees, the pond, even the strange beeping man in charge—it all amounted to a disappointing version of the place they'd left behind.

Maybe it was a mistake coming to town. Their mistake, but also Lernovski's. What did he know? He was always telling them how amazing they were, how beautiful, how special. But he'd also said they were the first cows he'd ever been around. He was a city boy (his words). It was exciting listening to him. They had never heard anyone talk like that. He made everything seem so important. But maybe it didn't mean much.

The cows had figured out one thing: for all his talk of unity and brotherhood, solidarity through organization, the stirring of the masses, Lernovski was a cull. He was isolated and friendless. He didn't even have a dog, and now Sarah was gone.

Who could blame her?

He told them he wasn't lonely, that ideas kept him occupied. He read a lot of books. But he'd seemed so solitary that morning, standing to one side as they headed single file into the woods, beginning their adventure. He'd been spending more and more time with them in the evenings, especially since Sarah went back to Cleveland. Now they had left him too.

Grazing not far from 74, 42 asked herself why grass inside the city was so bitter. It was true of rye they'd eaten as well as fescue. Even the clovers were bitter. That made her think the problem might be something other than the plants themselves—something city people were putting on the plants. But what? And why did they cut the grass so short? It looked like the farmer with the tiny tractor was making hay. Were they all doing that? Why?

She'd never had so many questions. They were bouncing around inside her like calves kicking to get out. This was after only one day away from the farm. She thought, *If these questions don't get answered, and tomorrow I have more and they don't get answered either, and each day brings more... How is that supposed to work?*

Everyone's shit was loose, but 106 and 102 were downright runny. When they lifted their tails to shit, a thin greenish liquid would squirt out of them. It was starting to crust up on their tails and rears.

Their mothers were concerned.

"When they're loose like this they don't get the benefit of what they eat," 68 said.

"Not that there's much benefit," 38 said. "This city grass is like bad hay."

27, overhearing them, said, "If you guys had listened to me, we wouldn't even be here. I tried to tell you. We should never have gotten on that path."

"27," 74 said. "That's enough."

"Enough of what? My being right?"

"You're here because you decided to stick with the herd. Nobody forced you."

"So now we can't discuss alternatives?"

"*I told you so* is not an alternative. You think you're the only one having second thoughts? Come on. The difference is you hold yourself apart."

"With you, it's always Big Me, little herd," 42 said.

"27 does make a point, though," 38 said. "What if—tomorrow—we turn around and head back?"

"To the farm?" 74 said.

"Winter's coming."

"Yeah," 68 said. "Time to hunker down."

"I'm not going back to the farm," 106 said. "I've already had more fun in one day than in my whole life."

"Your whole life?" 38 said. "You're not even a year old!"

42 said, "We need to review what to do. But first things first. We haven't had any water since the heaven place. Let's go to the pond. Then we can settle down for the night. We can talk in the morning, when we're rested."

TWENTY-SIX

FARMER TURNED in at the main entrance of Sutter Park. He followed the park's calm road into thick woods, keeping his truck at the posted limit of ten miles an hour. He was being watchful though he expected the cows were much farther ahead, in the open part of the park.

Still in woods, he came to a crossroads. Individual arrow-shaped signs pointed left, toward a Frisbee golf course and softball fields. Other arrow signs pointed right, toward picnic shelters, duck pond, deliveries. He turned right, toward where he and Sandy had been for a wedding a few years back. The road led to an open field-like area, fifteen or twenty acres, a broad sunny oasis sloping gently down to a pond. There was a parking lot near the pond and some picnic tables, a building with public restrooms attached. There were some big flower beds—the wedding had been in the midst of those—and a play area for little children with sand and a wooden climbing fort that looked like a pirate ship.

Farmer followed the little road as it passed several open-sided picnic shelters, each set in its own clearing and ready to host up to a hundred people. The shelters were named after famous Ohio State football players: the Eddie George Shelter, the Archie Griffin, the Jack Tatum. None were in use.

When Farmer reached the parking lot near the pond, he pulled in and parked facing the pond. And there they were! His cows! In the distance, at the top of the hill behind the pond grazing calmly, heads down, tails swishing. They seemed fine. Watching for several minutes, Farmer was able to get a count. They were all there.

For the first time since early that morning, he relaxed. Felt more like himself. Seeing the cows; being with them again, even like this—at a distance, without them knowing he was there—was at least a taste of the normalcy he'd been chasing all day.

He would take it.

There were no other people around. The park's day seemed done. It was five thirty, so the staff was gone. There were three other cars in the lot—a few last stragglers, probably out walking nature trails. In less than two hours it would be dark.

Not wanting to be spotted by the cattle, Farmer stayed in his truck.

He texted Nancy: "Found them. THX!!!"

Then he called Sandy.

"I found them," he said.

"Are they OK?"

"They seem fine."

"Where are they?"

"In Sutter Park. Remember? Where Bill and Jude got married."

"With the duck pond."

Farmer said, "I'm looking at them right now. They're grazing, like nothing's happened."

"Is Nancy there?"

"No, but she helped me find them."

"So, what now?"

"I'm coming home. They're calm here. When it starts getting dark, they'll settle down. I'll come back first thing in the morning."

"I'm glad they're OK," Sandy said.

Farmer could hear how tired she was. He hadn't noticed before. He realized it was her bad day too.

"I should be home in about an hour," he told her. "I was thinking about picking up a pizza. What do you think?"

"Just extra cheese on one half."

"OK. I'm on my way."

"Love you, Farmer."

"Same."

He hung up.

He'd been watching the cows while on the phone. They were working their way down the hill. It looked like they intended to drink from the pond before dark. If so, they would soon be close enough to recognize him. Preferring they didn't, he shifted into reverse, backed out of his parking space, and left the lot. He got on the park road leading back to Cherry Bottom.

TWENTY-SEVEN

THE MEETING with the Teachers Union had not gone well. Finally they left, lining up to collect parking passes from Sally as they exited the meeting room. Jenkins could hear them still grumbling as they headed down the corridor toward the elevators. He noticed they had pilfered all the pens, highlighters, and pads of paper that had been set out on the big table.

"What now?" he asked Sally when they were gone.

"While you were meeting, Mrs. Guildersnap called. She wants you to stop by before six."

Mrs. Guildersnap conducted all her business in person—never on the phone. She insisted on meeting one-on-one. She was old school, like a Mafia don. And when she sent for you, you went.

"Well, I better get over there," Jenkins said. "I'll drive myself, I guess. See, it's a good thing I have my car."

"I'll go down to the parking garage with you," Sally said. "We can talk on the way."

"Anything about those cows yet?"

"No sir, not yet. I'll let you know."

While they took the private elevator in his office down to parking level one, Sally prepped him for his meeting with Mrs. Guildersnap.

"She's holding a meeting of the Ladies' Society of Bexley later this week. She wants to squeeze you a little before proposing they endorse you."

The support of that group of no more than thirty wealthy older women—none of them older or wealthier than Martha Guildersnap, their founder—was critical. First, it meant a lot of cash. In Jenkins's first bid for office their contributions were 20 percent of his campaign funds. But they were influential in other ways too. One of the women, Eleanor Coyote, was the matriarch of the Coyote family, owners of the *Columbus Dispatch*. Her nephew George still ran the paper day-to-day.

"She likes her leverage," Jenkins said.

"Yes. And wields it like a baseball bat."

The elevator's doors slid open and Jenkins and Sally stepped out into the underground parking garage near where Jenkins's car was.

"What's on the old gal's mind?" Jenkins said.

"The library cutbacks. One of the branches slated for closure is a branch in Whitehall named after her husband."

"Can't we just leave it open?"

"It's the least utilized facility in the system."

"OK, I'll handle it. Anything else?"

"Not that I know of. But she'll come up with something. She always does before contributing money. And sir, we need that money. I need to be able to do a final push on TV and radio. Parnell's numbers are good but his campaign is running on fumes. A few more big contributions and we can bulldoze him."

Fifteen minutes later, Jenkins was driving east on Main Street. It was dusk as he crossed over I-71, at a standstill in both directions below him. He passed through several blocks of historic brownstones converted into law offices and headquarters for not-for-profits. Then he was in the slums. Old storefronts, nearly all abandoned, boarded up with plywood and covered with graffiti. Behind these, blasted neighborhoods where one house in three was vacant and not all the cars had tires. The only signs of life were occasional liquor stores or pawn shops. *Where*, Jenkins wondered, *do people who live here buy groceries?* The primary commerce left in this community was outdoors: shadowy figures standing on street corners watching for any car that might turn onto a pot-holed little side street and stop, window rolled down, looking for drugs.

Bexley was nestled deep inside these slums, some of the most dire in the city. It was an elegant old neighborhood, with a good number of stately mansions set under big trees. It was as if all the money in this part of town had been concentrated in these few fabulous households, leaving nothing but collapse and ruin all around them.

When Jenkins got to Mrs. Guildersnap's home, the wrought iron entry gate was open for him. He pulled in and parked in front of the imposing gothic home, made of stone, with leaded glass windows, towers, and a dark slate roof.

Thomas, Mrs. Guildersnap's man Friday, opened the mansion's big oak door before Jenkins could reach for the lion-head knocker.

"Mr. Mayor," he said, ushering Jenkins into the massive foyer and shutting the door behind him.

"Good to see you again, Thomas."

"Thank you. Good to see you too, sir."

"I hope she's in a good mood."

"Yes, of course," Thomas said, inscrutable as always. "I'll take you to her."

She was in her office. It had been her husband's, in deference to whom she had left hanging, at one end of the room, the mounted head of a rhinoceros. She was a small, frail woman, clearly diminished by age—shorter and thinner. Her skin was nearly translucent. But she still had a lively mind and spirit and an unmistakable air of command.

"Come in, come in," she said impatiently. Jenkins walked over to her as Thomas left, shutting the door. She did not offer to shake his hand. "I'm going out for dinner so we don't have long. Get yourself some scotch if you want it."

"I will have a little," he said. He walked over to the bar and served himself. "Shall I pour you some?"

"Never touch the stuff. Come, sit with me." She indicated two leather chairs over near the fireplace.

Glass in hand, he settled back into the leather chair—the most comfortable chair he'd ever sat in. He sipped the scotch, feeling the warmth of it spreading through him.

Mrs. Guildersnap said, "Andrew Carnegie believed a good library could uplift and enlighten like no other institution. I agree. They certainly do more good than churches. I am concerned that you are undermining the city's future by throttling the libraries."

"We're hardly throttling them," Jenkins said. "In fact, we're not even cutting the budget. We're simply reallocating funds, shifting resources, to get the biggest bang for our buck."

"Bang for the buck. As if the government knows anything about such things."

"It's unfortunate the library is closing the branch named after your husband. But, really, they had no choice. It's in such a bad neighborhood, it gets no traffic."

"It is precisely the poorest neighborhoods that need a library. A beacon in their midst."

"Well, I appreciate the sentiment," Jenkins said. "It's as fine and noble as this scotch. But, frankly, times have changed. Things are different now. No disrespect. The branch in Whitehall is mainly used by homeless people getting out of the weather. It's pointless to leave it open and even dangerous."

Mrs. Guildersnap stood, visibly shaken. She walked over to a large antique globe mounted on a wooden base. She stood contemplating it, then reached out and touched it, causing it to turn. Africa went by, then some of Asia.

Jenkins stood and joined her, holding his nearly empty glass. "I didn't mean to upset you. It's not a problem. We'll just rename some other branch, a much nicer and larger one, the Edgar Guildersnap Library."

"No, I think not. Times, as you say, have changed. I am persuaded. *Tempora mutantur…* Apparently libraries have exhausted their utility as remediators. Schools too, I would imagine. Oh well."

Jenkins was surprised to hear her being so reasonable.

Mrs. Guildersnap walked back to the leather chairs and sat. Jenkins followed her and sat again too.

She told him, "I am an idealist and there is no shame in that. But as my Edgar used to say, 'Sometimes it is time to cut bait.' An observation that served him well in real estate. The time has come for Plan B. If we cannot uplift the poor, then the priority must be protecting ourselves from them."

Wait. What? Jenkins thought.

"I've been told the police department has just opened a new SWAT Team Command Center. On the old Northland Mall property?"

"Yes, next to the gun range."

"Well, I want the naming rights to that facility. I will have it called the Edgar and Martha Guildersnap SWAT Team Command Center. We will establish a fund to provide ammunition, armored vehicles, whatever they need."

"Done," Jenkins said. "How generous."

He worried that the facility was already named, after a police officer who'd been killed in the line of duty heroically saving others. But this was the sort of detail he would not bother Mrs. Guildersnap with. "I'll get my staff on it. They'll call Thomas to schedule a ceremony."

"I suppose we should hurry. In case you are defeated by this Parnell fellow."

"With your help, and that of your friends, we will trounce him."

"I should hope so. My God, what a vapid man."

Jenkins's phone buzzed. He pulled it from his pocket, looked at it, and saw it was Sally. "Excuse me," he said. "This could be an emergency."

"Go right ahead."

"Sally," he said.

"Sir, I'm sorry to bother you. Can you do a breakfast at seven tomorrow with the Restaurant Association?"

"Sure, I guess so. If you're there."

"I'll let them know. Are you still with her?"

"Yes."

"Is she satisfied?"

Jenkins held the phone down and said, "Sally wants to know if you are satisfied."

"I am somewhat mollified. For the moment."

"I heard," Sally said. "I'll let you go. Call me when you're in your car. Oh, and the police didn't see any cows. Chief Jackson says maybe they were deer."

"No, they were not deer," Jenkins said, irritated. "I know what deer look like. They were cows. You tell him to keep checking."

He hung up.

"I swear," he muttered, putting his phone away.

"What's this about cows?" Mrs. Guildersnap said.

"It's the damndest thing. This afternoon I was driving in New Albany and all of a sudden, out of nowhere, I see a bunch of cows. They're on their own, just walking around. They crossed the street right in front of me."

"A bunch of them, you say?"

"Half a dozen or so."

"How odd. What kind of cows? Were they dairy cows?"

"Heck, I don't know," Jenkins said.

"My God, Jenkins. Are you unable to distinguish between beef and dairy cattle?"

Jenkins shrugged.

"What color were they?"

"Black mostly. Some had white faces."

"Baldies," she said. "An Angus-Hereford cross. They can be damn fine animals. And most certainly beef producing."

"Mrs. Guildersnap, I'm confused. How is it you know about cows?"

"That's how Edgar and I got started. When we married, we moved onto his family's farm. He took over the dairy herd and we did the milking."

"You milked cows?"

"Come now, Jenkins. I am not a royal. With lots of hard work and, yes, some manure on our shoes, Edgar and I fought for everything we have. We worked till there was not light enough to see. We'd be up again before dawn, having meat for breakfast, lacing up our boots.

"Back then, there was no safety net. You had to be tough and smart. And even then you had to count on family and neighbors. And they relied on you.

"There were times when we would get two or three feet of snow. Edgar and other farmers would get together and work day and night to keep the roads open—so the milk truck could get through. In our township, nobody ever had to pour out even a single gallon."

"I had no idea." Jenkins had trouble relating to what she was describing. He and his two sisters had been raised on less than half an acre, and a lawn service company had come to take care of that.

"Certainly," Mrs. Guildersnap said. "Then they built I-270 along the southern edge of our farm. His parents had passed by then. Just like that we had two miles of prime frontage. There's a Walmart now where our milking parlor was. All that good ground paved. Beaver Creek, where we swam, was forced underground, channeled through galvanized pipes so they could squeeze in a few more fried meat franchises.

"Edgar dealt with all those people, lawyers and money men, flying in from New York with their proposals: here a hotel, there a mall with escalators and fountains. He was good at it. Parlayed a thousand acres into the fortune I have now."

"I knew he was in real estate," Jenkins said.

"I do not mean to over romanticize the years we spent farming," Mrs. Guildersnap said. "The work was brutal. It never ended. We were like mules in harness when I look back on it. Edgar had back troubles all his life. That's why he was never any good at golf.

"But I will tell you this: I miss the cows. To this day I miss them. Such gentle, trusting creatures. When cattle are content, Jenkins— when you've finished your chores and they have everything they need—there's no better feeling in the world. A kind of peace comes over you. An equilibrium.

"Come," she said, standing. "I want to show you something."

Jenkins stood and walked with her over to her big desk. She went behind the desk, to a formal portrait of Edgar that was on the wall, and slid the portrait to one side, revealing a round metal safe. She opened the safe and reached inside.

"Here it is," she said. She turned and came to Jenkins holding a curled little black-and-white photograph two inches square. She handed it to him.

He looked and saw a young man in overalls standing next to a wooden cart. The cart was parked on the side of a dirt road, next to a rural mailbox. On the cart stood a young boy, maybe six years old, with the same face as the man—the same nose and chin—and wearing overalls made of the same material. He was no taller than the metal containers on the cart beside him.

"What are those metal things?" Jenkins said.

"Milk cans, of course. That is a photo of Edgar and his father. They're out by the road, waiting for the milkman to come collect the day's milk. That's from 1931."

Jenkins handed the photo back to her.

She spent some time looking at it.

"This was always Edgar's favorite photo of his father."

She put it back in the safe, shut the thick door and locked it. She slid Edgar's portrait back in place.

When she turned around, Jenkins thought he saw the smallest trace of a tear welling in one of her eyes. It was hard to be sure.

TWENTY-EIGHT

WHEN DANNY GOT TO THE PARK, he found the cows standing in the pond, in water up to their stomachs. He parked in the empty parking lot, got out of his car, grabbed his Coke and his sack of food and headed toward the pond.

38 saw him first.

"Look! It's Danny!"

"Hey, Danny," several cows said.

"Greetings, cows. What are you doing?"

"We're drinking," 74 said.

"Oh, OK. Cool. I thought maybe you were taking a bath." He sat cross-legged on the grass near the pond. "I thought I would come over, see how you guys are making out. I brought my dinner."

"Your burrito?" 38 said.

"Yes." Danny was surprised she remembered. "And some Funyuns."

"Funyuns?" 27 said.

"Yeah, they're kind of like…" He realized he didn't know what they were. "Well, they're really tasty, and they're fun to eat."

He unwrapped one end of his burrito and took a bite. It was still warm inside and delicious. He drank some Coke.

"Did you guys get enough to eat?" he said.

"Yes," 74 said. "The grass here is better."

"I'm glad. It's kind of rough being around you guys when you're hungry."

74 said, "We're not meant to be hungry. There should always be more ahead of us than we need."

"I feel you," Danny said, taking another bite of his burrito.

The cows finished drinking and one by one climbed up out of the pond. They came over and stood in a circle around Danny, watching him.

"Jeez, you guys are huge," he said, looking up at them. "From this angle, you're like monsters."

68, one of the cows in front of him, started cleaning out her nostrils with her tongue.

"68! What are you doing?" Danny said.

"What?" She stepped back.

"Just the craziest thing I've ever seen. And the coolest. How can you do that?"

"What?" she said.

"You totally just put your tongue inside your nose. Like all the way in."

"Oh. I was cleaning it."

"Cleaning it?!" Danny said. "Do it again!"

68 obliged, sliding her tongue inside her left nostril. She didn't see the point. She'd already got everything out of there.

"Can all you guys do that?"

"Sure," several cows said. Some of them started sticking their tongues inside their nostrils.

"OK, this is absolutely my new favorite thing about cows."

"It's easy," 38 said. "You can do it."

"Well, you know? I've never tried. It never occurred to me. Hold on. I'm going for it."

The cows watched as Danny tried, the ones behind him crowding around to the sides so they could see. He stuck his tongue straight out as far as he could, then curled it up toward his nose. He couldn't touch his nose, much less slide his tongue deep inside it.

He tried again, then gave up.

"Not even close," he said.

"How do you clean your nose out?" 106 said.

"I use a finger."

"Well, that's just as good," 74 said.

"No way. Using your tongue is way better. Like say I'm carrying something really heavy with both hands. Or I'm hanging from a cliff. Or I'm tied up. Or I've been in some heinous accident and I'm paralyzed from the neck down. No problem; just send in the tongue."

"Maybe if you practice," 38 said. "Each day get a little closer."

"No. It's not going to happen… But hey, you know what? I could make a video of you guys doing it. People would love that. It would be immense."

He put his burrito down. Soon he had his phone ready.

"OK, who wants to?"

"Me!" 106 said. He came around and shoved in next to 38, in front of Danny.

Danny held up the phone. "OK, little dude. Go!"

He hit record. 106 stuck his tongue in his left nostril, then in the right one, then back and forth quickly.

Danny stopped recording. He reviewed the video, laughing. "Awesome! Good job, 106! This'll be show and tell supreme at the bookstore tomorrow."

He put the phone down and went back to eating his burrito.

The cows watched him with big calm unblinking eyes. When the burrito was gone, he opened the bag of Funyuns and ate some, making crunching sounds.

"I would offer you guys some, but I don't know if they'd be good for you. Hell, I don't know if they're good for me."

"You said they were delicious," 38 said.

"Oh yeah, beyond compare."

"We judge food by how good it tastes. The better it tastes the better it is for us."

"That might work for cows," Danny said. "But for people, the tastiness of something is lots of times the result of how it's been engineered by some mega food company. Taste is like a trick they know how to play on us. Stuff like this, it's not even really food exactly. It's more like something fun."

"It's fun to eat them?"

"Well not *now*. Not if we're *discussing* them."

He closed the bag, rolling it up so the contents would not get stale. He knew the crave for Funyuns would return. Probably later that night. Besides, he had almost three dollars invested in them.

"Danny, we're going back up the hill now," 74 said. "You're welcome to come."

"Sure. You guys go ahead. I've got to go to my car real quick. I'll catch up."

The cows started walking uphill toward the woods. Danny carried his Coke and rolled up bag of Funyuns to his car. He put the bag inside on the passenger seat. He put the Coke on the car's roof, then opened the back door and grabbed an Ohio State sweatshirt that was on the back seat. He slipped it on over his head. The sun was setting. It was early September and there would be plenty of warm sunny afternoons yet. But the evenings and early mornings were starting to get chilly. Summer was definitely over.

He rolled up his car's windows. Then, carrying his Coke, he left the parking lot and headed uphill toward the cows. They were already settling down near the woods. They were lying down, upright, their legs tucked under them, calmly chewing cud.

Half an hour later it was almost dark. Danny was stretched out, lying on his back in the grass, his hands cupped behind his head. He was looking up at the dark blue sky. He could see the silhouettes of treetops.

"OK, I want to ask you guys something," he said. "It's about these numbers you have. What's up with that?"

"What do you mean?" 74 said.

"OK, like you're 74. That's your number. But don't you have a name?"

"74 *is* my name."

"No, that's your number. It tells you apart from other cows. But it's not a name."

"I guess names are for people."

42 said, "Farmer's dogs have names. Max and Chloe. He doesn't call them one and two."

"Maybe because they live in the house," 74 said.

68 said, "That doesn't explain Sandy's horse, Valentine."

"Right, but Valentine's the only horse. There's a bunch of us so we need to have numbers. To keep things straight. All our medical information, our histories—everything's connected to our numbers."

"I get it," Danny said. "It makes sense you have numbers. I'm just saying it feels weird, hanging out, to not have names to call you. You see what I'm saying? I mean, people have both—names *and* numbers."

"Really?" 42 said.

"Sure. There's lots of people and only so many names, so there ends up being a bunch of Dannys and Sallies and Joes. But for official business, like you're saying—medical records, stuff like that—they use numbers to keep track of us."

"Like the boy we met," 102 said. "He was 4½, but that man called him Mason."

"Wait. What boy?" Danny said.

"A boy we met. He said he was 4½."

Danny laughed. "A real little guy, was he?"

"Yes."

"Four-and-a-half is how old he is. He was telling you he's four-and-a-half years old."

"Oh," 102 said.

106 said, "Oh wow. How embarrassing."

"Shut up, 106."

38 said, "What's your number, Danny?"

"230-71-4823."

"You're lucky you don't have to wear an ear tag. It would be huge."

Danny laughed. "You're right. But we don't wear our numbers. We keep them secret. So nobody can steal them."

"Why would someone steal your number?" 42 said.

"So they can pretend to be me." Danny could tell the cows were confused. "It's like people steal other people's numbers. But it's not the numbers they want. They're trying to steal their identities."

"Danny, I'm pretty sure you're blowing our minds right now," 74 said.

A while later, they'd fallen silent again. It was totally dark. Still lying stretched out on his back, Danny could hear the cows chewing. The earthy smell of dew was in the grass. In the distance was the noise of highway traffic on I-270.

"Hey, Danny?" one of the cows said.

"Yeah? What?"

"Do you want to go to heaven?"

"What?!" Danny said, surprised. Then, speaking carefully, he said, "Well, for me, and this is just what I think, OK—I don't believe in heaven. As far as I'm concerned, there's no such place."

"But it's in Ohio, isn't it?"

Heaven in Ohio, Danny thought. *Man, these cows are a trip. Where in Ohio?* he wondered. *If it was in Dayton it shut down and moved away a long time ago. If it was in Cincinnati it would be Mt. Heaven. In Cleveland, Heaven Heights. Yeah, Heaven Heights; over on the east side.*

Danny started giggling.

People in Shaker Heights would insist Shaker is better—closer in, more diverse.

He thought about Pittsburg then, where he'd lived as a little kid. *Heaven, PA. Yes! Almost West Virginia!*

He said, "What makes you guys think it's in Ohio?"

"We were told it's not far."

"OK, but didn't it sound a little too perfect? Too good to be true?"

"It sounded wonderful."

"Well, in my experience, if someone is telling you about heaven, it's because they want something from you."

"That's kind of what we thought, but I had to ask."

There was another long silence, then one of the cows said, "What about Cuba, Danny? Is Cuba real?"

"Yeah, sure, Cuba's real."

"Yes! And free, thanks to Fidel."

Another cow called out, "Hasta la Victoria!"

TWENTY-NINE

IT WAS NEARLY DARK when Ron Jackson pulled the big black-domed BBQ grill out of his garage. He parked it in the driveway. With its dome and grill set aside, he dumped half a bag of charcoal in. He squirted lighter fluid on the briquettes, then threw a lit match at them. A huge flame leapt up into the evening air—a fireball that whooshed up over his head. Then the flames settled down, starting to consume the charcoal. Jackson held his hands above the fire to check its progress. It would be a while, another ten minutes at least, before it was hot enough. He needed a strong fire tonight. He wasn't roasting weenies.

Behind him, Mrs. Jackson opened the kitchen door. She was holding the cordless phone. "Ron, honey, you have a phone call."

"Can you please take a message?"

She said, "If I understood, I think it's someone from the mayor's office."

"The mayor's office?!"

"I think that's what she said." She held the phone out as he came to take it from her. "It's on mute."

He pushed the mute button and held the phone up. "Hello?"

"Mr. Jackson?"

"This is Ronald Jackson."

"Hi. I hate to bother you. I got your number from Commissioner Jarvis. My name is Sally Martinez. I work with Mayor Jenkins."

"Yes?"

"I'm the mayor's chief of staff... Mr. Jackson, you're in charge of Sutter Park, is that correct?"

"Yes I am."

"Were you over there today? This afternoon?"

"Yes."

"Do you have any knowledge of cows being in the park?"

"Yes! They showed up about the time I was leaving. Around four thirty."

He could hear her telling someone who was with her, "He saw them." Then she spoke into the phone again. "Do you know whose cows they are, Mr. Jackson?"

"No, they just showed up. Nobody was with them."

"Sir? I'm going to put you on hold for a minute. Is that all right?"

"Sure."

Jackson, holding the phone aside, whispered to Mrs. Jackson, who was hovering nearby, "It's about the cows."

Her eyes opened wide with surprise.

Sally Martinez came back on the line. "Sir, I am putting the mayor on."

Then the mayor—Jackson recognized his voice!—said, "This is Bart Jenkins."

"Your Honor."

"You saw cows in Sutter Park today?"

"Yes, sir."

"Describe them."

"There were five adult individuals and two juveniles. They were unaccompanied. Mostly black, but a couple brownish red, some with—"

"What the hell are they doing there?" the mayor said.

"Sir, I am unable to explain their presence."

"We need to get rid of them!"

"Sir?"

"We need them gone, Jackson. And not just out of the park. Out of town altogether. Gone! As if they'd never been there! Immediately! Do you understand?"

"Yes, sir."

"Those damn cows…"

"I have to tell you, sir, I did try talking to them. I asked them to leave but they refused. They're very stubborn, sir."

"Stubborn?!" the mayor said. "Is that what you're saying? The cows are stubborn?"

"Sir, I—"

"Listen, Jackson, are you going to be able to take care of this or not? Maybe you're badly placed over there. Sally!" he shouted. Then Jackson could hear muffled voices and some other noises—like there was a scuffle. Then Sally Martinez came on the line.

"Mr. Jackson?"

"Yes?"

"We're quite tense here. We're preparing for tomorrow night's debate."

"I understand," Jackson said.

"The mayor has every confidence in you."

"Tell him not to worry. I'm exactly the right guy for this. Those cows are history."

"We are encouraged to hear you say that, Mr. Jackson. And of course grateful. Now, I must stress how important discretion is when it comes to a matter like this. The less attention the better. You can appreciate that, can't you?"

"Yes, ma'am."

"Will you call me, please, at this number when the cows are gone? This is my cell."

"I sure will."

"Thank you, Mr. Jackson. Goodbye."

She hung up.

"What in the heck is going on?" Mrs. Jackson said.

"The mayor wants me to get rid of those cows. He just authorized me to handle the situation by any means necessary. And it will be my pleasure."

"Oh, Ron, you can't get all upset, you know that's dangerous."

"Don't worry, I'll be professional," he said. "But that doesn't mean I can't enjoy it."

Mrs. Jackson said, "What if you lose control? You need to keep it in the cage, honey."

"The fire should be ready now," Jackson said. "I won't be long."

He went outside. It was completely dark. The heap of charcoal inside the Weber was bright red. He could feel the extreme heat coming off the grill from twenty feet away. It was ready.

He walked to his Jeep, which was parked on the driveway closer to the street. He opened its rear hatch. Inside was the black plastic trash bag. He grabbed it and shut the hatch, walked back to the grill.

He opened the bag and pulled out the flag. It was still folded in a triangle.

"This flag," he said, "has served well and long. But now it is desecrated. It has cow shit on it and can no longer represent the nation."

He stepped up to the grill, into its fierce blasting heat, and dropped the flag on top of the charcoal, retreating quickly as flames engulfed it.

When he was a good twenty feet back, he turned and snapped to attention, saluting the flag as it burned.

He put his right hand over his heart and pledged allegiance to it: "I pledge allegiance to the flag of the United States of America, and to the Republic for which it stands, one nation, indivisible, with liberty and justice for all."

Then he stood watching the flames in silence.

Yes, with liberty and justice for all, he thought. For all *people*.

THIRTY

BY THE TIME FARMER GOT HOME it was dark. Sandy had left the outside light on for him. He got out of his truck, then leaned back in, collecting the warm pizza box and the twelve-pack of beer. Walking to the mudroom, he could hear the dogs inside the house barking and scrabbling at the windows.

The day had turned out to be a big departure from his settled lifestyle. He'd been thrust into the role of hunter-gatherer: out all day tracking animals across the open landscape; returning home with provisions he'd collected at the Beverage Barn and the pick-up window at Johnny's Villa Pizza.

He was exhausted, but not discouraged—nowhere as rough as he would have been had he not found the cows.

By seven thirty—the pizza mostly eaten, its surviving pieces scattered in the grease-stained box—Farmer was well into his telling of the day. He'd consumed three or four beers, giving momentum and emphasis to his presentation.

The dogs were under the table, their noses aquiver with pizza smells.

Sandy, drinking water, was sitting at the table with half of her second piece of pizza on a plate in front of her. She was listening. Occasionally she would add a comment or question, but she understood this was a monologue—not a conversation.

Earlier, getting plates out for the pizza, bringing a roll of paper towels to the table, Sandy told Farmer about Lernovski's visit. ("You know, it's such an old expression, you don't think of it as being literal; like cars having horsepower. But to actually throw rotten tomatoes at someone? Someone who deserves it? Oh man, it's awesome!")

That was some time ago, before Farmer got going. Now he was like a fast-moving freight train coming off the mountain.

"I'm not kidding you. I opened the door and that freak was standing right there. You should have seen the look on his face. If I'd reacted a little faster, I probably could have grabbed him."

"I'm glad you didn't."

"I don't know what I would have done."

And a bit later: "I just know that shifty son of a bitch meant to steal them." Meaning Pastor Rod. "He had these beady little eyes. I asked him how he was going to find me if he got them loaded. I came right out and asked him point-blank. He had nothing."

Farmer was up, walking around, holding a can of beer—gesturing with it as he talked.

"I swear to God," he said. "That drone shot up like two hundred feet and took off doing fifty miles an hour! At *least* fifty miles an hour! It was incredible! We need to get one!"

Another beer in, he told Sandy, "It was so great to finally see them. I can't tell you."

He came back to the table and sat across from her, the pizza box between them. He wanted more pizza, but was already full. When he was younger he could have finished a pie like that by himself and still be hungry for breakfast the next morning.

"So, what now?" Sandy said. This far into the evening, taking into account the beers and his belly full of pizza, she figured Farmer would be asleep in less than half an hour. He would be out cold, flat on his back, as if he'd been carried to the bed and left there. If she wanted any information she needed to get it quick.

"What do we do now?"

"I don't know," Farmer said, vaguely irritated.

"You could hire Dave Monroe, like you said. You should call him. It's only eight o'clock. You could call Sonny and Brett, too."

"I'm not calling anyone," Farmer said.

"At least call Dave. Just to see if he's available."

"I probably should, you're right." He was surprised to see his beer was empty. How did that happen? He thought of getting up to get another one but that seemed unnecessary. He was already having trouble keeping his eyes open.

He stood and went over, leaned down to put an arm around Sandy and hugged her, then headed toward the bedroom to collapse.

Sandy dropped the last two pieces of pizza in the dogs' food bowls. When they'd finished, she let them out so they could pee. She went around turning off lights, shutting the house down for the night.

By the time she came in the bedroom, Farmer was dead to the world, snoring. The dogs were curled up against him looking at her.

THIRTY-ONE

BY SEVEN THIRTY, downtown Columbus was mostly deserted. Some COTA buses were still running—totally empty, like ghost ships passing through block after block of little daytime stores and sandwich shops, all shut down for the night. Security lights illuminated alleys and the service entrances of office buildings.

A gleaming black limousine came westbound on Broad Street, gliding calmly through all green lights. At Third Street it turned left and went by the State Capitol, then the Sheraton at Capitol Square. It pulled to the curb and stopped in front of a little restaurant on the east side of the street. There was a valet station next to its entrance. A red canopy with gold tassel trim extended to the curb, where a pair of planters held tightly trimmed shrubs.

Thomas, the driver of the limousine, got out. He went to the back door, opened it, and offered his hand to Martha Guildersnap. She took it, emerging from the back. She was wearing a black overcoat and a round green hat. As she steadied herself on Thomas's arm, the maître d' came outside to greet her.

"Good evening, Mrs. Guildersnap. Welcome to Le Canard Enchaîné."

"Hello, George," she said, taking his arm. "Thank you, Thomas."

"Yes, ma'am." Thomas walked back to the limo and stood beside it. He would wait until she was in the restaurant before leaving.

George walked Mrs. Guildersnap to the entrance, then inside the restaurant. It was small and intimate, dimly lit. Most of the linen-topped tables were occupied. Well-dressed patrons, many of them older, were talking quietly, sipping wine, lightly clinking their dinnerware as they ate.

Mrs. Guildersnap handed her hat and coat to one of the hostesses, and George led her across the dining room to her usual table. It was near the fireplace.

"Do you prefer the fire tonight or would you rather sit facing it?" he said.

"I'll have the fire."

He seated her with her back to the warmth of the small crackling fire.

Placing a menu on the table in front of her, he said, "Chef hopes you will take the prix fixe tonight. He made it with you in mind when he heard you were coming."

"Certainly. Other than my Edgar, and Thomas of course, Chef is the one reliable man I know."

George nodded.

"I'll be right back with your tea," he said.

"I'm expecting Eleanor Coyote."

"Yes, she called. She's running five, ten minutes late."

When George walked away, Mrs. Guildersnap looked down at the menu and studied the prix fixe. It suited her exactly. Chef had even included something with capers. Still, for some reason, she found herself wishing she could have a big bowl of chicken and noodles on mashed potatoes, with plenty of pepper. Or liver and onions smothered in gravy. *My God*, she wondered. *How long has it been since I tasted bacon?*

THIRTY-TWO

ONE MILE NORTH of the Ohio State campus, an old orange-and-white VW van with balding tires and dried tomato pulp on some of its windows parked along the curb in front of the Pita Hut and Grill. The van shook violently, sputtering and coughing to a stop.

Lernovski got out. It was eight o'clock, already as dark as it would get along that delinquent stretch of North High Street. He considered locking the van. He'd cleared anything he cared about out of that crappy little trailer earlier that day, and now it was all in the van, stuffed in his duffel bag. He caught himself—locking the van would be so bourgeois.

He went inside the restaurant. The brightly lit dining room was empty. There were cheaply framed travel posters for Beirut and Tripoli; a flat-screen TV showing a muted soccer game. The owner, Mohammed, was sitting on a stool behind the counter watching the soccer game half-heartedly.

Lernovski ordered a falafel with extra cucumber, paid, then sat at one of the tables to wait for his food.

He checked some local news sites on his phone for any mentions of the cows. There was nothing. The media, like some golem serving corporate interests and protecting the status quo, was never alert. They were so busy talking about the Auto Show or which Hollywood movie made the most money that anything spontaneous or unexpected, that actually *was* news, would go unnoticed. Still, if those cows made it to town, they would be hard to ignore. They would definitely get featured, at least in local media. It wasn't like they had anything else to report on.

Mohammed came out from behind the counter carrying Lernovski's pita on a plastic tray. "Here you go, my friend," he said, putting it on the table. "Falafel, extra cucumber. Enjoy."

Lernovski hadn't eaten all day. He ate the sandwich quickly.

He texted Sarah, letting her know he would be hitting the road soon and should be in Cleveland by 11:30. He would come straight to her dorm.

And so, he thought, getting up from the table to leave the restaurant, *this is how it ends.* His four-month foray into agriculture. Another chapter in his development. If those cows gained celebrity and could contribute to changing people's attitudes toward animal farming, that would nicely enhance his application to grad school. Of course, it would help if he had that journal.

He got behind the wheel of the van and started it. It ran but the engine didn't sound right. It was making a kind of high whine, and then it started shaking, rocking the back of the van. Dark horrible smoke was billowing up. It smelled awful. Finally there was a big explosion, accompanied by more smoke, and the engine died.

Oh no, Lernovski thought.

He turned the ignition key off, then tried turning it on again. Nothing.

Lernovski had been expecting an event like this ever since he bought the van. It was so cool, he had to have it. But it really needed an owner who was a mechanic—someone who could be tinkering with it, checking the oil and whatnot.

Well, so much for that, Lernovski told himself.

Leaving the key in the ignition, he got out of the van. He slid open the back door and pulled his duffel bag out. He grabbed the smaller knapsack and put it on his back, shut the van, and, picking up the duffel bag, started walking south on the sidewalk.

He would get to a COTA bus stop and look for a bus to take him downtown. He could spend the night at the Greyhound bus station, then in the morning catch a bus to Cleveland. A ticket would be like forty dollars.

He was sorry to lose the van. But maybe it was just as well. Parking around Case Western was really tough and he could just use Sarah's car.

THIRTY-THREE

WEDNESDAY

LONG BEFORE THE SUN CAME UP, Farmer was in the kitchen quietly fixing himself a breakfast of scrambled eggs, toast, and coffee. Sandy and the dogs were still asleep. He carried his food to the little table and sat down to eat. According to his weather app, it was fifty degrees. It was supposed to be a clear day, partly cloudy, high in the low-seventies. The first real chance of rain was Friday.

After all of yesterday's uncertainty, it felt good to be up early, getting ready to do his chores. They weren't exactly his normal chores. For one thing, he had to commute into Columbus to do them. But they were basically the same: check on the herd; see how they're doing; make sure they have what they need.

When he finished eating, Farmer put his plate and fork in the sink. Using the yellow pad of paper Sandy had for making lists, he wrote a note to leave on the table:

Columbus.

Back by lunch.

Love,

Farmer

He really did love her—after twenty-five years, more than ever. Felt lucky to be with her. She was smarter than he was. Read books instead of watching football or some gangster movie for the twentieth time. Drank hot tea instead of beer. For a snack, she would eat an actual piece of fruit.

She was the one who handled all the bills and bank accounts, kept files and did the taxes. Jim Grant, their accountant, said Sandy was the most organized client he had. Farmer was doing well if he could keep from losing his keys.

In her own quiet way, Sandy seemed as settled and content with farming as Farmer. She didn't get lonely. Didn't seem to mind the physicality of it—the ongoing chores, time spent outside in weather. He noticed, hearing her talk to others, that she took pride in the farm as he did: describing the barn they'd built, the uses they'd found for the new front-end loader.

She could be fierce in defending the farm, too. Lernovski had found that out. If the electric company sent a crew to trim trees close to the lines, she'd be there watching, ready to object. She confronted trespassing hunters as readily as Farmer did, escorting them off the property, giving them hell the whole way even though they were carrying loaded guns.

The cattle in particular were Farmer's thing. Sandy would help out when needed. But for her there was no special satisfaction in having cows. It was her horse, Valentine, that completed the farm for her, something that made no sense at all to Farmer. She hardly ever rode the horse. But what did it matter what he thought?

On a farm, everybody needs to have their own thing. Otherwise, they are badly rooted.

Farm life can come to seem like nothing more than a numbing sum of mud and chores, weeds, back problems and sunburns, insects, broken down equipment, shit on your shoe, mashed thumbs and poison ivy.

So many marriages are destroyed by farming. If either person starts to resent the farm—gets discouraged; starts daydreaming about living in town, with weekends and steady salaries, beyond the rough reach of nature—that's a divorce waiting to happen. There's no defense for farming. No explanation good enough. It'd be hard to imagine the marriage counselor who wouldn't conclude, "It sounds to me like the best way forward might be to sell the farm."

In the mudroom, putting on his boots, Farmer remembered a Valentine's Day card Sandy had given him years back. On the front it said: *I love you just the way you are.* Then, inside the card: *Just don't get any worse!*

He was trying!

It was hardly ideal, the situation he was in with his herd. They'd left him. But the fact that they'd gone through an open gate was natural. He knew better than to take it personally. If Sandy ever took off, it wouldn't be the farm she was leaving but his dumb ass. What could he do then? Post an advertisement for himself on farmersonly.com? Check to see if they had a singles night at the Tractor Supply store?

It was still dark when he let himself out the mudroom door and walked to his truck. He got in, put his travel mug of coffee in the center console cupholder, and started the engine. With his headlights on, he headed down the gravel driveway.

He didn't know exactly what would happen when he got to Sutter Park. He wasn't sure how he would get the cows back to the farm or when that could happen. He did need to call Dave Monroe. Sandy was right; he should have called last night.

The most important thing was to reestablish contact with the herd. Cattle are such creatures of habit. His had strayed and were on unfamiliar ground. All the more reason why they should be glad to see him. They were so used to him being around—bringing them stuff, hanging out and talking with them. They were comfortable with him.

He would just have to play things by ear. He would do what he could to get back into some kind of routine with them. Then he could see how things were.

THIRTY-FOUR

IN THE BLUE HALF-LIGHT OF EARLY MORNING, before sunrise, Donna Wilson was power walking on the bike path that bisected her neighborhood then entered Sutter Park. This was her routine morning exercise before going to the McConnell Wellness Center for yoga. She loved how the bike path passed through the shadowed calm of woods before coming out into the open grassy area, at the top of the hill overlooking the duck pond. She would walk another mile past there, maintaining peak pace. When she reached the bustling little Starbucks on Market Street, she would go in and order a grande no-caff-soy-latte and sit on one of the stuffed chairs for half an hour, checking her pulse and email.

She treasured the park. It was her personal bit of wilderness inside the city. She'd had memorable encounters there. She'd watched a red-tailed hawk hunting field mice once. She'd seen two wild turkeys, males, strutting around each other slowly, tails fanned out. She'd seen countless deer, mostly does and fawns, and one time found a shed antler. Her attempt to "turn it in" had only confused park staffers, so it was now displayed on her mantle beside the framed photo of her with Jimmy Carter (taken at a Habitat build). Even the time she was sprayed by a skunk had been positive in that it had been educational. Now she knew: a skunk staying put while you approach is not an invitation to stoop and pet.

This morning, coming out of the woods, she saw the cows grazing the dew-soaked grass about fifty yards ahead. They were so calm, moving around slowly as they ate. They seemed familiar to Donna, as if their presence were a reverberation of some prior life experience beyond her conscious memory.

Leaving the asphalt path, she came power walking straight toward them. The flashy iridescence of her exercise outfit and the odd exaggerated movement of her limbs alarmed the cows. They stopped eating and turned to watch her, poised to flee. Just when they might have bolted, she came to an abrupt stop, about thirty feet away. She was somewhat out of breath.

"My darlings!" she said. "My lovely, wonderful darlings! What a joy to see you!"

None of the cows said anything. The two calves moved slowly to be behind their mothers. They lowered their heads and watched the woman from between their mothers' legs.

"Such a wonderful surprise!" the woman said. "I have dreamed of this day, when the parks department would finally do something right."

The cows were confused by the tone of familiarity she was taking with them. They couldn't remember her ever being at the farm.

"Seeing you is one of the best things that's happened to me since I moved to Columbus. I'm *from* San Diego. I've lived in Boulder too. I came east to help my mother when she broke her hip. That was like five years ago and I just haven't gotten around to leaving. I mean, people here are nice. I've got some good friends. And I have my therapist and gynecologist and my yoga instructor. Sally is amazing! It's just that Columbus, the Midwest in general, is so conservative. And I don't mean politically conservative. I mean personally. Like people not wanting to try new things or go outside their comfort zone."

The cows went back to grazing while she talked. But they kept an eye and one ear on her.

"Columbus *is* changing. It is. There's so much more going on than when I first moved here. I helped start Sustainable New Albany and we've been able to effect change. There are lots of groups like that and now local government is starting to catch on. When I first came here there wasn't any recycling at all. I mean none. Can you imagine?

"So things are improving. But this—you guys—I am just blown away. I mean this is cutting edge. I only know about it because I read *Mother Earth*. They had an article about natural park maintenance in Austin: bringing animals in to graze the park; doing away with mechanical mowing and chemical fertilizers. Usually Columbus would need like another decade to come around to something so ahead of the curve.

"I'm taking pictures of you," she said, getting her phone out. "You are so adorable. Love the ears."

She held her phone up and took some photos.

"It's so perfect that you're here. The grass grows, you eat the grass, you shit…"

She took a picture of a fresh cow patty near where she was standing.

"Your shit feeds the grass, the grass keeps growing, you eat more… It's like this perfect cycle of hunger and growth, decay and regeneration. Kind of like my first marriage."

The cows, irritated by the woman's nonstop talking, started looking at each other. 42 caught 74's eye, then walked closer and said quietly, "What's wrong with her?"

"I don't know. I can hardly eat listening to her. I'm thinking of going in the woods until she leaves."

"She can't have much left to say."

"Maybe you're right."

"I'm putting you on my Facebook," Donna said. "I've already tweeted about you twice. I've been so critical of the parks department, I want to be sure and say something nice now that they've done something I approve of. Positive reinforcement! It feels like they've turned a corner—like maybe they finally woke up and realized we don't have to choose between recreation and survival of the planet… I'm going to call my friend Janet Jones. Her husband is the executive producer of Channel Four News. I bet they'd jump at the chance to do a story about you. Of course in Austin they used goats. They ultimately would be a more responsible choice. No offense. Yaks are cool too. There's lots of them in Colorado, but they're not really suited for the climate in central Ohio. They're mountain animals.

"I had a friend in Colorado who had yaks. She was so into them, she even traveled to Tibet to see them in their original habitat. It was hard to get inside Tibet too, because of the Chinese government, you know. She got across the border in the back of a pickup truck hiding under a tarp. I mean she was really into yaks. Most people don't know the CIA years ago tried to do a whole Bay of Pigs type thing with Tibetans. They brought them to Colorado to train them as insurgents. Because it worked out so well the first time, right? They figured the Tibetans might feel comfortable up in the Rocky Mountains. They brought yaks over too, to make it seem more like home. The program never amounted to anything, but that's how we ended up having so many yaks in Colorado—because of the CIA."

74 and 42, then all of the cows, stopped grazing and started

walking toward the woods. They did not hurry but neither did they linger.

"Oh, I see, you're done eating," Donna said. "Good for you. Take a break. You've earned it."

The cows, entering the woods, were so far away they probably could not hear her.

"I love you!" she called after them.

THIRTY-FIVE

AT EIGHT O'CLOCK, in the Tee Jaye's restaurant at Morse and High, off by themselves in a booth at the far end of the dining room, sat Ron Jackson and two friends he'd kept in touch with over the years since they'd been marines together—Jake Keller, now seasonally employed in the landscape and snow-removal industry; and Sam Van Scoy, a long divorced long-haul trucker.

Tee Jaye's, the Country Place, was a central Ohio chain of vaguely disreputable 24-hour breakfast joints claiming to serve "down home cooking at its best." Customers were greeted with a hardy "Howdy, folks!" whether coming in for breakfast after church or stumbling in drunk and sweaty when the bars shut down.

Ron, Jake, and Sam regularly met there.

This morning they'd all had the Barnyard Buster—biscuits, eggs, and home fries all heavily smothered with sausage gravy. They'd each had about six cups of coffee and had taken turns half-heartedly flirting with their waitress, Jenny, a no-nonsense pro in her forties whose ability to make a living from tips gleaned from tablefuls of tightwads like these guys was amazing.

Now, their dirty plates cleared, the men quit their chitchat and got down to business.

"Thanks for getting together on such short notice," Ron said. "So, basically, this is like that time we culled the deer at Blendon Woods Park."

Jake and Sam winced, remembering how that went. Ron had nearly lost his job.

"The difference is, this time it's sanctioned."

"Sanctioned?" Jake said. "Sanctioned by who?"

"The mayor of Columbus."

Jake and Sam stared at him.

"The mayor of Columbus," Sam said.

"That's right."

"Get the hell out of here."

"I'm serious. The whole thing is his idea. He called me at home last night to ask me to do it. *We're* doing *him* a favor."

"The mayor of Columbus."

"Yes. He wants them gone. The sooner the better. By any means necessary."

"He said that?"

"That's what I'm trying to tell you."

Ron understood their skepticism. The worst thing about military service was the way you got held back by politicians.

"We've got the green light this time, fellas."

"All right!" Sam said. "Oorah!"

He and Jake high-fived.

Ron picked up some manila envelopes he had on the bench seat beside him. He handed Sam and Jake each an envelope with their name written on it. Then, holding up his envelope, he said, "Gentlemen: Operation Charlie Oscar Whiskey."

"Nice," Jake said.

They opened their envelopes and started reviewing the materials inside.

"I've included a topographical map of the park. You can see there's tree cover along the ridgetop. There's an uninterrupted field of view available clear to the duck pond. My thought is we catch them near the pond. With the advantage of high ground, we can pin them down in a crossfire without the risk of friendly fire."

"Like the Battle of Dien Phu," Jake said.

"Exactly." It was a treat working with men who, like him, were students of tactical history.

"The three red dots indicate where I think we should take up our positions."

"We're going to need some serious stopping power," Jake said. "Thirty-ought-six? Is that what you're thinking?"

"Yes, with silencers."

They'd learned that the hard way at Blendon Woods.

"I included, in your packets, documentation that you've been retained by the parks department as independent contractors. You're each being paid one dollar. Here." He got his wallet out and handed each of them a one-dollar bill. "This will protect you from liability.

"There's a map of the park showing the roads and buildings. Also, I downloaded a drawing of a water buffalo—that's the closest thing I could find—showing where to aim for a kill shot. You've basically got the brain, the spinal column, or the heart. All three are indicated.

"And there's a timeline. My staff leaves at five, so I figure if you guys show up around five thirty, we can get organized and take up our positions by six thirty. Once the park clears out, we can start. It doesn't get dark before eight; that should give us plenty of time."

"I just bought these awesome night vision goggles at the Preppers' Show. You want me to bring them?" Jake said.

Ron said, "Sure. I'm bringing mine. I've arranged for a guy I know to come at seven thirty with a dump truck and a backhoe to dispose of the casualties, but it might be dark before we get done loading."

"You've really thought this through," Jake said. "Good job, Jackson!"

"I've been up half the night working it out."

"It's exciting to be able to use our marine training," Sam said.

"Yeah," Jake said. "And in a socially acceptable way."

THIRTY-SIX

NOT LONG AFTER WALKING AWAY from the woman who had too much to say—about the time it took the big orange sun to crest over I-270—the cows came back out of the woods. As they'd hoped, the woman was gone.

But they were not alone.

Now there was a man sitting cross-legged in the grass not far from where they were. His back was to them.

It was Farmer!

They hesitated, looking around to see if he was alone. The longer they held back, the more it seemed to them he was. Farmer sat perfectly still. His head and upper back were bent forward, as if he were studying something in his hands, too busy to notice them.

Right, the cows thought. As if Farmer just happened to be here of all places, sitting in the dew-soaked grass at dawn, for no particular reason.

Farmer and his cheap tricks.

"I wondered when he would show up," 42 said.

"It's nice to see him," 38 said.

"I'm curious to hear what he has to say," 74 said.

They walked toward Farmer slowly, ears swiveling. A few feet behind him, they stopped.

"Hello, Farmer," 74 said.

Farmer turned, twisting around to look up at them.

"Hey there! Good morning!"

74 said, "You found us."

"Yes. Finally." Farmer stood and faced the herd. "I've had a heck of a time. You guys really put me up against it."

"You're angry?"

"No. Mostly I've just been worried about you."

"You're always worrying," 38 said.

"Hey, I'm a farmer. That's what we do."

"It's nice to see you," 38 said.

"It's great seeing you guys. So, how is it with you? How's life in the big city?"

"We've met a lot of people," 68 said.

"You have?"

"Yes. We have a friend now. Danny."

"He lives next to Angel."

"We met Mason too," 106 said.

"That's terrific. And you've got a nice spot here… You guys are doing OK."

"It's hard finding enough to eat," 42 said. "We don't know where we'll go next."

"Looks like you've got enough to last another two or three days."

"We're getting runny," 74 said. "Something's wrong with the grass."

"They spray it with chemicals," Farmer said.

"And they cut it so short."

"They think it looks good like that."

"*Looks* good? Why do they care what it looks like?"

"That's just how it is in cities. They like everything neat and tidy… Now, when you say runny, how bad is it?"

"106 and 102 have it the worst. They practically have the squirts," 38 said. "Show Farmer."

The two calves turned around so he could see the shit crusted up on their backsides.

"Yeah, that's not good," Farmer said. "I'll tell you what. When I come back, I'll bring some hay. If you eat a little hay in between when you graze, it could help settle you."

"Hay?!" 106 said. "Yuck!"

"No, Farmer's right," his mother said. "A little hay will stiffen you up. That way you can get the benefit of what you're eating instead of it just running through you."

"Exactly," Farmer said.

"You're coming back?" 74 said.

"I figure I'll check in on you guys a couple times a day. See how you're doing. Bring you stuff you need."

"Can you bring us some salt?" 74 said.

"Sure."

"We might not want to come back to the farm, you know," 42 said.

"Yeah, I get that. You're city cows now. All sophisticated. Learning to take care of yourselves, making friends. It's like when I was in college."

"You hated college," 42 said.

"That's not true. It's just I was so busy trying to figure out who I was."

"You didn't know who you were?" 74 said.

"Did someone steal your identity?"

"What? No. It doesn't matter. All I'm saying is I understand. Even when things are tough—you can't find enough to eat or with winter coming—still, it's exciting to be on your own. The last thing on your mind is going home."

"Not the last thing…" 27 said.

"We're still sorting it out," 68 said.

"Well, whatever you decide, just let me know. I'm making arrangements to get some other cows if I have to."

"You are?" 27 said.

"Yep. I talked to a fellow over in Coshocton last night. He's got some Herefords. I'm going to go look at them this evening."

"You're not wasting any time," 74 said.

"The truth is, I need help keeping up with the pasture. There's that surge of fall regrowth coming on. It's so tender, especially the orchard grass. I hate to see it go to waste."

"Me too," 68 said.

"Well, I guess I've bothered you guys enough for now. You've got grazing to do. And I've got stuff to do back at the farm… I'm glad to see how well you're doing. I'm proud of you."

"When will you be back?" 74 said.

"In a few hours, around lunchtime."

"So, you'll bring some hay then?" 74 said.

"Yep. And salt."

"You better write it down," 38 said.

"Yeah, make a list so you don't forget, then put it with your truck keys."

"Really?" Farmer said. "Really? Are you kidding me?"

"Yes, we are kidding you," 38 said.

"Aw, you guys! I've missed you!"

38 stepped toward Farmer and said, "Come on. Give me a scratch."

Farmer started scratching her neck. She stretched her neck out, relishing it.

"We've missed you, too," 68 said, waiting her turn. "And this is the second morning in a row we haven't gotten any news. We don't know what's going on. Didn't the Calves play last night?"

"In Chicago. They beat the Bulls by twenty points."

"Yes!" 27 said.

"We should ask him about names," 68 said.

"Good idea," 74 said. "Farmer, we want names."

"You do?"

"People don't like calling us by our numbers. And anyway, it would be nice to have names."

"I like it," Farmer said.

"Really?"

"It's a great idea."

"OK, but how do we get them?" 74 said. "What do we have to do?"

"Nothing, really. You just decide what names you want. Have you thought about that?"

"No. We just had the idea."

"OK, I'll tell you what," Farmer said. "You guys think about what names you want. When I come back, I'll bring the ear tag kit. I've got blank tags and permanent ink markers. We can make name tags with your new names. How does that sound?"

"That would be immense," 27 said.

"All right then. See you guys. Take care. And don't go anywhere. I don't want to have to look for you again."

"We'll be here," 27 said.

"Thanks for stopping by," 68 said.

"We appreciate it."

"See you, Farmer."

Farmer walked down the hill to the parking lot. He was about to get in his truck when he saw a small red Toyota pull in and park a few spaces over. A woman got out. She was maybe fifty, deeply tanned, wearing shorts and a windbreaker. She had sneakers on. Farmer watched as she got a travel mug and a small knapsack from her car.

She saw Farmer watching her and nodded to him, giving him a half smile.

"Do you work here?" he said.

"Yes, I do. Why?"

"Those are my cows," he said, indicating the grazing herd in the distance.

"Oh. You mean the ones that have been walking through my flower beds?"

Farmer looked around at the mulched beds and saw—he hadn't noticed before—they'd been churned up quite a bit.

"I'm sorry about that. I'm working to get them back as soon as I can."

"I would hurry that right along," she said. "Mr. Jackson, the chief superintendent here, once he gets upset, it's not pretty. And he's none too happy about those cows of yours."

"Is he here? Can I talk to him?"

"No, he'll be a while. He had a breakfast meeting."

"Well, can you please tell him I'm working to get them out of here? And how sorry I am?"

"OK, hon, but really. The sooner the better. Mr. Jackson is kind of a control freak. I don't think your cows are a good match for him."

THIRTY-SEVEN

ANGELA LIND, intern at Channel Four News, was alone in the break area, cleaning a sinkful of dirty coffee mugs when Bob Jones, longtime executive producer, came rushing down the hall. Angela assumed he would hurry past her like he always did—tense and preoccupied, mumbling to himself. Instead, he suddenly stopped, leaned his head into the break area, and stared at her. It was eight o'clock in the morning, but already his suit was badly rumpled, his tie yanked loose. His hair was a mess. *Has he been up all night working?* Angela wondered.

"I'm making more coffee," she said. "It's almost ready."

He looked at her a little more, then said, "Who are you?"

"Angela Lind. I'm an intern. I just graduated from—"

"Oh for God's sake," he said. "Come with me."

Then he was gone.

She dried her hands and hurried up the hall to his office. By the time she got there and stood in the open doorway, he was already behind his desk talking on the phone.

"I don't care," he said. "Just deal with it. That's your problem."

He slammed the phone down.

"Look," he said to Angela. "Get in here. What are you doing?"

She entered the office.

"What's your name again?"

"Angela Lind."

"Look. Angela. I've got a story just came in. It's an exclusive if we hurry, but nobody else is here, so you're going to have to do it. Do you understand?"

Oh my God! she thought. *My big break!*

"I've got a cameraman coming around in a van. You'll go with him."

"You can count on me, sir."

"Are those the only clothes you have?"

She looked down at her jeans and blouse. "Well," she stammered.

"It'll be fine. Now listen. There are some cows. We got a tip they're in Sutter Park, over on the east side. The parks department apparently brought them in as part of some cockamamie natural park maintenance program. They never did a press release about it. Ducking the media as usual. Those guys are idiots. Sooner or later everything they do turns to shit and this will be no exception. And we'll be there for that story too. But, for now, we're the only ones who know about these cows. I've seen pictures of them and they're cute and you're doing a story on them for our midday newsbreak. An exclusive! Questions!"

It took Angela a moment to realize she'd been asked if she had any questions. By the time she was ready to ask the first of several, Jones said, "Good! Don't worry, you'll do fine. You better. This tip came in from my wife. If we screw it up, I'll never hear the end of it."

A thin young man wearing jeans and a T-shirt and sporting a goatee knocked on the open office door.

"All set," he told Jones. "I've got the van out front."

"Take her with you," Jones said. "Go! Go!"

"Come on," the young man said to Angela. She followed him into the hall.

"I'm Joey," he said.

"Angela," she said. "Pleased to meet you."

"Are those the only clothes you have?"

THIRTY-EIGHT

THE FARRIER was coming at nine. At eight thirty, after a bowl of cereal, Sandy put her muck boots on and walked to the barn. She slid the big doors open and went inside. She got a halter and the five-gallon bucket with grooming stuff in it, then went outside and let herself in the pen next to the barn.

She whistled for Valentine who was more than a hundred yards away, at the far end of the paddock. Instantly Valentine's ears perked up and she came galloping toward the barn, tail arched. When she reached Sandy, she stopped dramatically right in front of her. Valentine was a ten-year-old mare Sandy had rescued, a white Tennessee Walker with smooth gaits and an easy disposition. She waited while Sandy slipped the halter on.

"Good girl," Sandy said, patting Valentine.

She leaned down and got a curry comb from the bucket.

"I need to clean you up a little before the farrier gets here. So he won't know what slobs we are."

She started brushing Valentine, disturbing lots of dust. Valentine had a habit, when the flies were bad, of rolling in the dirt.

"So yesterday this college kid let Farmer's cows out," Sandy said while combing. "I don't know what he was thinking. And I'm saying that *after* reading his journal. As much of it as I could stand..."

Valentine nuzzled Sandy's jacket pocket, pushing against it to see if there was an apple. There wasn't.

"I'll get you an apple when the farrier is finished," Sandy said. "Farmer doesn't know how to ask for help is the problem. People want to help. He's done plenty for them over the years. But he's proud."

She walked around and started brushing Valentine's other side. The curry comb was pulling a lot of loose hair to the surface. She would follow up with the bristle brush when she was done, then start in on the mane. It looked to be pretty badly tangled. There were some burrs in it.

"Your coat is thickening up a little earlier than normal... I hope we're not going to have a hard winter."

Some time later, pulling a metal comb through Valentine's mane, Sandy thought about how, whenever she found a fallen bird's nest, or climbed a ladder to remove one from inside the barn, some of Valentine's white hairs were always woven into the encirclements of twigs and straw. The birds loved Valentine's hair—the suppleness and strength of it.

These were the kinds of things that amused Sandy about life on the farm.

She kept after the tangles in Valentine's mane. It was taking longer than she'd thought. She wasn't sure she could finish before the farrier showed up.

"The good news is, those cows know where they belong. That's what Frank says. They get tired of being out. They're curious, but not adventurous really."

When Farmer and Sandy had been on the farm only a year and got their first big animals—two rescue horses (Valentine, and an easygoing gelding, Shaundar, who two years later was killed by lightning) and a couple of steers Farmer bought from Frank—that winter's first big snowfall had taught them a lot about horses and cows. In the paddock where the horses were, every bit of the snow was trampled within a week. The horses were restless, walking off nervous energy. But in the steers' paddock, the six-inch-deep snow was hardly disturbed. Narrow muddy paths bisected it: from the shed to the hay rack, from the hay rack to the water tub, from the water tub to the shed. Otherwise the snow remained intact until, months later, a week of warmup melted it.

Even when they'd escaped, and with the whole world open to them, the cows had gotten on that bike path and followed it doggedly all day. Then they settled in Sutter Park which, as Sandy remembered it, was basically a pasture surrounded by trees. Wow! Such an adventure!

They were a lot like Farmer, she thought. No wonder he got along with them. If anything, he was *more* of a homebody.

She'd been trying to get him to take a vacation for years. They hadn't had one since they moved onto the farm, and she was starting to get restless. She wished it could be as simple as leaving a gate open, then following him through it.

Whenever she brought up the idea of taking a vacation he would immediately balk.

"I wouldn't be able to relax. I'd never stop worrying. What would be the point?"

"We could get someone to farm sit."

"Who? Someone who knows dogs and horses and cows? Who could stay in the house while we're gone? Who?"

"I don't know."

"Just go on your own," he would say. "Go see your mother."

"That's not a vacation. Besides, I want to go somewhere with you."

"I thought you liked living on the farm."

"I do. I love it here. It's just that sometimes—every once in a while—I want something different."

"Different? What do you mean different?"

"Like the ocean. I would like to see the ocean."

"Oh, well sure, the ocean…"

He would act crestfallen then, like he'd "lost." And she would relent. "I'm not in any hurry. Just keep it in mind. Let's work toward it, that's all I'm saying."

Every six months or so she would bring it up again, and each time it was like they had never talked about it.

"Isn't that something?" she said to Valentine. "The cows get to go on a vacation before I do."

Valentine didn't say anything.

THIRTY-NINE

AN HOUR AFTER RON JACKSON and his friends had finished their breakfast, a stretch black limousine westbound on Morse turned into the Tee Jaye's parking lot, rolling across the crumbling asphalt and stopping near its entrance.

The driver's door opened and out stepped Thomas, wearing a dark suit. He came around to the back door facing Tee Jaye's, opened the door, and helped Martha Guildersnap out.

She was incognito—a silk scarf tied down over her hair, large sunglasses obscuring part of her face.

"Thomas," she said. "Please stay close. I have no idea how long I will be. I don't know what to expect. If this place is too horrible, I will want to leave right away."

All the Tee Jaye's locations she'd researched had turned out to be in the worst parts of town. She'd picked this one, in Clintonville, because it seemed to her the safest.

Thomas took her arm and walked her to the entrance.

"I feel like Sir Hillary," she said.

Thomas held the door open for her.

"Have a good breakfast," he said.

Martha Guildersnap went inside. The hostess—standing near the Please Wait to be Seated sign—greeted her with an enthusiastic, "Howdy!"

"Yes. Hello."

"Will there be just one of you?"

"That is correct."

"Do you have a preference of table or booth?"

"A booth, please." She couldn't remember the last time she'd sat in a booth.

"Right this way, hon." The hostess headed out across a green carpet brightly patterned with little orange wagon wheels.

Martha followed, past mostly empty tables cluttered with ad cards and condiments, each surrounded by thick wooden chairs. The booths were along the back wall. The booth to which she was led had several places where its vinyl seats were patched with duct tape. A quick and intense review did assure her, however, that the booth was clean.

She scooted into the booth, then the hostess dropped a big plastic menu on the table in front of her.

"Jenny will be your server. She'll be along in a minute. Can I get you some coffee?"

"No, but tea would be most welcome. Green tea."

Martha took off her enormous sunglasses.

"We have Lipton's. Is that green?"

"You know, I will have, instead of tea, a glass of cold water. No ice. One slice of lemon."

"I'll be right back with that."

Martha looked around the dining room. It had the feel of an all-you-can-eat buffet even though there was no buffet. The furniture was cheaply veneered, pale and shiny. Decorations were simple: heavily patterned wallpaper, ruffled curtains framing the windows, and all around the dining room, a high wooden shelf displaying outmoded implements of rural life—watering cans and washboards, lanterns, metal buckets, hay hooks and fencing comealongs, all mixed in with antique labeled tins: saltine crackers, lard and coffee, cigarette tobacco, udder balm and oatmeal. The wagon wheel pattern of the carpet was echoed overhead by large wagon wheel chandeliers.

It seemed in sum much like a dining room aboard a very large and low-cost cruise ship—one perhaps partly owned by Dolly Parton or operating under a licensing agreement with *Hee Haw*.

It was not crowded this late in the morning. It was already ten o'clock. The patrons were mostly people from the neighborhood, all of whom seemed to know each other. Somewhat plump and cheerful folks in their sixties, many of them probably retired. They seemed to Martha like the people who went to casinos to play slots. She would not have been surprised if one of the women might have a Chihuahua in her purse, sneaking it little bits of food.

Looking over the menu, she saw several breakfasts that were positively obscene. It was going to be hard to decide.

Jenny brought her a plastic glass of ice water. There was no lemon.

"Here you go, sweetie. I'm Jenny. I'll be taking care of you. Have you been to a Tee Jaye's before?"

"No, this is my first time. I've heard the ads, of course."

"I've never seen you in here before is why I asked."

"It reminds me—so far—of a restaurant my husband and I used to frequent many years ago: Dink's Hillbilly Kitchen, out on Route Forty. Dink had the best biscuits—the closest I ever found to my mother's. Hers won second place at the West Virginia State Fair one year."

"Well, nothing here is *that* good," Jenny said. "But it's not bad for in-town. I'm from Kentucky," she added.

"What part?"

"Little place called Hand me Down Holler. Near Boone."

"My people came from Ripley," Martha said. "Near Loose Rock Gorge."

"Oh sure. That's where everybody goes bungee jumping. Well, welcome to Tee Jaye's, honey. You might like the corn pancakes, they're my favorite... I'll let you alone while you look things over."

"I'm ready now."

"Oh. OK. Shoot."

"I would like the Country Ham and Corncake Special. Eggs over easy. Sausage patty."

"Good choice," Jenny said, writing it down on her little pad.

"And I would like a piece of bacon with that."

"Just one piece?"

"Yes. And—the sausage gravy is good?"

"Pretty good."

"I would like a side of biscuits and gravy as well."

"That's an awful lot of food, honey. Are you sure you want all that?"

"I'm making up for lost time, Jenny. I haven't had anything for breakfast other than fresh fruit for over a decade. Oh, you have corn mush! I—no, I better not."

When Martha's food was ready, Jenny brought it to the booth on a big oval tray and put one plate after another on the table. "The Country Ham and Corncake, eggs over easy, sausage patty," she said. "Side of bacon. Biscuits and gravy."

The table was nearly covered with plates of hot steaming food.

"My goodness," Martha said. "It's positively apocalyptic."

"I'll be right back with some syrup."

Martha picked up a fork and knife.

She cut off a tiny bit of the sausage patty and put it in her mouth. She chewed it a while, enjoying it, then spit it discreetly into a paper napkin.

When the syrup arrived, she poured some on the corn pancakes, cut off a tiny piece of one and ate it. She decided to not in any way disturb the thick white sausage gravy covering the biscuits. Just the smell of it sufficed. She would not try the ham either. Using her fork and knife, she cut off a little bit of bacon and ate that. She could feel its grease entering her bloodstream.

After a sip of cold water, she ate another tiny bit of the corn cake. Then she was done. She put the knife and fork down and motioned for Jenny to come over.

"Jenny, how much do I owe?"

Jenny pulled a ticket from her apron pocket and put it on the table. "Nine dollars and forty cents," she said. "You've hardly touched anything. Is the food OK?"

"Oh, it's wonderful," Martha said. "Naturally I wasn't able to finish. But what a delight. I will cherish it for a long time."

She pulled a one-hundred-dollar bill from her purse and handed it to Jenny.

"Thank you so much, Jenny."

"I'll get your change."

"No, that's for you, darling."

When she came outside, Thomas was waiting. He helped her in the limo.

Minutes later, turning out of the parking lot, he asked, "Was it as you'd hoped?"

"Oh yes, it was wonderful. And horrifying of course."

He drove east on Morse Road, thinking they would be getting on I-71 south.

"Thomas," she said. "Call the mayor, would you, and ask him which park those cows are in."

FORTY

WHEN FARMER STARTED FARMING, he didn't have a livestock trailer. Brett gave him Dave Monroe's number. "Dave will haul for you. He's good with cattle and he shows up when he says he will." Farmer had never met Dave but had seen him around town—going by on the pike or filling up at the Circle K. It was hard to miss that rig of his: a red Chevy 3500 Duramax diesel dually pulling a long aluminum gooseneck trailer, the words "Bullshit Express" airbrushed on its sides.

Farmer had hired Dave three or four times a year until he bought a used trailer of his own. Looking back on it, he was glad he'd started out like that. He'd learned a lot from Dave—most of what he knew about handling cattle.

Dave was a big rough man, ruddy and unshaven, always wearing bib overalls and tall rubber boots. He kept a cheekful of juicy tobacco going all day, tending to it—part of why he was hard to understand. He roamed Licking County hauling livestock, his black lab Sam in the truck cab beside him.

Once, years before, Farmer looked inside the cab and saw a half-grown black lab puppy, sleek and shiny as a seal. He was confused. Sam was full-grown. "Who is this?" he'd said to Dave.

"This the new Sam," Dave said. "Old Sam's home. He retired."

Dave was gruff, but he was gentle. There was no anger in him. He had tremendous patience, with animals and with rookie farmers. "When it comes to cattle, there's no use hurrying. The best way to get them to do something is to let it be their idea," he'd taught Farmer. "Once you understand how they look at things, then you can get them to see things your way… They don't know how big and strong they are. You push them too hard, you might teach them they can kick your ass. Then what have you got?"

It'd been five, maybe six years since Farmer had talked to Dave. Driving home from the park, he called him.

"Hello!" Dave shouted. He was driving too, talking over the noise of his truck's diesel engine. It sounded like he might have a window open as well.

"Dave, this is Farmer, over on Cooper Road. I used to—"

"Yeah, Farmer!"

"I need some hauling done."

"Brett said you might call. Sounds like you're after the same bunch I tried to load yesterday. Kind of skittish."

"They're actually calm. I was just with them. They're settled down pretty good."

"When you thinking, Farmer?"

"Later today?"

"Well, let's see… I'm taking a load of fat cattle down to Zanesville. After that I got to get some calves loaded up near Dresden and take them to Gambier. Then I got to take Mom to the dentist. Could maybe do it after that."

"Maybe tomorrow morning would be better."

"That'd work."

"First thing tomorrow? About seven?"

"Seven's good. Where they at, Farmer?"

"They're in New Albany."

Dave whistled. "Getting around ain't they? How you figure on loading them?"

"Well, you know, I'll be hanging out with them, trying to get them used to the idea of going home. There's a pretty good chance they might walk in the trailer on their own."

"Way I remember, you always got along pretty good with your animals. Not like some of these yahoos. But that don't sound like much of a plan."

"I figure on having a couple other guys there too. If we need to, I think we can work them some with this white electric twine I use. They're so used to it being hot, I think we can walk with the twine stretched between us and corral them some that way."

"You're the boss, Farmer. But I tell fellas, there's ain't but two ways to bluff cattle: the wrong way and the lucky way."

"I don't know what else to do, Dave."

"Well, things might go our way. All we can do is try... Now, going clear into New Albany, I'd have to charge you extra. Sixty dollars be OK?"

"Yeah, that's fine. I was thinking of meeting at the feed mill. I could ride in with you from there."

"That'd do. You'd have to sit next to Sam. Didn't know if maybe Brett might be coming."

"I'm going to call him now."

"All right then, Farmer. You take her easy. See you in the morning."

FORTY-ONE

A NUMBER OF CARS had shown up since Farmer left. People got out of the cars and went in the building or into the woods, following paths they seemed to know. Some of the people had turned to look at the cows, but not for long; they went on. Even Ron Jackson, when he showed up, looked at them but did not come to visit. He must have been busy.

The cows were grazing the top of the hill when a white van turned into the parking lot. They didn't pay it much mind. But now they watched with interest as a young woman who got out of the van came walking toward them.

It was Angela Lind.

She was hurrying but having some trouble with her footing in the grass. The cows decided she was not a threat. They were more worried about the man who came in the van with her. He was still in the parking lot, holding a big complicated-looking piece of equipment. What was it? Why did he have it?

When Angela reached the cows, she said, "Whew. That was a hike." She caught her breath and, looking around, said, "Oh. I assumed there would be a shepherd up here, or a cowboy, I guess, actually."

"What do you want?" 42 said.

"You guys talk?" Mr. Jones hadn't mentioned that. This really *was* her big break! "This is incredible. Oh my God. Oh my God."

"What's wrong?" 74 said.

"I'm just excited. I get to interview you!" She flipped open a little notebook she was holding and clicked a ballpoint pen.

"You get to what?" 42 said.

"Interview you. Ask you questions."

"What kind of questions?"

"Like how you got here."

"We walked," 42 said.

"OK, but did the parks department send for you? Are you on loan? How does it work?" She wrote the word "cows" in the notebook and waited, ready to record what they told her.

"What do you mean?" 74 said.

"What did she say?" 68 asked 42.

"I'm confused," another cow said.

Angela saw, with dismay, that the cows being able to talk didn't necessarily mean much. She lowered her notebook and said, "I think I should talk with whoever is in charge. The person who takes care of you."

"You mean Farmer?"

"I guess so. Where is *he*?"

"At the farm. He's coming later."

"Shoot. I really need to talk to someone now. Who's the point person for the park?"

"Point person?" 74 said.

"Someone who represents the park."

"Ron Jackson is the chief superintendent."

Angela wrote Jackson's name in the notebook. "Where is Mr. Jackson?" she said.

"He's in that building. But he's very busy. He doesn't always have time to talk."

"Well, I should probably go see him. You guys don't go anywhere, I'll be back."

"You're in such a hurry… What is it you want?" 42 said.

"Yeah, and who is that man you came with?" 74 said.

Angela turned and saw Joey. He was sitting on a bench near the empty kids' playground, the video camera on his lap. He was smoking a cigarette, waiting for a signal from Angela.

"That's Joey," she said.

"Do *you* have a name?" 38 said.

"I forgot to introduce myself." Angela blushed. "I'm Angela Lind from Channel Four News. Real professional, huh."

"Angela," 68 said. "That's a pretty name."

"Thank you."

"What is that thing Joey has?" 74 said.

"What? Oh, his camera… That's why we're here. I'm a TV news reporter. Joey's my cameraman. We came to do a story about you… Actually, we should probably go ahead and at least get some video of you. That's the most important thing. You guys are so adorable. Especially you two," she said, pointing to 106 and 102. "I can ask you just a few simple questions. Then, after, I can talk to the parks people, get some context."

"Context?" 42 said.

"Just, you know, like what you're doing here."

"Eating grass," 38 said.

"But I mean, how you got here."

"We walked."

"We already told you that," 42 said. This woman asked a lot of questions, but she wasn't much of a listener.

"We left the farm," 38 said.

"Left a farm?"

"The gate was open," 38 said.

"Wait. So you just happened to end up here?"

74 said, "Actually, someone recommended it."

Great, Angela thought. *Instead of reporting on some cutting-edge parks department initiative, my story turns out to be: someone left a gate open.*

"We're just passing through," 68 said.

42 said, "Freedom is our natural state."

"What?!" Angela couldn't believe her ears. This cow, 42—had she just said freedom is a natural state? That was like a famous philosophy thing. She remembered it from some college lecture. Ben Franklin or John Adams or someone like that had said it.

Everyone told her college wasn't a waste of time for someone going into journalism!

"What did you say?" she asked 42.

"Freedom is our natural state. Just because people fence us in, doesn't mean we're meant to live that way. We're prey animals. We know that. We're vulnerable, OK? But we're wanderers by nature. So captivity, even when we're well taken care of, doesn't really suit us."

The other cows were impressed. Lernovski would be proud.

"*Were* you well taken care of?" Angela said.

"Well, yes. Things were OK that way. But that's what I'm saying: even so, we chose freedom."

"Are you kidding me?" Angela said.

"No, I am not kidding you," 42 said.

"Oh my God, you guys! Oh my God!"

Animal rights was such a hot topic. This had the potential to be huge! National, even! 42 was so articulate!

74 said, "We still might decide to go back to the farm."

But Angela didn't hear. She had turned away. She was waving frantically for Joey to come join her. He stood, picked up the camera, and started walking toward them.

Angela said to the cows, "OK, you guys, we're going to talk like we just did, OK? 42, you tell me some more about freedom. But this time Joey is going to video us so we can show it on TV. A lot of people will see it."

"Show and tell?" 38 said.

"Yes. Exactly. Show and tell."

74, watching Joey approach, said, "OK, but he should leave that machine behind."

"That's his camera. It's for the show and tell."

"No, he would just use a phone for that," 74 said. "I don't know what that thing is."

"It looks like a weapon," 42 said.

"I hate it!" 68 said.

"Oh no," 38 said, backing up, away from Joey and his terrible danger-maker.

"You're tricking us!" 27 said.

Angela could see the cows were starting to panic. If they got spooked and took off she would lose her story!

"Joey! Stop!" she called. He froze. He was maybe fifty feet away.

"Guys, for a bigger show and tell we need a bigger camera. OK? That's all it is. I swear. I'm not tricking you. We want to help you."

"You want to ask us questions," 74 said.

"Yes, but that's all. There's no trick."

"I don't know…" 74 said.

The cattle were so tense, they were ready to bolt at the slightest surprise.

Angela said, "Come on now. You guys trust me, right? Don't you?"

"Yes," 68 said.

"Well, Joey's my friend. That means he's your friend. I'm going to get him to show you the camera, so you can see it's nothing to be afraid of."

None of the cows said anything. They were all watching Joey.

"Joey?" Angela said. "The cows are afraid of the camera. Very slowly, come let them see it."

Joey—very slowly—walked toward Angela, lowering the camera from his shoulder. He held it out in front of the cows. They stared at it.

"Like this?" Joey said.

"Yes, just let them see it."

"I'm going to check it out," 42 said. She took a step forward. Then another step, then another. When she was maybe three feet from Joey, she stretched her neck, leaning forward till her big wet nose was just an inch or two from the camera. She touched the camera with her nose, then jerked back. When nothing happened, she touched it again. She licked it with her tongue.

Joey kept perfectly still. It was like going through security at the airport.

42 decided the camera was OK.

"All clear," she told the others.

38 said, "Are you sure?"

"I want to see," 74 said. She approached the camera as 42 had, until she too bumped it with her nose. She sniffed at it and licked it. Satisfied, she relaxed.

"False alarm," she said. "Better safe than sorry," she added.

"Whew," Angela said. "You guys are intense. I'm glad we got that sorted out. OK. Joey, let's start."

Joey said, "Hold up, I'm going to have to switch cameras. They totally slimed this one."

FORTY-TWO

LESS THAN NINE HOURS before his one and only televised debate, Mayor Jenkins was with his chief of staff, Sally Martinez, in the back of a Lincoln Town Car, eastbound on I-670. They were heading to the airport for a campaign event.

She filled him in on the way.

"It's a ribbon cutting. You'll be doing the honors, with Tom Bradley, a Northwest executive, and the airport manager Cheryl Grant."

Northwest Airlines was coming into John Glenn International. They were starting service that afternoon—ten flights daily, most notably non-stop service to San Francisco (a first for Columbus).

"We're just in and out of there," Sally said. "You don't need to make a speech. The TV stations just need a quote they can use."

"Columbus is taking off. The sky's the limit."

"Good."

"Columbus really is world class. No matter how pathetic it sounds every time we say it."

"I don't know about that one. Oh, be sure to mention the non-stop service to San Francisco."

"Yes, of course. The driving of the golden spike."

"You're in a mood." Sally turned off the tablet she'd been working on and focused more fully on the mayor. "Are you OK?"

"Just tired. I'll feel better when the debate is over."

"Sir, we're ready. You're going to do great. Bottom line is, you're a good mayor. You deserve to be reelected."

"I suppose… Sally, did you know Martha Guildersnap used to live on a farm?"

"Sir?"

"She took care of chickens."

"That's surprising."

"I know, right? And she misses the cows. To this day, that's what she told me. Still misses them. Not her dead husband, Sally. Cows!"

"Sir, is that what's bothering you? Those cows are history. The parks people will have them hauled away any time now. Forget about them. I'm just glad you didn't hit one of them with your car. You could have been hurt."

"No, they used the crosswalk," he mused.

Fifteen minutes later, he and Sally were walking through the modern concourse of the airport, not a minute to spare, heading for the Northwest Airlines counter where the ribbon cutting would be.

"It's the mayor!" a man in the crowd said.

Jenkins smiled at him without breaking stride, giving him a thumbs up.

"Hey, Jenkins!" another man called out. "Where you goin'? You skippin' town?"

"Look, Darlene," a mother told her little girl. "That's the mayor of Columbus."

Jenkins stopped and said hello to the mother. He shook her hand, then leaned down and patted the girl on the head. "Hi, Darlene," he said. "It's an honor to make your acquaintance."

"We voted for you," the mother said. "Wait till I tell my husband."

A young man came along and took a selfie of himself with Jenkins. "Thanks," he said, shaking Jenkins's hand. "Good luck with the debate."

Several other people gathered around.

"You ready for tonight?" someone asked.

"Now Town!" someone said.

The man who'd asked if Jenkins was leaving town pushed his way through the other people and confronted Jenkins. He was unshaven, pale and sweaty. He was wearing thick eyeglasses that made his eyes seem huge.

"The bridge on Fifth Street near my house has been shut down for a year," he said. "I have to go all the way to Ackerman to get on 315."

"I'm sure they're doing what they can."

"A whole year! There's weeks go by I don't see any work being done."

Sally said, "Thank you for bringing this forward, sir. We'll look into it as soon as we're back at city hall."

"Look, darling. Whoever you are. Don't blow smoke up my ass."

"Language!" the mother said. "My daughter's right here!"

"Screw you, lady," the man said. "I'm a veteran."

"OK, OK now," Jenkins said. "Fifth Street bridge. I'll look into it. I'm sorry for the inconvenience. Thanks, everybody. Don't forget to vote!" He flashed a big smile and gave two thumbs up. Then he and Sally were moving again, toward the Northwest ticket counter just ahead.

"Parnell's gonna kick your ass!" they could hear the man shouting behind them.

The Northwest ticket counter was decorated with dozens of helium balloons, some made of foil and saying things like *Congratulations!* and *Here We Grow!*

A uniformed woman who seemed in charge recognized the mayor and Sally. She ushered them behind the counter, then through a door marked *employees only*.

"Ms. Grant is already here," she told Sally as she led them down a corridor. She stopped at a door on the left and opened it. "You can wait in here."

Jenkins went through the door, entering a small harshly lit

room with no windows. In it was a small table and some upright chairs. A woman, Ms. Grant he presumed, was standing in front of one of the chairs, as if she'd been sitting and stood when she heard them coming.

"Hello," he said, reaching out to shake her hand.

"Your Honor."

Sally, reading something on her phone, looked up and said to Cheryl Grant and Jenkins, "I'll be back in ten minutes. I need to find out what's happening with Channel Ten."

"Come on, Abbie," she told the Northwest woman. She and Abbie hurried off.

Jenkins shut the door. "Please," he told Ms. Grant. "Have a seat."

They sat.

"Cheryl Grant," he said. "Did I appoint you?"

"You did. I've been managing the airport for two years."

"Well, you must be doing a good job or I would know all about you."

"I'm doing my best."

"Ohio State?"

"Northwestern."

"Are you *from* Chicago?"

"No, I just went to school there. I grew up in Cleveland."

"What part of Columbus are you in?"

"Clintonville, but we're looking for a place downtown."

He nodded.

"So, things are good at the airport. Anything I need to know, Cheryl?"

"No, sir. I appreciate your asking. No problems to report."

The door burst open and Sally appeared. She scanned the room frantically. "Has the guy from Northwest been here?"

"No," Jenkins said.

"I got you some waters." She handed each of them a small plastic bottle of water. "I'll be back. We can't find a ribbon."

The door shut and they were alone again.

"I hope everything will be OK," Cheryl Grant said.

"Don't worry. Trust in Sally." His phone rang. "Excuse me," he said. "Hello?"

"Sir, this is Thomas Reeves, calling for Mrs. Guildersnap."

"Yes?"

"Sir, I've been asked to inquire of you which of the city's parks you saw cattle in yesterday."

"Oh. Sutter Park. In New Albany."

"Thank you. And, sir—if I might—good luck with the debate tonight."

"Why does she want to know where the cows are?" Jenkins said, but the line was dead.

He put his phone away. *Those cows!* He saw again the look on the face of 60-something—the one that urinated in front of his car. She'd turned and looked right at him. She never even blinked. How quickly then they'd taken off, vanishing into the woods. But of course they hadn't vanished. They were still out there.

"What's that about cows?" Cheryl Grant said.

"Well, actually—"

"I love cows!"

Jenkins stared at her—this impressive professional in her thirties, smart, elegantly dressed, self-assured and well-educated. *She loves cows?* he thought. *OK, I am definitely missing something.* As much money as he'd spent buying analyses of the electorate, for all his consultations with demographic experts, all those hours watching focus groups through one-way mirrors—he couldn't be more perplexed.

As a kind of experiment, he said, "These were black with white faces."

"Baldies!"

"Look," he said. "I don't mean to be rude. But how is it you know anything about cows? You seem so urban. I mean it made sense to me when you said you were from Cleveland. You've got the accent…"

She laughed. "Yeah, I'm a city girl for sure. But every summer we would spend a month on my grandparents' dairy farm in Wisconsin. We loved it there."

Jenkins said, "I never had anything like that growing up."

"One summer I totally bonded with this one cow. Number 96. She just liked me, I don't know. I would brush her while she was getting milked. My father kept reminding me as a joke that we couldn't take her back to Cleveland with us—she wouldn't fit in the station wagon."

Jenkins watched, fascinated, as this clever, accomplished woman recounted these things.

"Do you go back to visit?"

"Oh no, they're both dead now. The farm got sold. That was a long time ago. My God," she said, dabbing at her eyes with a Kleenex she'd pulled from her purse. "I don't want to ruin my mascara." She got a makeup kit out to make sure she was ready to go on TV.

Sally came rushing into the room.

"It's just you two," she said. "We can't find the Northwest guy. You ready?"

Cheryl and Jenkins stood. Her eyes were dry and fixed up again, the makeup kit back in her purse.

"All the TV channels are here," Sally said. "There's quite a crowd. They're handing out pieces of cake."

"That Fifth Street bridge guy isn't out there, is he?" Jenkins said.

"Oh no, sir. Not to worry. He's been arrested. Unpaid parking tickets."

FORTY-THREE

SANDY PAID THE FARRIER and gave Valentine—who'd been good—an apple. Then she got in her Subaru and headed for Johnstown. She had errands to do. She wanted to be available later if Farmer needed help.

She had to go to the bank. The propane tank was down to 15 percent. She'd locked in the price back in June, but even so, it was going to cost at least $1,000. She needed more money in the checking account.

Years earlier, Sandy had inherited money from her grandparents on her father's side. She'd paid off Farmer's pickup, bought him an eight-foot bush hog and herself a Bernina sewing machine. The rest of the money she'd put into CDs at Heartland Bank, where she and Farmer did their checking.

Every year or so she would cash in a CD, adding the money to their checking account to make ends meet. There was never a big crisis. Nothing dramatic. Just now and then they fell a little behind, usually because the propane tank needed to be filled or property taxes came due. She did this without talking to Farmer. Things weren't so bad that she needed him freaking out, getting all emotional. There was a reason why she did the financial stuff.

It wasn't like he could be more careful. He was a smart and thrifty farmer, keeping things simple. He'd learned from Frank, after all, who grew up during the Depression.

The problem with farming was that sometimes your best just wasn't good enough.

✱ ✱ ✱

In the bank lobby, at the tellers' counter cashing in her second-to-last CD, she decided to talk with Bob Germaine, the branch manager, about getting a home equity line of credit—something he'd recommended.

"He's in his office," Mary, the teller who'd been helping her, said.

Sandy went and looked through the open door. Bob was alone, at his desk looking through some papers. She knocked on the doorframe.

"Sandy!" he said. He got up and came over. They shook hands.

"How are you, Bob?"

"Can't complain. What about you and Farmer? Has he gotten those cows back in?"

Sandy seemed surprised enough that he added, "I just saw Brett."

"Farmer's working on it."

"They went quite a ways from what I hear."

"It'll be fine. Farmer's like a cow whisperer."

"Good. You tell him hey."

"I will. I wanted to ask you, Bob. You mentioned one time we might consider getting a home equity line of credit."

"Sure, sure…easy to do. Then it's just like having another checking account. You might never use it, but it's there if you need it."

"How are the fees?"

"Not bad. It's about a hundred dollars to set it up, then there's a minimum annual maintenance fee, but it's like ten dollars, I think."

"Well, we'd like to apply for one then. What do we have to do?"

"The application's simple. It's online. You can download it and bring it in. Or email it. We'll need about a week to process it is all. Now we do come out and inspect the residence as part of the approval process. We're old fashioned that way. It's just a quick walk-through."

"That's fine."

"Easy peasy. And you guys will like having it."

"OK. Thanks."

"Of course, you'll seem like less of a risk if the cattle happen to be home the day we visit—just kidding."

FORTY-FOUR

RON JACKSON was not doing well. Less than two hours after he'd sauntered out of Tee Jaye's—the man with a plan, feeling all was right with the world—he was cowering in his office, feeling sick to his stomach.

He'd worked so hard to get back on track since the intrusion of the cows.

He'd been solution-oriented, establishing what his therapist would call a framework—like a Christmas tree was how Ron liked to think of it. First you put the tree up; then you could decorate it, with things like patience and hope. His therapist liked to say, "All aboard the Solutions train: next stop Confidence City!" But Ron didn't approve of mass transit so he used the Christmas tree thing.

When he got to the park he'd stuck to his routine. He started by hoisting Old Glory up the flagpole in front of the maintenance building. A brand-new Old Glory. Pulling on the rope, raising the flag into the still grey haze, he looked beyond the pond, to where the herd was grazing. The cows seemed so relaxed. Not a care in the world. But he didn't let that bother him. They would be gone soon.

With just the slightest twitch starting up in his left eye, he'd gone back inside the maintenance building and held his morning meeting. The park's staff members were curious about the cows and started in with questions, something Ron discouraged. Betty Marsh, whose flower beds were getting trampled, was the most vocal. "Now hold up," Ron had said, signaling with both hands for them to stop. "Let me tell you about Operation Charlie Oscar Whiskey. I think that will answer any questions you have." And he'd laid it out for them, using the big dry-erase board to illustrate tactical detail. Of course they were impressed.

"In the meantime," he'd concluded, "we don't disturb the cows. The more relaxed they are, the easier things will go this evening. So—for now—no mowing. And Sally, just stay away from the flower beds. Let's concentrate on servicing our equipment, catching up on paperwork. There's that new video on diversity we never got around to."

"Operation Calm Before the Storm?" Sally had said. She could be such a smart-ass.

When the meeting was finished, he went in his office, shut the door, and did some breathing exercises. The twitch was still there, maybe a little more pronounced, but he felt calm.

Until, that is, he looked out the window and saw the Channel

Four News van. It was parked a few spaces from his Jeep Commander. *Holy God in heaven! What's a TV news crew doing at the park?* Fearing the worst, he went closer to the window so he could look toward where he last saw the cows. They were still there, a little closer to the pond. A young woman was with them. She was facing Ron's direction and he could see she was holding a big microphone. A young man with a video camera was filming her.

No! Not good! Ron thought. *Bad! Very bad!*

He called the number of the lady from the mayor's office. She answered and he said, "Hi, this is Ron Jackson."

"Mr. Jackson. What's happening? Are the cows gone?"

"No, not yet. I've made arrangements. But remember how you said you wanted things to be discreet?"

"Yes…"

"Well, there's a TV camera crew here. A reporter is with the cows. A cameraman is filming them."

"What channel, Mr. Jackson?"

"Channel Four."

"OK. They're probably trying to do a story in time for the midday news. Have they interviewed you yet?"

"Me? No, ma'am. Don't worry, I won't talk to them."

"But Mr. Jackson," Sally said. "You'll have to talk with them. They need a quote from the parks department. That should be you. You're the…what is your job?"

"Chief superintendent."

"Right. They're going to come looking for you. Don't worry. They'll be in a hurry, so you won't have to say much. It'll be over before you know it."

"But what do I say?"

"Just play it down. 'The cows are not a problem, they'll be gone soon, no big deal...' You'll do fine. I need to go now, Mr. Jackson. Hang in there."

"Should I—" he said, but she'd already hung up.

He could feel his left eye twitching erratically. *Oh yeah*, he thought. *That'll look good on TV.*

He went back to the window and crouched down, peering out from just above its bottom sill, as if dodging sniper fire. The cameraman had stopped filming. He and the woman were standing together talking, the cows some distance behind them.

This was when the trouble with his stomach started. What had been nagging indigestion—not uncommon after a big breakfast and free coffee refills at Tee Jaye's—quickly became more urgent. He felt woozy. Unexpectedly, he had the taste of sausage in his mouth.

He sat in his high-backed swivel chair and tried to steady himself by shutting his eyes. But moments later his stomach, lurching violently, lost control. Pushing the chair back and falling to his knees, he vomited into the metal trash can next to his desk. Most of the Barnyard Buster came up—all that sausage gravy.

He could hear someone knocking on his office door.

"Mr. Jackson?" It was Betty. "Sir, there's a TV news reporter here to see you. A Ms. Angela Lind, from Channel Four. She asked for you by name… I think she's here about the cows."

FORTY-FIVE

AT TEN O'CLOCK, inside the Greyhound bus station in downtown Columbus, Paul Lernovski was sitting on one of the plastic seats bolted in rows to the floor of the main room, waiting for the 2:10 to Cleveland. He'd already purchased his ticket. He had on a green army surplus jacket and a black beret, and was leaning forward, focused on a paperback book he was holding in both hands. His clothes, backpack, and the duffel bag by his feet smelled sharply of patchouli oil and campfire smoke.

"Where you headed?"

Lernovski looked up, irritated, to see, several seats down, a middle-aged man with a receded hairline and a light-grey wrinkle-free suit.

"Cleveland," Lernovski told him. Then he dove back into the paperback.

"Cleveland," the man said. "Going home?"

"Yes," Lernovski said, not looking up.

"Yeah, you don't look like you're from Columbus. That's how I guessed. I'm a good judge of people. My name's Lenny. Lenny Adams. I'm going to Buffalo."

"Never been there," Lernovski said.

"It's OK. They get all that lake-effect snow. You'd know about that, being from Cleveland."

When Lernovski did not respond, Lenny said, "I used to read. Is that a good book?"

"Yes, it is," Lernovski said.

"What's it about?"

"It's philosophy. I doubt I could explain it to you. It's by Wilhelm Reich." He pronounced Wilhelm as Vilhelm and gave an elaborate roll to the R in Reich.

"Oh. German fella?"

Lernovski did not answer.

"I always liked Stephen King myself."

"I don't read fiction," Lernovski said.

"I got a job interview in Buffalo. My kid sister lives up there."

Lernovski said, "Come on, Lenny. I just want to be left alone."

"Yeah, you from Cleveland all right… I'm going to the Wendy's across the street. You want me to get you something?"

"What would you get me? Salmonella?"

"I never heard of that. What is it? A salmon sandwich? Sounds good—I like salmon. I usually just order from the value menu."

"No, salmonella," Lernovski said. "It's bacteria, you idiot. You're what's wrong with the food system. You eat garbage and don't know the difference. Just so long as it's cheap. Well, I got involved in agriculture. I'm making a difference. I've set some things in motion, and pretty soon you're going to know all about it. 'The center cannot hold! Anarchy is loosed upon the world as some rude beast slouches towards Bethlehem!'"

"Anarchy?! What are you talking about?"

"The (Moo)vement has begun! POW! BAM! BOOM!"

Lenny stood up. He extended the handle on his suitcase so he could pull it along behind him. He walked away, toward the station's main entrance. Outside the double doors, across the street, was Wendy's. The doors whooshed open and he stepped outside. He saw a pair of uniformed police officers lounging nearby on the sidewalk and went up to them.

"Excuse me," he said. "I hate to bother you."

"What is it, sir?" said the younger officer, a woman with red hair.

"It might be nothing. But you know with all the homeland security stuff, and they say if you see something you should say something…"

"Do you have something suspicious to report?" the other officer said. He was older and had the look of a veteran.

"Well, I was talking with this young fellah inside there. He's from Cleveland, he said. He was a real jerk. Anyway, I asked him if he wanted anything from Wendy's and he got all upset. He started talking about anarchy, said he was setting things in motion. Then he made some noises that were like explosions."

"Nothing more specific?" the female officer said.

"Something about agriculture. And that made me think. I saw this thing on *Sixty Minutes* or somewhere, about guys using fertilizer to make bombs. Like in Oklahoma City. That bomb was a rental truck full of fertilizer, wasn't it?"

"Maybe he was kidding," the older officer said.

"I don't know. He wasn't much of a kidder. He said pretty soon I would know all about it. I mean, it could be nothing. But I thought I should report it."

"Point him out to us," the female officer said.

Lenny turned and went back inside through the automatic doors, the police officers following him. "Over there," he said, pointing to Lernovski. "The guy reading a book."

"OK, thank you, sir. We'll take it from here. Please go on about your business."

Lenny went back outside.

The police officers walked across the big room to where Lernovski sat reading.

"Excuse me," the female officer said.

Lernovski looked up. "What?"

"Sir, we've had a tip that you've been talking about setting off a bomb?"

"What?! No! That's ridiculous! Oh, I see. It's Lenny. That moron."

"Please don't get upset."

"Don't get upset?!"

The female officer took a step back, watching Lernovski closely. Her partner unsnapped the holster holding his pistol.

"Sir, it's important that you keep calm," he said. "Please make no sudden moves."

"Sure, because I'm like some mad bomber, right? Oh no! Better be careful! For all you know this duffel bag is a bomb."

The older officer pulled his pistol out and, crouching down, aimed it at Lernovski's chest.

"Sir," the female officer said. "We are placing you under arrest."

He started to protest but she suddenly reached forward and Tasered him.

With a muffled scream, he lurched forward and collapsed on the floor of the waiting room. The paperback he'd been holding went flying through the air and landed near him.

FORTY-SIX

SANDY LEFT MAX AND CHLOE in the front yard when she went to Johnstown.

When Farmer got home, there they were—front paws up on the board fence, barking at him, their tails wagging. He let himself in at the gate and stopped to pet them, then opened the front door and went inside. The dogs came in too.

Farmer was hungry. It was only ten o'clock, but he'd left the house at six. Breakfast was four hours ago.

Dropping his keys on the kitchen table, he saw a note from Sandy:

Farmer—
In Johnstown doing errands. I'll be home by 11:30 and able
to help after that. Love you, Sweets.

—Sandy

He went to the fridge and opened it, scanning its brightly lit interior. There wasn't much. A Tupperware with meatballs in spaghetti sauce. Half a pecan pie. Some individual yogurts. A sack of apples and some carrots were in the crisper. He opened the Tupperware and fished around in the red sauce with his fingers for a meatball. He found one and, cupping his other hand under it so he wouldn't spill sauce, brought the meatball to his mouth and put it in. He licked the red sauce off his fingers and shut the Tupperware. A few minutes later he opened the fridge and did the same thing again. This time some sauce spilled on the floor. Max, lurking nearby, rushed in and licked it up. Farmer did not touch the pecan pie. He would pretend to be the kind of adult partner Sandy deserved, who could sit down at the table after dinner and have pie with her *like a civilized human being* instead of hacking and swiping at it randomly while she was napping or outside mowing or in Johnstown doing errands. It was bad enough that when she went to reheat the spaghetti sauce someday soon for lunch, she would find there were no meatballs.

He made a peanut butter and jelly sandwich and left the kitchen with it, eating as he crossed the yard. After lunch—the last of the sandwich gone—he backed his truck up to the shed.

He went inside the shed, got a fifty-pound block of salt, and put it in his truck's bed. He got two square bales of hay and loaded them too. The bales were second-cutting timothy that Sandy fed Valentine—better than what the cows were used to. They should be pleased.

The ear tag kit was on a high shelf in the back of the shed. He put the kit in one of the five-gallon buckets he had there, then put the bucket inside the truck, on the front passenger seat.

He shut the shed doors and got in the truck. Before heading out, he called Sandy.

"Farmer," she said.

"Hey, Sandy. I'm home. I ate lunch and grabbed some stuff I need. I'm going back to the park. You want me to leave the dogs out?"

"Yeah, I'll be home soon. Everything's OK? What's happening?"

"The cows are fine. They're calm and have plenty to eat and drink. I called Dave Monroe. He and Brett are going to help me load tomorrow morning."

"Good!"

"I'm thinking I'll stay with the cows tonight. It feels weird to leave them."

"If you want, I can bring you stuff. Something to eat, a pillow and blanket, whatever. Just let me know."

"OK, I'll call you when I know what I'm doing."

FORTY-SEVEN

CHRIS HEUING hadn't sold a vehicle in weeks.

The closest he came, Monday morning, fell apart because of a credit check he ran for a young couple wanting to buy a Focus. They couldn't afford a bicycle built for two. He felt bad for them. He himself was still in his twenties and just starting out. He knew what it was like.

Chris looked more like a well-meaning Boy Scout leader or youth minister than a car salesman. He had a nice smile and kind eyes. He worked hard at his job—studying the models' different features and trim packages, warranty terms—but he wasn't the most competitive person. If his luck didn't change soon, he would be selling used cars at the satellite lot in Pataskala.

He didn't know what to make of the odd couple that came in the showroom about ten thirty. The old woman was well dressed and looked like she had money. But she was so old, it seemed unlikely she still drove. A man in his forties, much taller, accompanied her—

held the door open for her, followed her inside and walked close beside her. He wore a dark suit. Her grandson? If so, a serious one. He didn't exhibit any of the signs of excitement people show when someone is about to buy them a car.

Nick Faber, the senior salesman on duty, had already spotted the couple, decided they were not worth his time, and turned away—leaving them to Chris.

"Hey now," Chris said, walking up to them. "How are you folks?"

"We are well," the woman said.

"Glad to hear it. What a wonderful day to be alive. My name is Chris. What brings you into Finkle Ford?"

"I want a pickup truck," the woman said.

"Well, you've come to the right place. We're central Ohio's truck headquarters. Ford trucks are America's best-selling pickup, as you may know. They're built Ford tough. The F-150 is Motor Trend's Truck of the Year."

"Young man, I want to buy a truck. I do not want to discuss them."

"All right! I like your style! And you picked the right day. We've got a great selection. We just took delivery of a new shipment. I'll take you guys over in the golf cart. Let me grab my windbreaker."

"What about this one?" the woman said, indicating the massive black F-250 Super Duty at the far end of the showroom. It was next to a white convertible Mustang with red leather seats.

"Well, it's a beaut. It's the nicest truck we have. It's a King Ranch

Edition, with the Mesa leather seats and wood grain detail. We hardly ever see these. But it's a 250 and a V-8 turbo diesel. That's an awful lot of truck—maybe more than you need."

"Show it to me," the woman said.

She and her companion and Chris walked over to the truck. It was huge. It had a full-sized four-door crew cab plus an eight-foot bed.

"It's four-wheel drive?" the woman said.

"Yes. And like I was saying, it has the six-point-seven liter V-8 Powerstroke. It'll get you out of anything you might get into, believe me. Check out the interior," he added, opening the front and back doors on the passenger side. It was gorgeous inside. The leather of the seats was top grade—like saddle leather. You could smell it.

The woman walked over to the opened back door and peered inside. The cab's floor was higher than her waist.

"Yes, it is nice," she said.

"If you want to take it for a spin, I can have this puppy outside curbside in fifteen minutes."

"I want to see the tailgate."

"Oh. OK. Sure." He walked them around to the back of the truck. "This truck has the full eight-foot bed. It's got the tow package and the fifth wheel hitch kit already installed. This year Ford has added a backup camera in the handle of the tailgate. It's good for backing up in general, but it's also perfectly placed for zooming in when you're backing up to a hitch ball. And check this out. Tailgate down." The tailgate swung out and down slowly till it was flat. "Voice activated. You can also raise or lower it using the key fob."

"Thomas, if you would, please lift me onto it."

"Yes, ma'am." He leaned down and deftly scooped her up, sitting her on the tailgate.

She sat there quietly, hands folded in her lap, her legs swinging gently forward and back.

Chris didn't know what to do. Finally realizing it was best to do nothing, he stood beside Thomas, trying to match his calm. He heard a phone ringing in the background. Then a voice over the intercom telling a Mr. Jones his car was ready. A horn honked in the service area.

Finally, Martha Guildersnap said, "I'll take it."

"Really?" Chris said. "You haven't even asked me the price. It's over seventy thousand dollars."

"Give me your best price now, Chris. Do you understand? I will not haggle."

"Sixty-four-five," Chris said.

"Fine. Use this." She handed him an American Express card. "Thomas and I will take the truck now. Kindly have it ready in fifteen minutes. Thomas will do whatever paperwork is needed. He has power of attorney."

Chris and Thomas left her sitting on the tailgate. As they walked across the showroom toward Chris's cubicle, Chris said, "Your grandmother doesn't mess around."

"I am her driver. And, yes, she does not, as you say, mess around."

That was when Chris saw the stretch black limousine parked outside the side entrance. "Is this your car?" he said.

"It is hers."

"You're her driver… Who is she? Would I know her?"

"I don't think so."

Chris looked at the American Express card and read the name on it: The Guildersnap Fund. The name seemed familiar but he couldn't place it. Then he realized—the Guildersnap Building. One of the tallest towers in downtown Columbus. And here he'd been wondering if the AmEx would go through.

"Is she looking to trade the limo in?" he asked.

"No. We'll leave it for now. I'll come get it later. You know, we really should hurry, Chris. She meant fifteen minutes—not twenty, believe me."

"You bet." Chris ushered him into his cubicle.

Nick Faber showed up suddenly. "Nick Faber," he said to Thomas, reaching to shake his hand. "Senior salesman. Is Chris here taking care of you?"

"Yes, he is."

"They're buying the King Ranch," Chris said. He held up the American Express card to show Nick. The bastard.

Precisely fifteen minutes later, with Martha Guildersnap in the back seat, Thomas climbed in behind the wheel of the truck, started its powerful engine, and backed it carefully out of its parking space. Chris was there, hovering, happy, even a little giddy. He waved cheerfully as the truck drove away.

He wondered if Thomas or Mrs. Guildersnap had any idea what that truck could do. Would they ever even take it off-road?

He went back inside the showroom. He would go ahead and write the post-sale thank you card and get it in the mail to them. The newest members of the Finkle Ford family.

FORTY-EIGHT

BACK AT CHANNEL FOUR, Angela went straight to Bob Jones's office. He was waiting for her. He waved her in through the open door and into the chair facing his desk.

"Angela," he said. "It is Angela, isn't it?"

"Yes, sir."

"I'm told you and Joey got some stuff we can run?"

"Yes, sir."

"Outstanding! Give me a full report!"

"Well, the story has changed. Sir, the cows talk."

"They talk? What do you mean?"

"They talk, sir. I interviewed them."

"Where did the parks department get talking cows?"

"Well, it turns out the cows aren't part of any parks department initiative. They're runaways, from some farm. They just happened to show up at the park."

"Talking cows…and you got the interview. So, what do they say?"

"It's a mixed bag. Everything's kind of confused. But this one cow—wait till you hear. She's like this spokescow. She's incredible. She was like quoting philosophy, talking about justice and liberty. She says they want to live on their own, and they think their best chance is in town, with city people."

"My God, Angela. Do you know what this means?"

"It's a bigger story?"

"You got that right. One minute we're talking about the fact that idiots are in charge of the parks department. That hack Jarvis and his golfing buddies. Now we're talking about what could be a seminal event for animal rights—an issue that's been bubbling up forever.

"Animal rights has it all: Hot-headed activists on both sides; special interests; big business versus grassroots do-gooders. There's a religious component—man's dominion and whatnot. It ties into the whole sustainability thing... This story is like Roe v. Wade meets *Animal Farm* meets Frank Capra meets *Silent Spring*! An Inconvenient Herd! And we have the exclusive? I only have one question for you."

"Sir?"

"Are you ready?"

"Yes, I think so."

"OK. Here we go."

He hit a button on his desk phone and said, "Martha, send everybody in here! Ev-ery-body!"

Minutes later, with the entire news team assembled before him, Bob Jones said, "While you jagoffs were out of the building earlier today, having two-hour breakfast meetings with your agents, getting massages and haircuts, young Angela here saved the day by grabbing hold of what could be the biggest story of the year. She has grabbed it by the horns! So now we are all going to pitch in and help. Sam, you and Mitch look at the footage she and Joey took. We're going with it at noon. We're going to follow it up with some in-studio back-and-forth with Angela, so, Jackie, do something with her hair and get her down to wardrobe.

"What we've got is talking cows, people. They've come to town and want to stay. So first things first.

"They ran away from some farm. Probably out in Licking County. We need to find the jerk farmer who couldn't keep them in. What's his story? Was he not feeding them? Is he a drunk? Maybe he's in the wrong line of work. The cows are smarter than he is. He should be growing potatoes, this guy. Or he's sadistic. His wife left him so he starts taking it out on the cows. Or a pervert. Hangs out at barnyardlove-dot-com. We had that guy last year, remember? Wrote that book *Fourteen Shades of Consent*. Gail, find the stuff on him in case it's relevant. He was in Indiana somewhere.

"Now listen. Whatever his deal, this farmer is up against it. Everything his cows say can and will be used against him. He's in a world of shit. We need to be the ones to find him. We'll drag him through the streets.

"And as always, children—the best thing about this or any story—it gives us a chance to stick it to the mayor. He's out at the airport toasting the first non-stop flights between Columbus and San Francisco, as if we're some high-tech hub, and these cows come along and revive the whole cow town image he's trying to shed? It's like one step forward two steps back. And just before the debate? It's perfect!"

FORTY-NINE

THE COWS HAD MANAGED to get some serious grazing done, even with all the interruptions. It had been one thing after another all morning—a pattern they were starting to recognize as the hectic pace of big city life. Now, pleased to have a little quiet time, they settled down chewing cud, enjoying the warmth of the day. After a while they would graze some more, then go to the pond for water.

The sun was near the top of the sky. Farmer would be back soon.

"He probably won't come out and ask us, but he'll want to know if we've decided to go back to the farm," 74 said.

"I'm ready," 27 said.

"Farmer takes good care of us," 38 said.

"I get the feeling if we decide to stay in town he might try to trick us," 68 said.

"He's worried about us," 27 said.

38 said, "I agree he's acting sneaky. But I think he wants the best for us."

"You know my opinion," 42 said.

74 said, "This is an awesome adventure we're having. It's fun making friends. But Lernovski was wrong about the city being a good place for us. There's not enough to eat."

"Winter is coming," 68 said.

"I still think we should stay," 42 said. "We should do it for the greater herd."

"If you stay, I'll stay with you, 42," 106 said.

"No, I'll do whatever the herd decides. And so will you."

"Stupid herd."

38 said, "Either way we need to figure out what names we want. Farmer's bringing the ear tag kit, remember?"

FIFTY

HEADING BACK TO CITY HALL on I-670 after the ribbon cutting at the airport, Mayor Jenkins was brooding. After a long silence, he said, "Sally, I want to stop by Jack Franklin's."

"Sir?"

"I need a consult. Something's bugging me."

Jack Franklin: political consultant extraordinaire. He was practically a member of the campaign, they used him so much. He ran a little shop called Emerging Demographics. Sally thought of him as a kind of genius.

"Sir, we're on a tight schedule. You've still got two appointments before noon. Jack might not be available."

"As much money as we spend with him, he'll be available."

"I'll call him."

Sally got out her phone.

Jenkins leaned forward and said to the driver, "George, change of plans. North High and Spring Street."

George glanced up in the rearview mirror, looking for Sally. She caught his eye and nodded agreement.

"Yes, sir," George told the mayor. "North High and Spring."

"Hello, Jack?" Sally said into her phone. "The mayor would like to stop by. Is this a good time? We're in a car, maybe five minutes away... All right. See you."

She hung up. "I don't mean to second guess you, sir. I'm just trying to keep on schedule."

She made another call. "Todd, the people from the Children's Hospital are going to show up for an eleven o'clock. We're running fifteen minutes late. Let them in the conference room and offer them coffee. Tell them there's an emergency and we'll be there by eleven fifteen. Thanks."

They rode in silence, the mayor looking out at the traffic around them.

"It's about the cows, isn't it?" Sally said.

Jenkins didn't say anything.

"Oh my God! It is! Why can't you just forget about them? This is not the time for distractions."

"Are they a distraction, Sally? Or are they somehow the main point? I've been blindsided by cows more times than I can count in the past two days. Clearly I am missing something. I think you are too. We cannot have blind spots, Sally."

"A couple coincidences, sir…"

"Oh, really? Let's see." Jenkins leaned forward. "George?" he said.

"Yes, sir?"

"What are your feelings about cows?"

"Excuse me, sir?"

"Cows, George. Do you like them?"

"I guess so. They seem nice."

"*Seem* nice?" Sally said, leaning forward next to the mayor. "So you don't have any personal feelings for them?"

"No. I'm from New Jersey. It's my husband who loves them."

"Your husband loves cows?" Jenkins said.

"Yes. We have cow Christmas tree ornaments, a cow-shaped cream pitcher he brings out when we serve coffee to guests, cow silhouette dish towels. And some pajamas of his I'd as soon not talk about. He grew up in an awful little town in Indiana. Not that you'd know it to see him now. But he carries the scars."

Jenkins gave Sally an *I told you so* look.

"Thank you, George," he said.

He and Sally sat back just in time, as George took the steep exit ramp up to High Street. He waited at a red light, signaling a right turn.

"I'm telling you, Sally," Jenkins said. "People say they're sick of Columbus being a cow town. And we're promising them change—out with the old, in with the new—a brave new central Ohio. But just under the surface—the martini bars and Tesla superchargers;

valet parking and tapas and all-day spa treatments; gallery hops; fly-fishing shops; Asian fusions and downtown lofts, personal coaches and green spaces—under it all there remains this tremendous hidden aquafer of nostalgia. A longing for what has been left behind. I'm so busy being progressive, I've overlooked it. But not anymore. These cows are a trigger!"

Turning north on High, they entered the gauntlet of restaurants and boutiques that was the Short North, where aspirations hit the ground running. On the left, a modern furniture store selling cubist armchairs for $6,000. Next door, a FOR LEASE sign in the window of a shop that, one week earlier, was offering hemp hats from Italy. A little farther down: a wine bistro that had been featured in *Columbus Monthly*, a foreign languages bookstore, and a new place Sally had never noticed called Maggie Loo's.

"Sir, you've got a point. I'm just not sure it's something we need to focus on six hours before the debate."

George pulled over to the curb near the corner of High and Spring, stopping in front of a stationary store that specialized in fountain pens. Jack Franklin's office was upstairs.

"I'll just feel better if I can talk this through with Jack," Jenkins said. "This whole cow situation feels volatile."

"I'll wait in the car," Sally said. "Ten minutes, OK?"

Jenkins opened his door and got out. As he was being buzzed into the stairwell leading up to Jack's, Sally's phone rang. It was Ron

Jackson, calling from his office at Sutter Park. He'd just seen the Channel Four News reporter and was freaking out. He was a wreck. Sally tried to calm him down, but there wasn't much she could do.

Five minutes later, back from his consultation, Jenkins was pro-cow. He told Sally, "I've been focused on keeping the cows a secret, but that's not important. What matters is that they're safe. We can't let anything bad happen to them."

"Why, what did Jack say?"

"Basically, they poll much better than I do. Thirty points better. They rate up there with like panda bears and puppies."

The Lincoln was heading south on High Street, toward city hall.

Jenkins said, "Maybe you should call that guy at the park."

"I just talked to him, sir. The cows are fine. But they've been dis-covered. Channel Four News was just there taping them."

"Bob Jones. That bastard. He wants to rub my nose in it. But see, he's got it all wrong too."

Sally was reminded again of why she and Jenkins were such a good team. She was the organized expert; he had the reflexes of a cat that always landed on its feet.

FIFTY-ONE

JOE MARTIN, teeth in, emerged from Building D a little before eleven o'clock. He headed toward the clubhouse, where he was scheduled to meet up with two friends: George Parker, also in his eighties but still driving, and Bill Miller, ninety-three. Together, they comprised the Royal Crest Birding Club. Weather and various ailments and conditions permitting, they would meet in the clubhouse Wednesday mornings, then pile into George's Impala and go across the street to Sutter Park, where, sitting on a bench near the pond, they drank thermoses of coffee and talked. Bill had a nice pair of binoculars, which they took turns using to spot birds.

There were red-winged blackbirds and bobolinks, all sorts of warblers and sparrows and swallows, cardinals, bluebirds, bobwhites and mockingbirds, and red-tailed hawks. A pair of great blue herons sometimes visited the pond, which also drew kingfishers and several kinds of ducks. Sometimes they would catch a glimpse of wild turkeys that lived in the woods. Otherwise there were the damn geese, so many of them, honking loudly and shitting all over everything. And plenty of other birds the men could not identify.

They weren't dedicated birders. They just enjoyed being outside, having an appointment now and then that was not medically related. And they liked being together.

Truth be told, they were as likely to watch Betty Marsh, the parks employee who took care of the flower beds. She was constantly needing to squat and bend while working, no doubt part of why she was in such splendid shape.

When Joe Martin got to the clubhouse, Bill and George were waiting for him on the bench in the foyer. Joe told them, "We may have a little excitement today, fellas. Yesterday some cows showed up."

"Cows?" George said.

"What's that?" Bill said.

"Cows!" Joe said more loudly. "I think there's a good chance they'll be at the park."

"That'd be different," Bill said.

"Let's go," George said. He and Joe helped Bill to his feet. "We'll do some cow gazing."

They went outside and over to the Impala.

"They'll be grazing and we'll be gazing," Bill said.

Fifteen minutes later, the three friends were sitting on a bench near the duck pond, admiring the cows grazing in the distance.

They'd each taken a couple turns with the binoculars, which were too heavy to look through for very long.

"They're really something," George said.

Bill said, "We had sheep. I was ten years old before I realized everybody in the world didn't have mutton for dinner every night."

"I never knew sheep," Joe said.

"They're fragile."

"Cows have always been my favorite," Joe said. "And wait till you meet these. They're really nice. They'll let you scratch them if you want to. Whatever farm they came from, they must have been treated pretty well."

"I don't think I'll be scratching them," Bill said. "I'll leave that to you youngsters."

George said, "OK, guys, so today we are not the Royal Crest Birding Club. Today, we are the Former Farmers of America."

"Former Farmers. I like it," Joe said.

"We could have jackets," Bill said.

"Anymore, that's about the only kind of farmers left," Joe said.

"You got that right," George said. "My great-grandson joined the FFA last year. He lives with his mom now, just outside Mansfield. I asked him if he's going to be a farmer when he grows up, since he's in the Future Farmers. You know what he told me? FFA doesn't mean Future Farmers of America."

"How can it not mean that?"

"They tell the kids it's just the FFA now; the FFA Organization. The letters don't stand for anything in particular—like UPS or IBM. Nobody cares what the letters used to mean. Most of those kids are never going to farm, so I guess the name got to be an embarrassment."

"That's a shame," Bill said.

"It's a bunch of BS is what it is," Joe said.

While the men were talking, a big black pickup truck turned into the parking lot and parked not far behind them.

"Jeez," Joe said. "That's some rig."

"It still has temporary tags," George said.

"Hey look. The cows are coming," Bill said. He hadn't turned around to look at the truck because of his neck.

George and Joe turned and saw the cows coming closer, heads bobbing, the two calves bringing up the rear. They passed through some flower beds on their way to the pond. They were about to step down into the water (to drink, Joe guessed) when one of them looked up and stared straight at the three men.

"Joe Martin?" the cow said. "Is that you?"

And just like that she made his day—heck, his whole month. He blushed with pride.

"Yes," he said. "Hello. Good to see you again."

The herd changed course and came over to the bench. When the cows got close, Joe could see it was 68 who had recognized him.

"Hi, Joe Martin," some of the cows said, not quite in unison.

"These are my friends, George and Bill."

That led to a clumsy chorus of "Hi, George! Hi, Bill!"

"Our friends now," one cow said.

"Heya," George said. Bill waved.

"They're as old as you are, Joe," 68 said.

"Well…"

"Danny came to see us last night," 38 said.

"That's nice," Joe said.

The driver's door of the black pickup truck opened and Thomas Reeves stepped out, still wearing his dark suit.

"Is he a friend of yours?" 74 said.

Joe turned and saw Thomas walking toward them.

"I don't know him," he said.

The cows were not at all spooked by Thomas when he came near. "Hello," he said. "Good morning. Do these cows belong to you gentlemen?"

"No, we're just talking to them," Joe said.

"We don't belong to anyone," 42 said.

"I beg your pardon," Thomas said, bowing slightly to the cows. "I meant no offense."

"That's some truck you've got there," George said.

"It belongs to my employer. She heard the cows were here and had me bring her to see them."

"She must have lived on a farm too. Tell her we're the Former

Farmers of America. We're the new FFA. She's welcome to come sit with us."

"I will tell her."

Thomas went to the truck. A rear window slid down and he spoke through it briefly. Then he opened the door. He helped Martha down out of the truck. She was wearing a dark coat and was incognito again—the silk scarf and big sunglasses giving her an air of mystery.

She took Thomas's arm and he walked her to the bench. "Gentlemen," she said when she was standing in front of the three men. "Hello. I am Martha Guildersnap. I am pleased to make your acquaintance."

Joe and George stood. They helped Bill up and, stammering and blushing, they managed to introduce themselves.

"Please, sit," she said. At their age, that's all it took. They sat a little closer together, leaving room for her at one end of the bench.

She sat too, next to Joe.

"Martha," Joe said. "These are the cows." He made a grand gesture of presentation with his right arm. "Cows, say hello to Martha."

"Hello, Martha!"

"Heya!"

"Welcome!"

Martha was positively beaming. She took off her big sunglasses and folded them. She handed them to Thomas. "Hello there, girls," she said. "I have been looking forward to meeting you."

"You have?" 74 said.

"Yes. And I am in no way disappointed. You are lovely. Absolutely lovely."

"You seem nice too," 74 said.

"And who is this?" Martha said, peering between the cows to look at 102, who was behind her mother.

"That's my daughter," 68 said.

"She's the cutest little calf I think I've ever seen."

"She's shy," 68 said. "102, come up here and say hello to the lady. You need to stop being so timid."

102 came up beside her mother.

"Hello," she said. She didn't look Martha in the eye, but added, "Very pleased to meet you."

"Oh, honey, you are as cute as a button."

"What about me?" 106 said. He came up next to 102.

"Yes, you're cute too," Martha said. "All of you are. OK, now listen. I have a surprise for you. I think you are going to like it. Do you want it now?"

The cows didn't say anything. Normally they would have said no. Cows hate surprises. But she had made it sound like a good thing and they were curious.

"On my way here, Thomas and I stopped and got you a gift. Thomas?" she said.

Thomas bowed slightly to the cows, then turned and went to

the back of the black truck. He lowered its tailgate, slipped on some thin leather gloves and, with everyone except Bill watching, pulled a bale of hay out onto the tailgate. He picked it up by its strings and carried it toward the cows.

The bale was dark green and pungent. The cows were all sniffing the air.

"What is it?" 38 said.

"It's not like any hay I've ever seen," 74 said. "It smells wonderful."

"It is a bale of pure alfalfa," Martha said. "A token of my esteem."

"*All* alfalfa?" 42 said.

"I am ready to do the honors," Thomas said. "Where would you like it?"

"Anywhere is fine," 74 said.

Thomas carried the bale out into the grass and put it down. With a small penknife, he cut the bale's strings. The bale sprung apart.

"Spread it out some if you would," 68 said.

Thomas obliged, picking up sheaves and tossing them ten feet or so in various directions. Then he walked back to the bench, avoiding the cows rushing toward the hay.

They tasted the hay. Within a bite or two all of them were eating greedily. It looked like the bale wouldn't last ten minutes. "Awesome!" "Wow!" "Alfalfa!" "Best hay ever!" were some of the things Thomas and Martha and the Former Farmers heard the cows saying as they ate.

"They really like it," Joe said.

"I wanted them to have the best," Martha said. "I swear, there is nothing more satisfying than watching cows eat."

It *was* entrancing. It was like watching a busy bird feeder.

"Mr. Martin, Thomas told me you and your friends are members of the Former Farmers of America. This is an organization I do not know. Is it national?"

Joe laughed. "No, that's just something we made up. It's a gag."

"I see. Well then, I should say you have made a rather good one. I am amused."

"We figure we're about the only kind of farmers left so we might as well stick together. Did you live on a farm?"

"I married a farmer. We milked for ten years."

"Well, consider yourself a full-fledged member in good standing. Bill here grew up with sheep. George was a hog farmer."

"I kept two hundred chickens," Martha said.

"Jeez."

"Man, that bale is already about done," George said.

"I'd forgotten how earnestly they eat," Martha said. "Thomas? How many bales did we bring?"

"Just the one, ma'am."

"Oh."

"I misunderstood," he said. "It seemed like a lot."

"Thomas is a good man. But not a former farmer," Martha said.

The cows, having finished the hay—there was hardly any trace of the alfalfa left—came back to the bench.

"Thanks for that," 74 said to Martha. "It was awesome."

"Oh, honey, you are very welcome. Believe me, seeing you enjoy it is all the thanks I need. It's been such a long time since I've been around cows."

"Alfalfa lady," 27 said. "What did you say your name was?"

"Martha."

"Martha. That's pretty," 38 said.

"Look out, Martha. 38 might steal your identity."

"No I won't. Danny says lots of people have the same name. It's the numbers that have to be different."

"What's all this?" Martha said.

"We're getting names," 68 said. "Farmer's going to help us do it when he comes back."

"When is your farmer coming?"

"Soon. Around lunchtime, he said."

"I should like to meet him," Martha said.

27 said, "He's nice. He worries a lot."

"Do you know what names he has chosen for you?"

"No, we're choosing them," 74 said. "That's the whole point."

"Cows are more independent these days," Joe told Martha.

"Yes, I can see that. Well, so what names do you have in mind?"

"I'm going to be Sandy," 38 said. "Either Sandy or Helen. Helen is Farmer's mother's name. Or Angela. What do you think?"

"They're all good," Joe said.

"They seem like fine choices," Martha said. "What about you, 27?"

"I haven't decided. I'm thinking Helen. I love how that sounds. But I like Sandy too."

"I like Sandy," 74 said.

"I'm going to be Joe Martin," 68 said.

"Really?" Joe said. Another unexpected honor.

"Sure," she said. "So I can remember you."

"Aw," Joe said. Then he said, "Oh hell." He was crying. He tried to stop, wiping the first tears away, but they kept coming.

"Thomas," Martha said. Thomas stepped forward and offered Joe a handkerchief.

"Thank you." Joe dabbed at his tears. When he was finished, he handed the handkerchief back to Thomas.

"He cries a lot," 74 told Martha.

"He's very sensitive," 68 said. "That's why he's such a good scratcher. Speaking of which…" She stretched out her neck.

"You betcha, sweetheart," Joe said.

FIFTY-TWO

DON MULLIGAN, anchor of the Midday Update, Channel Four News (the Hometown Team), nearing the conclusion of Wednesday's broadcast: "And finally…with winter coming…a lot of folks are making sure to take advantage of Columbus's metro parks—before it gets too cold. And not just people. From Sutter Park, Angela Lind reports."

Tape of Angela Lind (in park, the cows grazing behind her): "When the sun came up this morning, this herd of cattle was here in Sutter Park. They seem quite happy, grazing as you can see. But where did they come from? And how did they get here? Earlier, I spoke with Ron Jackson, chief superintendent of the park, about the bovine visitors."

Tape of Ron Jackson standing just outside the entrance to the Sutter Park maintenance building. He seems nervous as Angela—mic in hand—asks him questions.

Angela: "Mr. Jackson, can you explain why there are cows in the park?"

Jackson: "They just showed up is all. It's no big deal."

Angela: "Sir, I'm just trying to establish why the cows are here. One source claims they were brought in as part of an experiment with a more natural approach to park maintenance. Are you saying this is not the case?"

Jackson: "These bovines were not requisitioned."

Angela: "When did they get here?"

Jackson: "They appeared yesterday at about five o'clock. We have been monitoring them closely ever since. Citizens need not be concerned. I remain in full control. Anyone intending to utilize the park can do so knowing it is secure and available for their recreational needs. They will need to watch where they step, of course."

Angela: "So, in your opinion, these cows do not present any danger?"

Jackson: "No, they are large animals, but thoroughly domesticated, focused on the ingestion of forage."

Angela: "How long do you think the grass in the park can sustain them?"

Jackson: "Regardless, the bovines' presence here will soon expire. A plan for their removal—Operation Charlie Oscar Whiskey—has already been initiated."

Angela: "What does that mean?"

Jackson: "It means the park is for taxpaying citizens, not refugee livestock."

Angela: "Do you—"

Jackson: "Now, ma'am. I really am busy."

Jackson goes inside the maintenance building. The door closes behind him.

Angela (now alone): "That was Ron Jackson, chief superintendent of Sutter Park. He says the cows won't be here long. But I talked to the cows earlier and that's not what they said. And yes, you heard me right, Columbus. Hold onto your ball caps, because these cows talk!"

Tape of Angela standing in the grassy area with 42 and 74—the other cows nearby watching.

Angela: "Number 74, you and your cow friends seem quite at home here in Sutter Park."

74: "They are my herd mates. Yes, we like it here."

68: "Thanks, Joe Martin! Thanks, Danny!"

Angela: "Who are they?"

74: "Friends of ours. They recommended the park."

106 (suddenly appearing next to 74): "Show and tell!"

He starts sliding his tongue in and out of his nostrils, left-right-left-right, alternating quickly.

Angela: "Oh my!"

74 turns and lowers her head, then rams 106's midsection. 106 is lifted and thrown well beyond the camera's view.

74 (resuming): "Anyway, yes, it's nice here. But when we've eaten all the grass, of course, we'll move on."

Angela: "Where will you go?"

42: "We don't know yet."

Angela: "Will you stay in Columbus?"

42: "That's a decision we will make as a herd."

Angela: "But you won't go back to the farm you came from?"

42: "Speaking for myself, I am more inclined to pursue a post-agricultural lifestyle."

Angela: "So, is there anything you would like to tell people? A lot of them will be watching."

106 (from off camera): "Go Bucks!"

42: "Just respect us. That's the main thing. We understand people are predators, and we know we are delicious. It puts us in a tough position. But if people can rise above their appetites a little and give us a chance, they might find we can be good neighbors too. Freedom is a universal condition. We have as much right to it as anyone."

Angela: "OK. From Sutter Park, this is Angela Lind reporting."

Back in the studio live, Don Mulligan is talking with Angela, now resplendent in a tight red dress.

Don: "Well, it seems like *everyone* wants to move to Columbus these days. Who can blame them? Cute cows, Angela. Good job."

Angela: "Thanks, Don. It was amazing being able to talk with them, but also I really liked them. They're nice animals."

Don: "That one was quite the politician. Very articulate for a cow."

Angela: "Yes."

Don: "Fascinating. Well, thanks for watching, Columbus. Don't forget, tonight at six o'clock is the mayoral debate. You can watch it right here on Channel Four. And we'll have an update for you about those cows on our five o'clock report—another Hometown Team Exclusive."

FIFTY-THREE

FARMER AND SANDY'S NEIGHBOR, Linda Green, was in her living room. She was in the upholstered chair Sonny had placed near the big window overlooking Cooper Road. Within reach on the cluttered table was the police scanner, her cell phone, a pair of camo binoculars that had belonged to her husband, the TV remote (aka the clicker), and an opened bag of hard red-and-white-striped peppermint candies.

She'd just gotten back from the foot doctor.

She turned on the big TV across the room, leaving it on mute. The twelve o'clock news on Channel Ten had already started. George Simmons was on vacation again—he was getting old—and this new one, Jimmy, was filling in. Mrs. Green hadn't made up her mind about Jimmy. He was from Minnesota.

Out the window, on Cooper Road, there was no traffic. There usually wasn't during lunchtime.

She unwrapped a peppermint candy and put it in her mouth.

The candies were her one weakness, which she permitted herself in a guarded way. She didn't want to end up having sugar like her sister.

She took up the binoculars and looked out across Cooper Road into Farmer's pasture. When she finally had the darn things focused, she scanned the gently rolling grass, looking for the cows. They weren't there. What a shame.

Refocusing the binoculars, she studied the Thompson place across the street. Their empty trash cans were still out by the road—three days after trash day. How people could live like that, she didn't know.

The phone rang. It was her cousin Martha.

"How'd it go?" Martha said.

"He ordered me some inserts. There's no point in surgery, he says. He's got a new receptionist. That Becky with the red hair is gone. I think he must have fired her. This new one now, by God, she's right on it. She doesn't miss a trick. You remember Hank and Betty Felton from up the pike, near the Homer turnoff? Their granddaughter."

"I just talked with Kathy. Jill Marlow fell last night."

"What happened?"

"Harry said she was walking across the living room. Turned to look at something on the TV and just went down. The squad took her to Licking Memorial."

"I hope she's OK," Mrs. Green said.

"She doesn't focus."

"Same as when she drove. My God she was a menace. I remember one time, she ended up in a ditch. She walked to the Lloyds' and called Harry. He took the tractor over there to pull the car out but she forgot to mention it was upside down. He never did figure out how she did that."

"Are you on Channel Four?" Martha said.

"No, Channel Ten. I don't like Don Mulligan." She looked at the TV and saw Samantha James, that nice girl who'd just had twins, standing in front of a big weather map. Her figure had come right back.

"Channel Four!" Martha said. "You've got to see this!"

Mrs. Green switched channels. She saw Angela Lind with the cows. Straight away she recognized them as Farmer's. She hung up the phone.

Oh my God, she thought, dialing Sandy's number.

"Hello?" Sandy said.

"Mrs. Farmer, this is Linda Green. I sure hate to bother you like this, but I thought you would want to know. Your cows are on TV."

"What?! Are they all right? Has something happened?"

"They seem fine. They're in some park, it looks like. In Columbus. How they got all that way without getting hit by a car I don't know."

"What channel, Mrs. Green?"

"Channel Four."

"Thank you." Sandy hung up.

Mrs. Green turned the TV sound up. The lady reporter was in the studio, talking with that awful Don Mulligan—telling him the cows wanted to stay in town. *They can have it*, she thought. She would no sooner move into a big city like Columbus than she would climb into a rocket ship headed to the moon.

FIFTY-FOUR

AT NOON, deep inside city hall, Sally Martinez and mayoral aides Todd and Lilly were in the Strategy Room watching the midday news. Four TVs were on, each showing a different network affiliate. They were set on low volume.

All the channels led with the ribbon cutting at the airport. It was a formula piece, pretty reliable, and it came out as expected. It was good news and made the mayor look good. He was gracious—crediting others—all the while occupying center stage. This was Sally's specialty—enhancing the mayor's brand without seeming to sell.

"Nice," Todd said.

Lilly said, "What is that? Like twenty thousand dollars' worth of airtime?"

"At least," Sally said. "OK. Now mute the others and turn up Channel Four. Let's see about these cows."

Toward the end of the broadcast—as a final feel-good feature— the anchor went to Angela Lind, reporting from Sutter Park. She was standing outside in an open grassy area. Behind her, in the distance, cows were grazing.

Then she was standing near a building, with a man she introduced as Ronald Jackson, chief superintendent of the park.

"Come on, Jackson. You can do this," Sally muttered.

But he looked shaky. Also, now that she was seeing him, something was bugging her. He looked familiar somehow.

"I know him but I can't put my finger on it," she said.

Todd said, "Why is he sweating like that? Jeez. He looks like De Niro in *Taxi Driver*."

"'He's in control of the park'? Who talks like that?" Lilly said.

The door burst open and Jenkins came in. His jacket was off, his tie loosened. "Are you watching this?" he said. He stood behind their chairs and fell silent, watching with them.

"Oh my God!" Sally said when Jackson mentioned Operation Charlie Oscar Whiskey. "What's wrong with this guy?"

"I know him…" Jenkins said.

"Me too," Sally said. She relaxed, knowing it would come to the mayor. He was uncanny like that.

Todd said, "Are other cities using cows for park maintenance? Is that a thing?"

"Look into it," Sally said. "It sounds good. In fact—you know? It's one of the greenest things I've ever heard of. We could end up taking credit. If life gives you a herd of cattle…"

"She's interviewing the cows?!" Jenkins said. "They talk?! Since when do cows talk?!"

He had a flash of panic: the cow he had almost hit with his car describing what happened. "Oh, it was no accident. He *tried* to hit me. I don't know why anyone would vote for a person like that."

Sally and the interns were as surprised as the mayor. In fact, in front of TVs all over central Ohio, thousands of people were transfixed, watching with open-mouthed wonderment as the cows conversed with Angela.

"Post-agricultural lifestyle…" Todd mumbled. He wondered if 42 could use an intern.

"I never even knew I liked cows," Lilly said.

"This certainly makes things more interesting," Sally said. She wondered about the possibility of getting an endorsement from the cows. And naturally worried that Parnell's people could be having the same thought. She needed to reach out to the cows.

When the story was over, Sally turned the TV off.

"OK, so, talking cows," she said. "That's one heck of a wild card."

"Austin is using goats," Todd said, reading from his phone. "… part of an initiative to reduce the city's carbon footprint. They just won a big grant from the EPA… San Diego's using cows."

"Call San Diego," Sally said. "Let's find out what—"

"Son of a bitch!" Jenkins said. "I know who he is! He's that guy who killed the deer in Blendon Woods!"

"Yes!" Sally said. Then, realizing the implications of Operation Charlie Oscar Whiskey, she added, "Oh no."

"What?" Todd and Lilly said.

"He's like an ex-marine or something," Jenkins said. "Guy's a nut. I thought we had him fired."

"No, Jarvis said he'd keep him under control. They must have reassigned him to Sutter Park."

"You can't control crazy," Jenkins said.

"What?" Lilly said. "What did he do?"

Sally said, "Three years ago there was an overpopulation of deer. It was a problem all over Ohio. There were way too many deer in Blendon Woods Park, and there was concern they would become this horrible spectacle during the winter, slowly starving to death. This guy, he ran the park, and he decided to thin the herd, which his bosses approved. They must have thought he would relocate them or something.

"So he told the media he would be closing the park on Monday to thin the herd. He told everyone. Then, that morning, he brought in snipers. Folks started hearing shots coming from the park. Someone called the police and they went in and made the snipers stop."

"But they didn't stop," Jenkins said. "He had those guys put silencers on their guns and they kept shooting."

"What's he going to do to those cows?" Todd asked.

Jenkins told Sally, "Damn it, we should have fired that freak when we had the chance. Get Jarvis on the phone."

FIFTY-FIVE

WHEN FARMER got to the park at noon, it was calm and mostly deserted. The cows were in the pond drinking. They didn't see him turn into the parking lot. There were only a few cars, most of them near the building. One of them was the red Toyota that belonged to the park employee he'd met that morning.

Closer to the pond, at the other end of the lot, an imposing black pickup truck was backed into a parking space. It was an F-250 with big tires. It was so new it still had temporary tags. Farmer carefully backed in beside the truck so that his tailgate would face the open grassy area.

A man was sitting behind the wheel of the other truck. He was reading a magazine. He looked up, saw Farmer, and nodded to him. Farmer opened his door and got out. He went around to the back of his truck.

The tailgate of the other truck was down. An older and distinguished-looking woman was sitting on it. She had a silk scarf tied down over her hair. She was watching the cows.

"Hello," Farmer said.

She looked over at him and smiled.

"You must be their farmer," she said. "The cows told me you'd be coming. I would get up to say hello but I need Thomas's help to get down off this tailgate. I am Martha Guildersnap."

"I'm Farmer."

"I've been enjoying your cows. I am a charter member of the Former Farmers of America. You just missed the others. My husband Edgar and I milked a small herd for ten years. Not far from here, actually. A long time ago."

"That's the hardest kind of farming. I'm glad I don't have dairy cows."

"It's all relative. Many people, seeing what you do, wouldn't want any part of it. They might even think you're mad. Whereas I rather envy you."

"You do?"

"I am a wealthy woman, Farmer. And I have power. I am one of the Masters. But suddenly I am feeling more like a caged bird. I miss being outdoors. You don't have to go to a park to visit nature; it is at your doorstep. And you get to spend your days with cattle. Such magnificent creatures. I'd forgotten about them."

Farmer, who'd been keeping an eye on the cows, now focused

on them more fully, trying to see them from this woman's point of view. 27 had her back arched and was pissing into the pond only a few feet from where 74 was drinking. As he watched, 106 squirted out some thin manure, the last of it dribbling down his rear.

"I don't know. They're not for everyone," Farmer said. "They suit me. I can't say why. My wife Sandy's the same way with horses."

"Your wife's name is Sandy," Martha said. "I guess that explains why your cows all want to be named Sandy. Or Helen."

"That's my mother's name."

"Yes, I know."

"I promised them they could have names. It seems to mean a lot to them."

"It's all they could talk about earlier. They're very excited about it."

"Hey, whatever makes them happy."

Martha said, "Farmer, I think these cows must have a good home with you."

"Well, they're meat animals. No way around that. I just do everything I can to make sure they have lots of good days and just one bad one."

"At this point in my life, that's a deal I might accept myself."

The cows were coming out of the pond. They'd seen Farmer and were coming over.

"Hey, Farmer," 74 said.

"Hey, you guys."

"You've met Martha."

"She says we're magnificent," 68 said.

"Yes, she's a real fan," Farmer said. "So, I brought that hay we talked about. And the salt. I didn't forget."

"Oh. OK," 74 said.

"Sure."

"Thanks, Farmer."

They weren't very enthusiastic.

Farmer dropped his tailgate so they could see the hay.

"Come on now," he said. "I brought the good stuff. This is Valentine hay."

"We already had the good stuff," 106 said.

"Pure alfalfa," 68 said.

"Best hay ever!"

"Someone brought you hay?"

"Well…I did," Martha said.

"But alfalfa is way too rich. That's the last thing they need."

Farmer was so used to controlling and knowing exactly what they ate, it never occurred to him they might be eating things other people gave them. Next thing he knew, someone would bring them corn. They might as well come home addicted to crack cocaine. Just one more reason why he needed to stay with them until he could get them home.

"I'm sorry," Martha said. "I just wanted to do something nice. I shouldn't have fed your animals."

"It's just that they're runny. I was hoping some starchy hay like this, mixed in with the grazing, could help."

"I see." Martha told the cows, "You eat this hay Farmer was good enough to bring you."

Then she said to Farmer, "Thomas will help." She rapped on the metal of the tailgate, and in a moment Thomas was out of the truck, standing beside her.

"Ma'am?" he said.

"Thomas, Farmer brought some hay for the cows. Would you please help him? Farmer, this is Thomas."

"That's OK," Farmer said. "You're all dressed up."

But Thomas already had his leather gloves on and was pulling one of the bales out onto Farmer's tailgate. Farmer grabbed the other one. They walked, each carrying a bale, out into the grass. They put the bales down. Thomas got his little penknife out. "I can serve," he told Farmer.

Farmer went to his truck and got the salt block. He carried it to where Thomas was spreading out the hay and dropped it. It fell with a thud.

When he got back to his truck, he sat on his tailgate. It was like he and Martha were neighbors, sitting on their porches.

The cows stood looking at them.

"Go on, eat your hay," Farmer said.

The cows didn't move.

Thomas finished spreading the bales out and came back carrying coiled pieces of twine.

"Go on now," Farmer said.

The cows begrudgingly turned and walked to the hay. They nosed it around half-heartedly. 74 went to the salt block and started licking it. 38 stood nearby, waiting her turn.

"You need to eat some hay. This kind of hay—not alfalfa. You calves more than anyone."

102 started eating. 106 chewed some but spat it out.

Martha said, "That's enough fooling now. Eat your hay."

The cows started eating then.

"Thank you, Thomas," Martha said. He left her, going back to the front of the truck. He opened the truck's door and got in behind the wheel.

Martha and Farmer, sitting on their tailgates, watched the cows picking through the hay.

"You need to get them home," Martha said.

"I'm working on it."

"The city is no place for them. Where is your farm?"

"Just north of Johnstown."

"Such a long way."

"Well, what happened is, there's this bike path that goes by our farm. They got on that and it led them straight into Columbus."

"Hmm…their yellow brick road…"

Farmer's phone rang. It was Sandy.

"Excuse me," he said. "It's my wife… Hey. What's up?"

"Farmer, the cows were on TV."

"What?"

"They were on Channel Four. On the noon news."

"Hold on," he said. He called to the cows, "Hey! Did you guys see a TV news crew?"

"Show and tell!" 106 said.

"Angela Lind reporting."

"Channel Four, the Hometown Team."

Farmer said, "Martha, did you see them?"

"It must have been before we got here."

"Who's Martha?" Sandy said.

"Sandy?" Farmer said.

"Who's Martha?"

"She came to see the cows. Did you see them on TV?"

"No, Mrs. Green called. I tried to catch it but I missed it. Farmer, I know you have Dave Monroe lined up for tomorrow, but I think it would be better to get him there this afternoon. There's no way he can do that?"

"I don't know. I could call him back."

"I'm worried things might get out of hand. Remember how it was when Nancy got interviewed on TV at the farmers' market?"

She'd told the reporter she needed more farmers. Within a couple days she'd gotten like a hundred phone calls. All these people saying, "I saw you on TV." And not only farmers. There were insurance agents; men who thought she was cute and wanted to ask her out. She thought she was going to have to change her number.

"I remember," Farmer said.

"We need to get them home. The sooner the better."

FIFTY-SIX

RODERICK JONES—of the Devon's Glenn Neighborhood Watch Committee—was somewhat slight, had flat feet and a touch of asthma. But he worked hard to keep in shape. He needed to be fit for duty.

During his years patrolling for the NWC, he'd seen it all: drug addicts desperate for a fix, quick-talking con men, craven pedophiles, serial arsonists and limousine call girls, burglars on the prowl. Most of the cases he was familiar with were episodes of *Law and Order*, but those were based on actual events.

A nice neighborhood like Devon's Glenn was such a tempting target. Luckily, thanks to the vigilance of the NWC, the Glenn was essentially safe.

There were still problems, of course.

The most persistent crime was a kind of bio-terror taking place along the tree-lined sidewalks and grassy curb strips—people, walking dogs, standing by while their canine counterparts poop, the pair then moving on, leaving the poop behind. Roderick considered such behavior heinous. He was always on the lookout for fresh evidence.

Many of these poop-and-runs, or poop-skips, took place in Lawnview Park, which dog walkers favored as a turnabout. It wasn't much of a park—a quarter acre or so of grass and a couple benches at the end of Lawnview Avenue, where a right-of-way to the New Albany bike path was.

It was approximately one o'clock when Roderick, midway through his patrol, entered Lawnview park. He found Mason Ferguson already there, sitting on a bench, holding a red plastic dump truck. Mason was one of the Glenn's younger residents. He was pre-school—his indoctrination not yet started. He lived in a home adjacent to the park.

"Hello, Mason," Roderick said, coming over to the bench. "What have you got there?"

"One of the wheels came off."

Roderick sat on the bench. "Let me see," he said. Mason handed him the truck and a black tire. Roderick looked things over, then pushed the tire (left front) back onto the axle. There was a click when the tire was in place. "I believe that's it," he told Mason, giving him back the truck.

"Thanks!"

"Have you got a permit for that vehicle?" Roderick said.

"A permit?"

"Just a joke."

"No. Jokes are funny."

"Listen," Roderick said. "Did any dogs come to the park today?"

"Just Snowball." A toy poodle who lived in a split level over on Conifer. Her owner was such a scofflaw, it probably would disappoint him if Snowball *didn't* poop while out for a walk.

"Did she poop?"

"Pee-pee, but no poop."

"Good job, Mason."

Roderick relaxed. He would rest on the bench for a few minutes before heading back out. That's when he noticed something was wrong with the park's sign.

"What the hell?" he said, standing and walking over to the sign. Its top board, with the name of the park inscribed on it, had been knocked off. It was lying nearby in the grass. Long nails protruded from it, mangled and twisted. Squatting to get a closer look, Roderick could see no evidence of tools having been used—no marks on the board from hammering or prying. *My God*, he thought. Someone had done this with sheer brute force. Superhuman strength. Potentially some fiend hopped up on PCP or bath salts.

"You cussed," he heard Mason say from close behind him. He'd followed Roderick.

"Keep back," Roderick said. "This is a crime scene. We need to preserve the evidence. You haven't touched the sign or that board, have you?"

"No."

"Good. See those nails? They're dangerous. I'm calling the police." He got his phone out.

"I thought *you* were the police."

"I help the police, but no. I'm just a citizen, same as you."

"I'm a citizen?"

"Maybe you should go home, Mason. Whoever did this might still be around."

"No, they were here yesterday."

"They? You saw them? How many were there?"

"There were seven." Mason held out both his hands, one showing five fingers, the other two.

A gang! Maybe one member was forced to damage the sign as part of an initiation. That's what they did. New members had to "make their bones."

Great. He'd wondered when gang activity would come to the Glenn. Soon there would be tagging—the gang word for graffiti. *Up here in the DG.* Maybe he should move. Get away from these urban problems. He could buy a house in a suburb farther out. There were some new developments going in near Johnstown.

"They were nice."

"You talked with them? Mason, I told you—never talk with strangers."

"They weren't strangers. They were cows."

"Cows?!" *Is that what they call themselves?* Roderick wondered. *What kind of sick twisted shit is this? Is milk their code for drugs? When they rumble it's because they have a beef with someone?*

It was one thing to hear about stuff like this on the Discovery Channel; it was another to have it happening in your own backyard.

"Some of them pooped," Mason said. "Over there." He pointed toward the entrance to the bike path.

OK, this was way hardcore—beyond anything Roderick knew about. He really needed to just call the police and let them handle it. They could send the Gang Unit.

"Over here?" Roderick walked toward the bike path slowly, watching the ground. Not far from the bike path, he saw some excrement. It was not turds, but a single round disc about a foot in diameter and one inch thick. He recognized its form and aroma now that he was standing over it. He'd seen this before, at the State Fair. It was a cow patty.

"This is cow poop," he told Mason.

"That's what I just told you."

"So cows were here? Real actual cows?"

Mason nodded.

Looking around, Roderick saw three other patties, any one of them equivalent to a month's worth of Pomeranian poop.

"Seven of them… What did they look like, Mason?"

"I've got pictures. You want to see?"

"Oh. You do? Yes. That *would* be helpful."

"Mason?" a woman's voice called. It was Mason's mother, standing on the back patio of her house.

"Here, Mom."

She looked over and saw Mason and Roderick. She walked toward them.

"Hello, Mr. Jones," she said.

"Morning, ma'am."

"How are things? Is all well in the Glenn?"

"Well, Mason was just telling me about the cows he saw."

"Oh." She frowned. "Mason," she said, "why don't you go in the house. I'll be right there. We're going to the grocery."

"All right. See ya, Mr. Jones." Carrying his red dump truck, he walked to the back of the house and went inside.

"I'm actually taking him to see a child psychologist," Mason's mother told Roderick. "I called this morning to make an appointment and they're able to see him right away. Yesterday he started talking about seeing cows. They say it's a good thing when children have imaginary friends. It develops their verbal skills. I've even been kind of hoping he would get one. I mean, he's alone a lot. But cows? What good could that do? I have no idea what they represent or why all of a sudden they've appeared like this. What did he tell *you*?"

"Ma'am, I don't think there's anything wrong with Mason. I

think he saw some cows who were here in this park. Look," he said, leading her to the nearest cow patty. "That's not imaginary."

She gasped when she saw the patty. "Mason saw real cows…he really did…and I didn't believe him." She hung her head. "What kind of mother am I? I gave him this whole lecture last night about telling the truth. God. Maybe *I* should see a therapist."

"No, you're fine," Roderick said. "Mason's a good kid. I can tell you, he's one of the only children around here who'll look me in the eye and talk right to me."

Just then, Mason came running out of the house holding some pieces of paper.

"Mr. Jones! Here they are!" He handed Roderick three pieces of paper, each a colorful and somewhat abstract crayon drawing.

His pictures of the cows.

They were black and brown and white, with cherry-red noses and big toothy grins. They had stick legs and were basking under a yellow sun that took up a fifth of the page. Mason's house was there, simpler and a little crooked, smoke coming from its chimney. In one picture, a cow was standing in the bed of a big red dump truck. It had a numbered ear tag: 106. Looking back through the other pictures, Roderick saw there were more ear tag numbers: 74, 38, 27. That was good solid information. The police would be impressed. Well, maybe.

"Outstanding, Mason."

"I'm a good drawer," Mason said matter-of-factly.

"You certainly are. Is it OK if I keep these for a while? I'll get them back to you."

"Sure. You want me to make you some more?"

"No, this is plenty."

"And what do you want them for?" Mason's mother said.

"They could help with the investigation. These are powerful, dangerous animals. We really need to get them off the streets."

Not wanting to alarm her, he did not mention that, presuming the drawings were accurate, at least one of the animals—106—was a bull.

FIFTY-SEVEN

WHEN FARMER GOT OFF THE PHONE with Sandy, he told Martha Guildersnap, "My wife is worried the cows are attracting too much attention."

Martha, still sitting on the tailgate of her truck, said, "She's not wrong, Farmer."

"I guess." He watched the cows picking listlessly through the hay he'd brought.

"Did she say they were on TV?"

"Yes. Channel Four was here." Farmer sat on his tailgate. "She wants me to call the hauler I lined up for tomorrow and see if he can come now."

"Good. Call him. What's the problem?"

"I was counting on having more time to talk with them, to bring them around to the idea of coming home. There's no use in Dave bringing his trailer if they won't get in it. I don't have any way to corral them. It needs to be what *they* want."

"Well, as time is suddenly short, how lucky that you are a good farmer and have built up a reserve of goodwill with your animals."

Martha cupped her hands on either side of her mouth and called, "Cows!"

They lifted their heads and looked at her, ears swiveled forward.

"Announcement to make. Lots at stake. Come here, please."

They were only too happy to step over the disappointing hay and gather in front of Farmer and Martha.

"Farmer has something important he needs to tell you."

"What is it, Farmer?" 74 said.

"It's time for you guys to come home. I don't mean to be rude about it. I've been waiting for you to come around to that way of thinking, and I think you would have sooner or later."

"We're considering it," 74 said.

"We're running out of time."

"What do you mean?" 42 said.

"Well, the main thing is, you were on TV. What did you call it?"

"Show and tell," 38 said.

"A lot of people are going to see that."

"Angela said the more people who know about us, the safer we'll be," 38 said.

"But I think that's wrong. See, there are lots of people in Columbus who are..." Farmer hesitated, then started over. "OK, it's like...you know how you guys always say that safety is when you can see everything and nothing sees you?"

"Yes," 74 said.

"Well, this show and tell is the opposite. Now, a whole city full of people can see you, but you can't see any of them."

"He's got a point," 68 said.

42 said, "There's more to life than being safe." But even she realized how lame that sounded.

"I'm worried some of the people who see the show and tell are going to want to come here to get a closer look."

"A lot of people?" 38 said.

"Yes. Way too many. Don't you think so, Martha?"

"I agree completely. Even though Channel Four is dead last in the ratings."

"They don't get a lot of cows in town," Farmer said.

74 said, "That's easy to understand. The city is not very nice. Maybe it suits people, but I can't see how it's a good place for them either. Why do you like it, Martha?"

"What makes you think I like it?"

"Don't you?"

Martha said, "I'm a lot like you. I was living on a farm. I was curious about the world. I liked the idea of getting out and having new experiences. When I could, I left, and I don't regret it. I've had a heck of a run. But now I'm starting to think it's time for me to go home. Back where I belong."

"Really?" 38 said.

"Yes, honey. I'm tired. I just want to relax. I can't really do that in the city."

"That's how I feel," 68 said. "I miss my comfort zone."

74 said, "If we decide to go home, Farmer, how would it work?"

"I'd call Dave Monroe—he's the man I told you about who has a trailer big enough. I'd see if he can be here in an hour or two. We get you loaded up and head for home, you could be back on pasture before the sun goes down."

"I'm ready," 27 said.

"Me too," 68 said.

74 said, "I'll go along with whatever the herd decides."

"Me too. Whatever the herd decides," 38 said.

"That's what I meant to say," 68 said.

Jeez, Farmer thought. They were about like the township trustees.

"42?" 74 said. "What do you think?"

"It's time. Let's go home."

"No!" 106 said.

"This is an adult conversation," 38 said.

106 said, "Does this mean we don't get names?"

"We can still do names," Farmer said.

"What about all the friends we've made?" 106 said. "We'll just never see them again?"

"They can come visit us at the farm," 74 said. "Can't they, Farmer?"

"Sure. We'd have to have some rules. Maybe set visiting times. We wouldn't want them coming after dark."

"That makes sense," 68 said.

Farmer said, "And no Lernovski. Ever."

"I'll come see you," Martha said. "And, if Farmer says it's OK, I can bring you a bale of alfalfa once in a while."

"OK. If that's what you guys want," Farmer said. "I guess I'll call Dave. I just hope he's available."

Martha said, "Actually, Farmer, you know what? I can get a trailer. Where Thomas and I picked up the hay earlier, there were several trailers that would do. They're just sitting there. Thomas and I can borrow one, and we'd be back in an hour at the most."

"Are you sure? I hate to put you out."

"It would be my pleasure."

"And you're certain the trailers you're thinking of are big enough?"

"Absolutely."

"Well, that would be ideal..."

"It's decided, then." Martha rapped on her tailgate. A moment later Thomas stood beside her.

"Ma'am?"

"Thomas, get me down from here, please. We're going."

He helped her down and shut the tailgate.

He walked her to the back door of the truck's cab, opened it, helped her up and inside.

When the door was shut, she slid the window down and called to Farmer.

"Yes?" he said.

"Thomas will exchange phone numbers with you. Take care and do not worry. We'll be back soon."

FIFTY-EIGHT

A LITTLE AFTER ONE O'CLOCK, Ron Jackson emerged from his office, where he'd been holed up since his interview with Angela Lind. He'd just gotten off the phone with his boss, parks commissioner Frank Jarvis. It was starting to look like vomiting into a trash can might not be the low point of his day.

He found Betty in the break area serving herself some coffee.

"Betty, we need to have a staff meeting. Please proceed to the conference area. Have you seen Vincent?"

"He's working on the mower."

Jackson walked to the far end of the big room, where the zero turn Kubota was parked. A plastic drain pan full of black oil was under its engine.

Vincent came from the supply room carrying plastic pints of 10-W30.

"Mr. Jackson," Vincent said. "What's up?"

"We're having a staff meeting."

"Good. I'm running out of stuff to do. When is it?"

"Right now."

"OK. I need to clean my hands real quick."

Jackson turned and walked back to the end of the room where his office and the bathroom and break area were. In front of some pallets of fertilizer, there was a freestanding dry-erase board and some metal folding chairs arranged in a semi-circle. Betty was sitting on one of the chairs.

Standing in front of the dry-erase board, Jackson opened the meeting with a roll call.

"Betty Marsh," he said.

"Here."

"Vincent Morales."

Vincent, arriving, sat next to Betty. "Hola," he said. "I'm here, Boss."

"All right, team. Now listen. As you know, today is supposed to be C-Day, when we liberate the park. I have an update to provide you on this matter."

Betty and Vincent had attended so many of Jackson's meetings, they were used to what Vincent called his "high talking."

"Apparently, it is wrong to think of these bovine visitors as intruders. I have been informed by Frank Jarvis—my commander—that we are to stand down regarding Operation Charlie Oscar Whiskey."

"He called you? Just now?" Betty said.

"Affirmative. Soon after my interview appeared on Channel Four."

"Well, what does he suggest we do?" Betty said.

"Until further notice we are to consider the cows part of the parks maintenance team."

"Say what?" Vincent said.

"This from his honor, the mayor of Columbus. The cows will eat the grass, meaning we don't mow. They will shit on the grass, meaning we don't fertilize. And, in this way, the park will be kept in tip-top condition without resorting to the use of fossil fuels which, as you know, are causing our planet to warm."

"They're destroying my flower beds," Betty said.

"It would somehow never occur to folks at city hall that we might know more than they do about what's best for this park."

"Still, I never did understand that whole Oscar Charlie deal," Vincent said. "That was a little wack. Come on, Mr. Jackson, you can see that, right?"

"This is ridiculous," Betty said. "Just because they got on TV."

"So, when do I mow?" Vincent said. "I got to get back on schedule."

"Sorry, Vincent. For now, the cows are in charge of mowing."

"Whoa, hold up," Vincent said. "I spent all morning doing busy work. What am I supposed to do now?"

"Perhaps you can assist Betty somehow."

"This ain't right," Vincent said. "I mow the park. And I been doing a good job. All my performance evals have been positive. Now I'm being replaced? It's seasonal as it is. Next thing they gonna call and tell you to lay me off."

"Vince is right," Betty said. "Vince, you should call the union."

"Yeah, I'm gonna call my steward. They bringing in scabs."

"As you know, I consider unions un-American," Jackson said. "But perhaps it could be useful to involve them. Maybe the mayor needs to hear another point of view."

"Dios mío," Vincent said, shaking his head.

"OK, meeting adjourned," Jackson said. "I have to go to headquarters now and meet with my boss."

FIFTY-NINE

AFTER MARTHA AND THOMAS DROVE OFF, Farmer sat again on his tailgate. He watched the cows grazing in the distance, well beyond the neglected hay he'd brought.

Sandy called. "What's going on?" she said. "Did you call Dave?"

"No, Martha's bringing a trailer. She should be back in an hour."

"Who is this Martha?" Sandy said.

"She's pretty intense. She's older, really rich I think. She loves cows. She was here visiting them when I got back to the park."

"What do you mean, older?"

Sandy was just checking.

"At least eighty. I don't think she drives anymore. She has this guy with her who drives; he's like her chauffeur. Anyway, she thinks you're right—that the cows being on TV is trouble. She said she knew where she could borrow a trailer and offered to go get it."

"Well, good. And everything's OK? Still calm?"

328

"So far. And the cows have decided they want to come home, so that's good. I'd feel better if you were here."

"I'm leaving now. What about Brett?"

"I don't know. I was hoping you could call him. If he can make it, you could stop at the mill and give him a ride. And you can tell him it's called off for tomorrow."

"All right, I'm on my way. You need anything?"

"No, just come."

He hung up. Things were working out.

He couldn't relax completely. But he did allow himself the pleasure of imagining how good it would feel to finally have the cows home, him standing at the back end of the trailer—he imagined Dave's because he knew it—swinging open the back door and standing by as the cows stepped out, then watching as they started to graze in the shining last light of day. Shadows would be lengthening as the truck and trailer, running lights on, bumped back onto Cooper Road and drove away. It was a pretty picture. And something of a beer ad—the rest of last night's twelve-pack waiting in the fridge.

Farmer stood and stretched. He wished he'd asked Sandy to stop off at the Circle K and grab him something to eat: a chocolate bar, a honey bun or Little Debbie oatmeal pie.

He was thinking of calling her back when an older Chevy S-10 pickup truck came into the parking lot, drove toward Farmer, and parked nearby. A young man got out of the truck. He was tall and slim, dressed like a cowboy, with snakeskin boots, a white felt hat, and a colorful rodeo shirt featuring a collage of American flags, soaring eagles and snow-capped mountains.

The young man nodded to Farmer. "Howdy," he said. He had snuff tucked up inside his lower lip. He spat some brown saliva onto the parking lot, then turned to the bed of his truck and pulled out a lasso. It was brand new, so stiff it was in a perfect circle resting in his hands.

"Who does a fella talk to about signing on to help round up these critters?"

"What?" Farmer said.

"I wouldn't expect to get paid. Are they your cows?"

"Yes. But there's not going to be any roundup."

"I could help you keep an eye on them. Make sure they don't stampede."

"Have you ever been around cattle?"

"No, but I'm willing to learn. Just tell me where you need me and what to do."

"I appreciate your offer. What's your name?"

"Kyle."

"Kyle, the thing is, cows get nervous around people they don't know, so it's best if you keep your distance."

"Do they bite?"

"No, but—just stay here in the parking lot, OK? You can watch them from here."

"OK," Kyle said, disappointed. He put the lasso back in his truck's bed.

A green Toyota Corolla pulled in and parked next to Kyle's truck. A young woman got out. She was wearing a short white leather dress with lots of fringe, pink cowboy boots and a matching hat.

"Hey, Kyle," she said, coming over.

"Hey, Cindy."

"You two know each other?" Farmer said.

"Yeah, from line dancing."

"I figured you might be here," Cindy said. "Who's your friend?"

"He's the guy whose cows they are," Kyle said.

"Carrying your brand, are they, mister? What's the name of your ranch?"

"I don't have a ranch. Just my farm. Out by Johnstown."

"The Triple-J!"

"Good one," Kyle said.

They high-fived.

"Your cows are even cuter in person," Cindy said to Farmer. "Can I pet them?"

"They get nervous around people they don't know," Kyle told her.

Farmer saw a man come out of the park's maintenance building. Something told him it was Ron Jackson. He excused himself from

Kyle and Cindy and walked over to introduce himself. The man did not look well. He was pale and out of focus or something. He was gazing at the cows. When Farmer came up to him, he heard him mumbling, "Someone brought them hay? Now there's cowboys?"

"Excuse me. Sir?" Farmer said.

"Yes?" The man did not look away from the cows.

"Sir, you're Mr. Jackson, aren't you? I'm sorry about my cows ending up in your park like this."

"Your cows?" Jackson said—as if the words had no meaning. "My park?"

"I'll have them out of here in just a couple hours, sir. I'm sorry for the inconvenience."

"The inconvenience…" He turned and looked at Farmer. "You're sorry for the inconvenience. Is that what you said?"

"Yes."

"But they've been wonderful guests. Here at Cow Patty Park, all are welcome. Now if you'll excuse me, *I* am the one who needs to leave. I have to go see my boss."

He walked over to a black Jeep Commander, beeped it with his key fob, and got in. He started the Jeep and drove away.

Another man came out of the maintenance building. He was wearing a light-blue uniform shirt with the name Vincent embroidered on its chest. As soon as he was outside, he lit a cigarette and took a long deep draw on it, blowing smoke out slowly. Seeing

Farmer nearby, and indicating Kyle with his cigarette, he said, "Is that cowboy dude here to get his cows?"

"No, they're my cows," Farmer said.

"For real? Who are those cowboy people? They work for you?"

"No, I think they just like dressing up like cowboys."

"Whoa. Like Halloween... Hey, listen. Get your cows out of here. I'm not kidding. I can't do any mowing till they leave."

"They'll be gone in a couple hours."

"Mr. Jackson is wack. He got told by the mayor to leave the cows alone and now he's in trouble with his boss."

"The mayor? Of Columbus?" Farmer said.

"Your cows got friends in high places."

SIXTY

PRISONER 7451, wearing an orange jumpsuit, shuffled up the corridor, hands cuffed in front, ankles loosely shackled. The uniformed guard at his side stopped him when they got to the interrogation room.

"Here you go," the guard said, ushering him inside. "Take a seat."

The prisoner sat on a chair facing a wooden table. A tape recorder was on the table.

Two detectives wearing suits came in.

"Thanks, Jerry," one of them told the guard, who then left.

The detectives sat across the table from 7451. One of them turned the tape recorder on and said, "September fifteenth. One thirty p.m. I am Detective Saul Murkowski. Detective Jim Green and I are interviewing inmate seven-four-five-one. Seven-four-five-one, please state your name."

"Paul Lernovski."

The irony, Lernovski thought. The cows were free and he, their liberator, was in prison. *He* was being called a number. Was this what martyrdom felt like? Earlier, alone in his cell, he had felt himself getting the blues. But martyrs were supposed to feel a kind of elation. Weren't they? It was all so intense and confusing.

"Your address?"

"I'm kind of in between residences."

"The subject is homeless," Murkowski said. Then, sitting back in his chair, speaking less formally, he said, "So, you're the terrorist from the bus station this morning."

"That's absurd."

"Absurd? Really? You made a threat, kid. You said your duffel bag was a bomb."

"No. To be precise, what I said was—"

"Maybe you should get an attorney before you say anything. Would you like that? We can appoint you one."

"I didn't do anything."

"Let him talk," Green said.

"My reference to my duffel bag being a bomb was purely hypothetical. I was making a point."

"Well, you got that done."

"You shut down the bus station," Green said.

"What are you talking about?"

Murkowski said, "After they arrested you, the police evacuated the building. They called the bomb squad. A robot pulled your duffel bag outside and detonated it. And see, that's because—hypothetically—if police officers ignore a bomb threat and then a bomb goes off, they get in trouble."

"Hypothetically," Green said.

"I didn't mean for that to happen."

"Well, there wasn't a bomb in your duffel bag. We know that now. But making a threat like you did is still a serious matter. It's called inducing panic. That's a first-degree misdemeanor. But then you got the economic harm caused by the evacuation of the bus station. You add to that the cost of the bomb squad, I think the prosecutors will probably ask for third- or fourth-degree felony charges. You could end up doing time, kid."

"Maybe I *should* get an attorney," Lernovski said.

"He's clamming up," Green said.

"We just need to know, kid. What else do you and your comrades have planned? Is this part of a coordinated series of attacks?"

Lernovski, bewildered, stared at the detectives without saying anything.

"We found the commie literature you had in your backpack. *Mao's Little Red Book*; *The Communist Manifesto*."

"I own books. Is that a crime?"

"The crime is hating America," Green said.

"A witness quoted you as saying you 'set things in motion; pretty soon he would know all about it.' Does that sound familiar?"

"Yeah. That idiot Lenny."

"Why the bus station?" Murkowski said. "That's what we can't figure. Why not the airport? If there's no real bomb, why not call it in instead of making the threat in person?"

"I'm not a terrorist," Lernovski said.

"Come clean," Green said. "It's over."

"I want an attorney," Lernovski said.

"Was the bus station thing a way to test how the police respond? What's the real target?"

"No comment," Lernovski said.

"Thinks he's in a press conference," Green said.

"Look, Paul. If you don't talk to us, we're going to turn you over to the FBI. And that's not a good thing. Believe me. We're trying to help you here."

"They got different parameters," Green said.

Murkowski said, "It's not right the things they do. Not when it comes to American citizens."

"Congress approved," Green said.

"We're better than that, or we used to be. Besides, the information they get isn't reliable. People will say anything to make them stop."

"What kinds of things?" Lernovski said.

"You don't want to know, kid."

"Look, I lost my temper with the police officers. I was rude. I'm sorry! OK? I'm sorry! I don't know what you want from me."

"What got set in motion, Paul?"

"All right. What I did was, yesterday, out near Johnstown, I opened a gate and let some cows out. OK? That's it. I let some cows out."

"Cows?" Murkowski said. "Is that what you're saying? Like on a farm?"

"Yes. I know it was against the law but that's what I did. I felt sorry for them. And that's *all* I did. I'm not part of any terrorist organization or anything like that."

"What do you think, Green?" Murkowski said.

"There were those cows on TV today at lunch. Remember? In New Albany. They were in that park."

"That's right. You think those could be your cows, kid?"

"Could be," Lernovski said, trying to hide his excitement.

Green said, "There were five or six of them—not very many."

"That's about right," Lernovski said. *It* was *them! They'd made it to Columbus! They'd been on TV!*

"Yeah, they were something," Murkowski said. "One of them in particular—very articulate for a cow."

Number 42, Lernovski thought. His best pupil.

"OK. Well, I guess that does it. I'm satisfied. Green?"

"The kid's no terrorist. He's an arrogant little shit but that's no crime. Needs to tuck in the attitude."

"I concur," Murkowski said. "This concludes the interview." He turned the tape recorder off. "Kid, you're going to have to pay some damages. You should be able to get out of lockup tomorrow. You'll get a court date and if you show up for that and pay what you owe, you should be OK."

"Thank you," Lernovski said. "I'm sorry I was rude to those police officers."

"A little respect goes a long way, kid."

The detectives stood to go.

"What about the cows thing?" Green said.

"We'll file a report," Murkowski said. "He confessed he let them out."

"Yeah, on account of he's a cow-moo-nist," Green said.

SIXTY-ONE

VINCENT AND FARMER watched a yellow Honda Civic pull in and park on the far side of the lot. Two young men, both dressed like cowboys, got out. They walked over to Kyle and Cindy, spurs jingling. They greeted each other enthusiastically, high-fiving all around.

"More cowboys," Vincent said. "Looking like a rodeo."

The cows were about fifty yards past the pond, off by themselves. But, as Farmer watched, 74 left the herd and came walking toward the parking lot. He tensed as he realized she was heading toward the cowboys. When she reached the edge of the parking lot and stepped up onto its asphalt, Kyle and his friends, frightened, ran around behind Kyle's truck and kind of half crouched there together.

"Every rodeo got its clowns," Vincent said.

74 walked by the truck without seeming to notice them. She was coming to see Farmer.

"Hey, Farmer," she said when she reached him. "I hate to bother you."

"No, you're fine," Farmer said.

Vincent started laughing.

"What's funny?" 74 said.

"You talk. Shit." He couldn't stop laughing. "Now I know why Mr. Jackson got it in for you. He don't like anybody talking but him."

"You know Ron Jackson?"

"Oh yeah, I know him," Vincent said.

"What does it mean when he starts beeping?"

Vincent stopped laughing. "He was beeping? Listen. When Mr. Jackson starts beeping, that's when you got to be careful. I'm Vincent, by the way."

"Helen," 74 said. "Pleased to meet you."

"Hablas español?" Vincent said.

74 looked at Farmer.

Farmer told Vincent, "I don't think so." Then he said, "Helen. That's the name you've chosen?"

"I've always liked it."

"Elena," Vincent said. "It's a beautiful name."

"Thank you, Vincent. Farmer, we were wondering—did you bring the ear tag kit?"

"Yes, it's in the truck."

"Can we get our names now?"

"Has everyone decided what names they want?"

"Pretty much. I think if we get started we can sort it out."

"OK. I'll be right there."

"Thanks. Nice meeting you, Vincent." She turned and walked back across the parking lot, returning to the herd.

The cowboy people cowered behind Kyle's truck again as she passed. She turned her head and looked at them but said nothing and did not stop.

"Oh my God! It looked right at me," Farmer could hear Cindy telling Kyle and the other cowboys. "I have goosebumps. Look."

"Your cows seem nice," Vincent said. "Cows know how to take it easy."

A Columbus Police cruiser entered the parking lot. It pulled up near Farmer and Vincent. The driver's side window slid down. A uniformed officer behind the wheel said, "What you know, Vincent?"

"Officer Perkins. What's up?"

"Nothing. Just cruising around. You got a smoke?"

"Sure."

Officer Perkins opened the cruiser's door and got out. He was maybe fifty. He was much bigger than Vincent or Farmer—tall, broad-shouldered, and big through the chest.

Vincent handed him a cigarette. He lit it and took a deep draw.

"What's with the cows?" he said.

"They're his," Vincent said.

"Is that right?" Perkins said to Farmer.

"Yes, sir."

"Well, here's a thought. Maybe you should get a farm."

"I have a farm."

"OK. Another thought. And I'm just spitballing here. Maybe keep the cows on the farm. What do you think?"

Farmer didn't say anything.

"You need to get them out of here. They're a shit storm waiting to happen. Believe me, I know how it goes. Are those cowboys with you?"

"No. They saw the cows on TV and came here to see them in person."

"Yep. Shit storm," Perkins said. "Add freaks and stir."

"I've got someone coming with a trailer. We should have them loaded up and gone in an hour or so."

While Perkins smoked his cigarette, more cars came into the parking lot. A family with a bunch of kids got out of one car. The parents headed to a picnic table carrying a big cooler while the kids, squealing, raced toward the pirate ship playground. A woman from another car went to a bench near the pond and stood on it, holding her phone out in front with both hands to take pictures of the cows. A man who had come in a minivan walked up to Perkins.

"Excuse me," he said. "Officer? Do you know where the protest is?"

"Protest. What do you mean?"

"Humans First. It's all over Facebook. It said two o'clock at Sutter Park, but I don't see anyone."

"Humans First?" Perkins said.

"Yeah. Times are tough. Our species has its own problems. We can't afford to be nice to animals."

"I think you're just early," Perkins said. "Are you expecting a lot of people?"

"It depends. Our last rally, downtown, we had like sixty. That's about average. But this being a weekday and with short notice, I don't know."

"My cows aren't bothering anyone," Farmer said.

"All rights are human rights! Hashtag mansdominion!"

"OK, settle down," Perkins said.

"Do you have a preference where we set up?" the man asked Perkins.

"Just stay around the parking lot. Don't bother the cows."

"Thanks, officer."

The man went to his minivan, opened its rear hatch, and got out a wood-handled white protest sign that said EAT THEM! He went over to a bench and sat down, the sign resting next to him.

More cars were coming down the park's little road and pulling into the parking lot, one after the other. The park was getting busy.

"There's a lot of people," Farmer said.

"I never seen this many on a weekday afternoon," Vincent said. "It's only like two o'clock."

"Just my luck," Perkins said. "I stopped by for a cigarette. Hell, I can't leave now. I'm gonna have to call for backup."

"I'm going back to my cattle," Farmer said. "If you can keep these people away from my cows, I'd appreciate it."

Farmer headed across the parking lot, back to his truck. He fell in step with several people walking along carrying binoculars, cameras, and water bottles. An older man wearing a beret had set up a wooden easel at the edge of the parking lot and was sketching the cows. Another protester had arrived; he was getting a sign out of his car. He said to Farmer, "Do you know where the protest is?"

Farmer pointed to the other protester sitting on the bench.

A couple more cowboys had shown up. Now all of them were dancing in unison, stepping forward till they all hopped and clapped hands, then several steps back, pivot to the left, pivot to the right. They seemed to be having fun.

Farmer went to his truck. Sandy was right again. Things were turning out just like she said. *You'd think I'd get used to it*, he thought. If he could stop forgetting she was the smart one, he would probably get along a little better.

He got the five-gallon bucket with the ear tag kit in it from the truck, then shut and locked the truck's door.

A woman with two young children in tow said, "Hey, mister. Are those your cows?"

"Yes."

"Are they tame? I was hoping I could get a picture of my kids sitting on one. I'd be willing to pay. I don't know, like five dollars? For both."

"It's not a good idea," Farmer said. "They bite."

"Oh. Sorry, kids. Mommy tried."

Carrying the bucket, Farmer walked out into the grassy area toward the cows. They'd stopped grazing and were standing fairly close together, facing in different directions, their ears turning this way and that.

"Hey, you guys," he said, joining them. "Don't worry, those people are going to stay with the cars, over by the building."

"There are so many," 68 said. "And new ones keep coming."

"There could be lots more on the way, too," Farmer said. "But we're fine. We just need to stick together and keep our distance. Before we know it, Martha will be here with the trailer. Meanwhile, how about those names? I've got the ear tag kit." He indicated the white five-gallon bucket.

"Someone is coming," 102 said.

Farmer and the herd looked toward the parking lot. A young man wearing jeans and a tie-dyed T-shirt had emerged from the crowd and was coming toward them.

When he got closer, 106 said, "It's Danny! Hi, Danny!"

"Hi, Danny!" all the cows said.

"Greetings and salutations, cows," Danny said. "How's it going?" Then he said to Farmer, "I'm Danny."

"Yes, so it seems. I'm Farmer."

They shook hands.

"I knew these guys before they got all famous," Danny said.

"We're getting names, Danny," 38 said.

"That's awesome!"

"It's immense!" 106 said.

"You just missed Joe Martin," 68 said.

"Farmer, it was Danny who had the idea for us to get names."

"It just seemed weird calling them numbers," Danny said.

"We're going back to the farm!" 27 said.

"But you can visit us there. Right, Farmer?"

"Sure." Farmer said to Danny, "I'm about to make them some name tags. You want to help?"

"Well yeah."

SIXTY-TWO

WHEN MASON AND HIS MOM went back in their house, Roderick Jones called the non-emergency number for the Seventh Precinct. It was in his contacts.

"Columbus Police. How may I help you?" a woman's voice said.

"Hi, I'm calling to report some cows that are on the loose."

"Cows, sir? Is that what you said?"

"Yes."

"Hold please."

She came back on the line.

"Are the cows with you now?"

"No. They came through here yesterday."

"Where exactly are you, sir?"

"Lawnview Park, in Devon's Glenn. They did some damage to government property here. Plus they left behind manure—a possible Code 10-24A."

After a slight pause, the woman said, "Is this Mr. Jones?"

"Yes, ma'am. I've secured the scene; collected eyewitness testimony; and I have some pictures of the cows which could be useful."

"Mr. Jones, I am dispatching an officer. When he arrives, please identify yourself to him. Thank you." She hung up.

They're sending an officer! Yes! And they should be pleased, Roderick thought. There was some solid evidence. Plus he had Mason's eyewitness account and drawings. He'd done all the legwork. This was the kind of citizen/police partnership the Neighborhood Watch Committee was all about. The police were too busy to do a good job; everybody knew that. They needed help.

As he was putting his phone away, he saw the overhead garage door of Mason's house opening. A bright red VW Bug backed out. Mason's mom was driving. Mason was in the back seat, strapped in.

Roderick walked toward the car. Mason's mom slid her window down.

"I talked to the police," Roderick told her. "They're sending an officer."

"Good. I hope they find those cows."

"Don't worry, they will. Thanks to Mason."

"My little hero."

"We're going for ice cream!" Mason said from the back seat. "I'm getting two scoops!"

"That's right. And then you can play on the pirate ship."

"You two be careful out there," Roderick said.

"Bye, Mr. Jones," Mason and his mom said. Then the car backed into the street, turned, and drove away.

★ ★ ★

As soon as she hung up on Roderick Jones, the police dispatcher called Officer Chris McCarthy. She figured he was parked behind the Walmart on Morse Road.

"McCarthy?" she said.

"What? I'm kind of busy."

"You are now. Sarge told me you're the go-to until further notice for anything cow-related."

"What?!"

"All bovine matters. That's what he told me this morning. He said you're in the middle of an ongoing investigation?"

"Oh, for God's sake. He's just getting back at me because I gave him a little attitude yesterday."

"Be that as it may…"

"What are you saying? You got a call about cows?"

"You got it, Einstein. Lawnview Park. You know where that is?"

"Sure."

"There's a guy there waiting for you. He says cows were there and did some damage. He has the scene secured and has some photos of them for you."

"Wait, is it that neighborhood watch guy? Jones?"

"Bingo. Get over there, McCarthy. No kidding. The chief is taking an interest in these cows. Word is the mayor's office is asking about them."

"All right, all right, I'm on my way."

McCarthy *was* parked behind the Walmart on Morse Road—in the shade of a compacting dumpster. It was one of his favorite spots. Soon he was eastbound on Morse in light afternoon traffic. He was not in a good mood. That morning he was told his application to work security at the mayoral debate was denied. That would have been a nice little piece of overtime. Yesterday he'd screwed up at the gun range. Now Sarge was mad at him and had him chasing cows.

It was two thirty when he got to Lawnview Park. He pulled over to the curb, got out, and entered the park on foot. He approached Roderick, who was standing near one of the benches.

He said, "You're Jones, right?"

"Yes. Good to see you again. We worked together on that abandoned minivan last summer."

"Yeah, I remember. I don't see any cows."

"They were here yesterday. Come on, I'll get you up to speed."

He led McCarthy to the damaged sign. "They did this. You can see how powerful they are. And over here," he said, leading McCarthy to the cow patties. "These are the calling cards they left behind."

"Don't you have a job? What are you, disabled or something?"

"Officer, that's a question of a personal nature I don't feel you have the right to ask."

"Sorry," McCarthy said. "OK. So, they came through here yesterday. What time would you say?"

"They hadn't been here yet when I came through on patrol. That was about one. Judging from the crusting of this manure, I'd say they were here between two and four o'clock."

McCarthy pulled a tiny notebook from one of the breast pockets on his shirt and flipped it open. He got a pen out and wrote something.

"OK," he said. "And how many were there?"

"Seven."

"We had a report some cows were sighted late yesterday in Sutter Park. You think these could be them? I mean, they'd have to be, right?"

"Makes sense. It looks to me like they got here on the bike path. Assuming they got back on the path heading west, it would lead them straight into Sutter. It's about a quarter mile from here."

McCarthy shut his little notebook and put it away. "I guess I'll head over to the park and look around. Thank you for your cooperation, Mr. Jones. Oh wait. Don't you have pictures of them?"

"Yes. On the bench."

He led McCarthy to the bench and picked up Mason's drawings. "Here you go," he said, handing them over.

McCarthy looked at the top drawing. It was the one of 106. He flipped through the drawings quickly, just long enough to see they were all in crayon.

"What is this, a joke?" He handed the drawings back.

"I realize they're a bit crude," Roderick said. "But just look at them. Look," he said, holding up one that depicted several cows. "Ear tag numbers. See?" He pointed to them as he called them out. "Seventy-four... Thirty-eight... Forty-two... See?"

McCarthy got his notebook out. "What are the numbers?"

Roderick flipped through the drawings, calling numbers out as McCarthy wrote them down. "That's all of them," he said when he was finished. "But there's something else."

He flipped back to the picture of 106 and, pointing a finger toward 106's back legs, said, "You see these? Down here?"

McCarthy wasn't getting it.

"Testicles," Roderick said finally. "They're intact, meaning we are dealing with at least one bull."

"Bulls are dangerous," McCarthy said.

Just a few weeks earlier he'd watched bull riding on TV. Those bulls were violent. They threw the riders off, sending them flying through the air. Then they attacked the fallen riders, looking for payback. They were mean! And powerful as hell!

He could feel his heart speeding up. He involuntarily reached down and touched the handle of his holstered pistol.

"A bull wandering around in town… Well, thanks for your help, Mr. Jones."

Taking the picture of 106 with him, he hurried back to his cruiser, then drove away at a high rate of speed.

SIXTY-THREE

FARMER TURNED the five-gallon bucket upside down and put it on the ground. He sat on it. He opened the ear tag kit, got out the new tag applicator and the cutting tool for removing old tags, then put the kit down within reach. Inside it were dozens of blank tags and two black permanent markers.

It was like the cows had pierced ears. Farmer would insert new tags through the same holes the old tags were in. It was simple: clamp down on the applicator tool, which looked like a pair of pliers, and the front and back pieces of the tag would snap together like a rivet.

The cows were gathered in front of Farmer, watching closely. All had one ear swiveled toward the parking lot and the many people there.

Farmer said to Danny, "Are you ready?"

"I guess so."

"You can do it, Danny!" 38 said.

"You'll be fine. The cows trust you, and that's the main thing. Just remember, there's no hurry. No reason to get excited. If something goes wrong, it's OK. We'll just come back around and do it again."

"OK."

"You're going to remove the old tags. You see this cutter? It has this slot with blades inside. You put it between the tag and the ear, then go like this." He pulled the cutter straight down. "It'll cut the old tag off. It won't hurt them. Then I'll put a new tag on." He handed the cutter to Danny.

"OK, who's first?" Farmer said.

"Me!" 106 said.

"All right. Come on up here, 106. What's your name?"

"Mason."

"OK." Farmer got a marker and a blank tag from the box. Working on his knee, he wrote MASON on the tag. He loaded the tag into the applicator tool.

"You're up, Danny," he said.

Danny put the cutter behind 106's ear tag. "Hold still, little dude," he said and he pulled the cutter down. The tag fell to the grass. "This is easy," he told Farmer.

Farmer lined up the pliers with the hole in 106's ear, then squeezed, securing the new tag.

"There you go, Mason," he said. Mason (106) was so excited he ran around in circles, kicking and twirling.

74 stepped up. "I'm Helen," she told Farmer.

"OK."

Danny removed her old tag, and Farmer, as soon as the ink had dried, attached the new one.

Next was 68. Farmer had to write smaller to get JOE MARTIN to fit on the tag.

38 stepped up and announced that she was Sandy.

"OK," Farmer said. "But if Sandy asks you about it, be sure and tell her it was your idea."

He made a tag for her and put it on. "What about you, 27?" he said.

"I don't know. All the good names are taken. Sandy was my first choice."

"What about Sarah?" Helen (74) said.

"I don't know…"

"Angela?" Helen (74) said.

"No, my next favorite is Martha."

"That's going to be 102's name," Joe Martin (68) said.

Helen said, "Danny told us different people can have the same name. Is that right, Farmer?"

"Sure. As long as you don't look the same."

"That means you can pick any name you want," Helen told 27.

"Then I want to be Sandy."

"OK," Farmer said. He made the tag. Danny cut the old tag off and Farmer replaced it. "So, I'm thinking of you as Sandy Short Tail.

And you," talking to 38, "Sandy White Face. OK?" They both agreed.

102 stepped up then.

"Martha's the name you want?" Farmer said. She nodded. "You're sure?"

"Yes."

"Oh, for God's sake," Joe Martin (68) said. "It was her idea. Tell him, honey."

"It's a positively magnificent name," 102 said.

Danny and Farmer went to work and Martha (102) walked away wearing her new tag.

"That just leaves you, 42," Farmer said.

"I don't want a name."

"You don't?"

"I've decided against it."

"You have to have a name," Helen said.

"Why?"

"You just do."

"I had to have a number. Now instead of a number I have to have a name. What's the difference?"

"You get to choose your name," Sandy White Face (38) said.

"Well, I choose not to have one."

Farmer didn't know what to say.

Danny said, "Do you want me to remove your old tag, 42? Then you would just not have a tag? Is that what you want?"

42 was thinking. "Or I could have a new tag with nothing on it…" Then she knew. She told Farmer, "I'll keep my old tag. But I want you to mark the number out."

Danny said, "42, you are so deep. So, you're like The Cow Formerly Known as 42?"

"I'm Not 42."

"OK," Farmer said. 42 stepped closer and Farmer made a black line through her number. "I think that's got it."

"How does it look, Danny?" she said.

"It's perfect. You can still tell it was a 42, but it's like canceled."

"Awesome! Thanks, Farmer!"

"You bet, Not 42."

Farmer stood. He turned the five-gallon bucket over and put the ear tag kit and tools back inside it.

What he needed to do, he thought, was make a chart showing each cow's name and number. It would look like this:

106 Mason

102 Martha

38   Sandy White Face

68   Joe Martin

27   Sandy Short Tail

74   Helen

42   ~~42~~

"Someone else is coming, Farmer," Joe Martin said.

Farmer turned and saw a woman he did not know coming across the grass toward them. He said, "Danny, hang out here with the cattle. I'll go see what she wants."

He walked out to meet her.

"Hello," he said. "Can I help you?"

"Are these your cows?"

"Yes."

"Hi. I'm Sally Martinez. I'm chief of staff for mayor Jenkins."

She extended her hand and she and Farmer shook.

"I'm Farmer."

"Nice to meet you, Farmer. I need to tell you, these cows of yours have made quite an impression on the mayor."

"They have?"

"I'll say. He would hope the cows see him as a friend. He sends his warmest wishes, and regrets he could not come himself. He is preparing for tonight's debate. I've brought the cows a gift on his behalf."

"It's not hay, is it?"

"No."

"I don't feed them corn—no grain of any kind."

"It's not something to eat, Farmer. The mayor has authorized me to present the cows with the key to the city, as a symbol of gratitude for the privilege their visit has been, and an indication that they are always welcome."

"Well," Farmer said, struggling through the turbulence of such talk. "I mean… You want to give them a key?"

"It's ceremonial," she said. She held up a rectangular box Farmer hadn't noticed. She opened it to show him a shining gold key about a foot long. "Keys like this one have been given to a number of visitors over the years: Princess Diana; Frank Sinatra; Mother Teresa; LeBron."

"Well, OK," Farmer said. "Thanks." He reached for the box.

"No, I need to present it to you," Sally said. "I have a photographer. Can we do it now?"

"Sure, I guess."

Sally waved her arm toward the crowd of people lining the edge of the parking lot. A young man with several cameras hanging from straps around his neck stepped out onto the grass and came over.

"Jack Prine," he said to Farmer. "*Columbus Dispatch*."

He and Sally walked with Farmer over to Danny and the cows.

"Danny, this is Sally Martinez, from the mayor's office. Jack is with the *Dispatch*."

"Right on. I'm Danny."

"You guys!" Farmer called to the cows. "Can you come here, please?"

The cows, curious about these new people and eager to show off their name tags, came right over.

"This is Sally. She brought a gift for you."

"We like gifts," Sandy White Face (38) said.

"I could get used to this," Joe Martin said.

"Is it wonderful alfalfa hay like we got from Martha and Thomas?" Sandy Short Tail (27) said.

"No. Sally wants to present you the key to the city."

"Martha and Thomas," Sally said. "Do you mean Martha Guildersnap?"

"Do you know her too?" Helen said.

"Yes, I do."

"She's so nice. My daughter is named after her. Come show the lady, Martha," Joe Martin said.

Martha (102) stepped forward.

Sally was a little irritated. Her calls to Martha Guildersnap were going to voicemail. Sally was working hard to get that big check the campaign needed. Meanwhile Martha was over here handing stuff out to cows?

"We're already in the city," 42 said. "Why do we need a key?"

"It's just to make you know you're welcome," Sally said.

"Anyway, we're leaving. We're going back to the farm," Helen said. "The city is not very nice."

"It's crowded and busy," Sandy Short Tail (27) said.

"Yeah, and the grass is terrible," Mason (106) said.

Get the photo; just get the photo, Sally thought. She said, "Well, with this key, you can come back any time you want."

"It's the same key they gave LeBron," Farmer said. He was trying to help Sally out.

"LeBron is the man," Sandy White Face said.

"Go Calves!"

"Well, are you going to give it to us?" 42 said.

Sally told the photographer, "Stand over there." Then she said, "Farmer, how about I present the key to you in front of the cows?"

"OK."

Sally held out the box with its lid off to show the big key. She showed Farmer how he should have a hand on the box too, as if they were frozen in the act of her handing it over.

"Big smiles," the photographer said.

Sally smiled.

When it was over, she handed the box to Farmer. He put it in the five-gallon bucket with the ear tag kit.

"Well, goodbye, cows," she said. "I hope you have a nice trip home."

"Thanks, Sally," Helen said.

"Bye, Sally!" several cows said.

"Thanks for giving us LeBron's key."

"You tell the mayor he can come see us any time," Sandy White Face said. "He doesn't need a key."

"Thanks, Jack," Sally told the photographer.

"No problem. It'll be in tomorrow's edition. I'll have it online tonight." He got out a small notebook and said to Farmer, "How do you spell your name?"

Farmer spelled it and Jack wrote it down. "Here's my card," he said. "If you want some prints, let me know. I'll make you a deal."

Jack left.

"Farmer, can I talk with you a minute?" Sally said. Some of the cows were still standing nearby, in the afterglow of the ceremony. "In private?" she added.

"Danny, I'll be right back," he said.

Farmer walked several paces away with Sally.

"I just wanted to let you know we have terminated Ron Jackson. He was chief superintendent of this park."

"Really?"

"I don't know how familiar you are with him."

"I just met him for the first time like an hour ago."

"The mayor determined that Mr. Jackson presented a danger to the cows. He is a deeply troubled man. As soon as we realized there was an issue, we took action. I don't know if you or the cows experienced any tension with Mr. Jackson. If so, we apologize."

"I talked with a park employee, Vincent, who said we should be careful around Mr. Jackson."

"Vincent Morales. I just spoke with him. He's co-acting chief superintendent now. I just wanted you and the cows to know that your safety and well-being is of paramount importance to us."

"I'm happy to hear that. I have to say, I'm getting a little nervous with all the people here." He indicated the parking lot, where now there were at least two hundred people. The big policeman Perkins and several other uniformed officers were in front of them, keeping them from coming closer. There was kind of a traffic jam on the park's little road. The parking lot was full, so cars, unable to park, were turning around and pulling over to park on the shoulder of the road. Clusters of people were walking down the road to join the crowd in the parking lot.

"We've arranged for some barricades to be put up," Sally said. "More police are on the way. Don't worry."

"I appreciate it," Farmer said.

Sally handed him a card. "Call me anytime for any reason whatsoever, Mr. Farmer. You said you have someone coming with a trailer?"

"Yes. Martha Guildersnap, actually."

"Martha Guildersnap," Sally said. She looked at her phone to see the time. "How long do you think she'll be?"

"Not long. Maybe half an hour."

"Well, you know? I think I'll stick around. If that's all right with you. I'll go wait in my car and make some calls."

"Sure," Farmer said.

Sally shook Farmer's hand, then turned and walked toward the crowded parking lot.

Farmer walked back to the herd. He told Danny, "I really appreciate your help."

"Are you kidding? I love hanging out with these guys."

"Well, they're comfortable with you. And that's helping keep them calm. I can't believe all those people."

"Truthfully though, the crowd has a mellow vibe, Farmer," Danny said. "It's like festive. You know? Like they're just happy digging on the cows."

Now there was a flatbed truck parked on the grass near the parking lot, its hazard lights blinking. Half a dozen men in green jumpsuits were pulling wooden pieces of barricades from the truck and setting them up along the edge of the parking lot. They were barricades like they used at Red White and Boom, the Fourth of July fireworks, to restrain the crowd in its eager celebration of freedom.

Farmer called Sandy.

"Hey, Farmer," she said. "I'm just turning onto 305. Brett couldn't come. Is everything OK?"

"Yeah. Still waiting on the trailer to show. You were right, though. There are a lot of people here. It's kind of a wild scene. You won't be able to drive all the way in. People are parking along the road because the parking lot's full."

"There are that many people?"

"The police are setting up barricades, Sandy. A few are protesters, but mainly they're just people who want to see the cows."

"Protesters?!"

"Don't ask. The mayor's office just gave the cows the key to the city. And they fired the guy who runs the park. They said he was like a danger to the cows or something."

"The cows are OK though? They're calm?"

"They don't care. They're still grazing. I named them," he added. "I replaced their numbered tags with name tags. They were asking about it and it was something I could do to keep busy while we wait for the trailer."

"That's different."

"Well…just so you know, the number one name they wanted was Sandy."

"You didn't name one of them Sandy, Farmer."

"Actually, two of them."

There was silence on the phone.

"Sandy?" Farmer said.

More silence.

"Sandy? Are you there?"

"Oh. Are you talking to me?" she said.

"It's a compliment. It's because they've heard so many good things about you."

"Uh-huh."

"One of them chose Helen," he said.

"Won't your mother be proud. OK, I'm hanging up. I'll be there soon."

SIXTY-FOUR

SOMEHOW THE PETA PEOPLE—maybe a dozen of them—ended up next to the Humans First protesters. That was causing some excitement Perkins didn't need. The two groups had gotten into a kind of angry call-and-response: the PETA people shouting, "Meat is Murder!" and the Humans First guys, "Yum! Yum! Yum!"

Both groups were essentially a bunch of nerds, so violence didn't seem likely. But Perkins grabbed a couple younger officers and went over to separate them. For one thing, they were near the playground where a lot of young children were playing.

"All right now," Perkins said, walking into the middle of the brouhaha. "Simmer down." He blew a whistle he had with him. "Listen up!" When he had their attention, he said, "You're all welcome to stay as long as you like. You've every right to express yourselves. But you need to be on opposite sides of the parking lot. OK? Now, Humans First was here first so you guys stay where you are. PETA—we're moving you to the entrance of the parking lot."

He and the two younger officers escorted the PETA protesters through the crowd. They cut a wide swath around the line dancers in cowboy outfits, who were putting on quite a show.

Perkins's wife had tried to get him to go line dancing once.

"This is your spot," he told the PETA people. He'd brought them to the landscaped base of the big flagpole, in front of the maintenance building.

He was turning to go back to the barricades when he saw a police cruiser coming down the park's road. *It's going a little too fast*, he thought. *Who is showing up now*, he wondered. He already had ten officers on site—all that he'd asked for.

He walked up to where the cruiser had come to a stop. It was Officer Chris McCarthy, riding solo.

"Hey, Chris," he said.

McCarthy got out of the cruiser. "Perkins," he said. "What the heck is going on? Is all this because of the cows?"

Perkins nodded.

McCarthy said, "I am so screwed. Sarge has been asking me since yesterday to find these cows. I been blowing him off. I figure to hell with him. What am I, an animal warden? So, I'm telling him I can't find them. Meanwhile, there's this huge crowd…"

"It's OK," Perkins said. "The farmer's with them. He's got a trailer coming any minute."

"One of them is a bull, Perkins. They're freaking monsters. You ever watch bull riding? Or like in Spain, where people run with them? They're mean!"

"I haven't seen a bull. It's just some cows and a couple calves. I'm more worried about some of these yahoos in the crowd."

"Check it out," McCarthy said. He reached inside his cruiser and got Mason's drawing of 106. He handed it to Perkins. "It's just a sketch," he said. "But it's pretty good. Look here." He pointed to the testicles.

"Chris, we were in the academy together, so I'm going to do you a favor. Never show this to anybody ever again." He handed the drawing back. "What's wrong with you?"

"I can't afford any more demerits. I'm teetering as it is. I'm teetering, Perkins. A couple months ago I got reprimanded for a fender bender. I rear-ended some guy in a Wendy's drive-thru. He got upset, so I Tasered him, and then he had a stroke or something. Yesterday, at the gun range, I shot every civilian that popped up. I'm telling you, one more problem and they'll put me on parking meters."

"Get hold of yourself. I got your back. Come work the barricade. If anyone asks, you were the first one here. OK? You alerted me."

McCarthy smiled for the first time.

"Thanks, Jack," he said. "You've always been a standup guy."

SIXTY-FIVE

FARMER ASKED DANNY if he would watch the cows for a few minutes. He wanted to go back to his truck and put away the five-gallon bucket with the ear tag kit and the key to Columbus in it.

"Sure, Farmer. No problem. But can you do me a favor and get me a funnel cake? I'm totally jonesing for one."

"Where are there funnel cakes?"

"Over there."

Farmer looked and saw behind the crowd at the barricades—so many smart phones in the air, little children on parents' shoulders, down at the far end some protest signs bobbing, the thin line of uniformed police across the front of all this—there were several food vendors set up in a row. Where did they come from? One was selling pizza slices and stromboli; another, Italian sausages and corn dogs. There was a lemon shakeup stand and the funnel cake vendor.

"Sure, I can do that," Farmer said.

Danny started to give him money, but Farmer said, "That's OK, I got it."

Farmer told the cows, "You guys, I'm leaving you with Danny for a while. Take it easy on him. Stay here and keep calm, OK? I'll be right back."

Carrying the five-gallon bucket, he walked to the barricades. When he got there, he nodded to one of the policemen and went between two stanchions. The crowd parted to let him through, some people taking his picture. He unlocked his truck, put the bucket inside on the front seat, then locked it again.

He walked through the milling crowd to the funnel cake stand. Somehow there was no line. He ordered a funnel cake and paid for it. Waiting for it to be made, he saw a big van coming down the park's road. It pulled off onto the grass just before the parking lot. It was a Channel Four News van.

A young woman got out. She was pretty, wearing a red dress with a jean jacket over it. She was holding a big mic with the Channel Four logo on it. Joining her was a goateed young man with a professional-looking video camera.

"Here you go," the funnel cake guy said. Farmer turned and got the funnel cake. It was warm, on a greasy paper plate, with too much powdery sugar on top. He grabbed a bunch of napkins.

When he turned to go back to the cows, the Channel Four people were gone. Farmer walked around their van and saw them well out in the grass, heading toward Danny and the herd.

Damn, he thought. He wasn't sure how, but he had to stop them. No more show and tell!

He hurried but, even so, by the time he caught up, they were already talking with Danny.

"No, I'm not the farmer of them," Danny was telling the woman. "I'm Danny."

"I'm Farmer," Farmer said. "Is there some way I can help you?"

The woman turned and said, "Hi, I'm Angela Lind from Channel Four. I interviewed your cows this morning. I'm here to do a follow-up."

"Here, Danny," Farmer said, handing him the funnel cake and napkins.

"Thanks!"

"Go ahead, eat it while it's warm."

Danny walked off a ways. After a close examination of the grass, he sat cross-legged and started eating.

"Can't you just leave my cows alone?" Farmer said to Angela. "They've had enough excitement."

"Maybe—if you wanted to keep them out of the limelight—you shouldn't have named them. How am I not reporting that? I notice you have two Sandys. Who is Sandy?"

Both Sandys perked up.

"That's my wife's name," Farmer said.

"You named them after your wife?"

"No!" Just like that, Farmer was in over his head. "*They* chose their names. It's a compliment—because of all the good things they've heard about her."

"She can win an argument even when she's wrong," Sandy White Face said.

"She's just like her mother," Sandy Short Tail said.

"Hey!" Farmer said. "Look, Angela. Is that your name? Can I talk to you for a minute?"

She walked with him a little.

"Why can't you just leave them alone?" he said.

"I could interview you instead."

"I've got nothing to say."

"Just a couple questions." She motioned for Joey to come over with his camera. "So people can know *your* side of the story."

"I don't have a story. I'm just trying to get them home."

"Over there, Joey," she said. "So you can get the cows in the background." She turned and called to the cows, "Can you guys act like you're grazing? Just act natural. I'm going to interview Farmer."

"Farmer's doing a show and tell!" one of them said.

Then, clumsily, they started "acting like they were grazing."

Jesus, Farmer thought, watching them.

Angela said, "Ever been on TV, Mr. Farmer?"

"No." His heart was speeding up.

"There's nothing to it. This is a mic," she said, showing it to him. It was tiny. "I'm just going to clip this to your shirt." She stepped closer and attached it to his shirt.

"Have you been farming long?"

"About twenty years."

"It must have been a shock when you discovered they were gone."

She took off her jean jacket and lay it on the ground near her feet, did a quick adjustment of her dress, and touched her hair to make sure it was OK.

"All right. Now don't be nervous, Mr. Farmer. We're just having a conversation. Just talk to me… Joey? You ready?"

"Yes." The camera was on his shoulder.

Looking back, Farmer saw Danny had finished the funnel cake. He was licking the plate.

Angela cleared her throat, then held up the big microphone with the Channel Four logo on it.

"This is Angela Lind, reporting from Sutter Park, where a herd of cows has taken refuge. Channel Four broke this story earlier today—another Hometown Team Exclusive. With me now is the owner of the farm the cows came from. Mr. Farmer, why were your cows so desperate to escape?"

"I wouldn't say they were desperate. They—"

"Was it because of abusive conditions?"

"No!"

"Have you been letting them go hungry? When animals are in your care, sir, you have a responsibility to provide them adequate food and water."

"They always have enough to eat. I take good care of them. Someone opened the gate and let them out, that's all."

"A good Samaritan. Someone who witnessed the abuse and decided to do something about it."

SIXTY-SIX

MASON'S MOM decided to bring Mason to Sutter Park *before* getting ice cream. The playground would be less crowded if they got there before school let out. If other parents were there with preschool kids, they could have the run of the pirate ship. She hoped Mason would not be the only child there.

She needn't have worried about that.

When she turned at the park entrance at two thirty, she drove about halfway in when she saw cars parked bumper-to-bumper along the road. She had to wait while a car coming toward her pulled over and parked. She decided to park there too. She maneuvered her car around till it was facing the way she'd come in and pulled off onto the dirt shoulder.

She didn't know what was happening in the park. She'd seen a lot of people there before, once for a Frisbee golf tournament, another time because of a big family reunion. But never anything like this.

She held Mason's hand and they walked down the little road toward where the playground was.

When they came out of the woods, she saw the crowd, the parking lot full of cars, the barricades and police. At the far end of all the excitement as many as fifty kids were swarming over the pirate ship.

"Look, Mom," Mason said. He was pointing at the field behind the pond. "The cows are here!"

And so they were. They were a good distance from the crowd. Two men were with them.

"Can we go see them?" Mason said. "They're really nice." Then his face clouded over. "I wish I had my truck to show 106."

Mason's mom said, "I think maybe we should leave. The park is too crowded."

"But Mom," he said. "They're my friends."

"Well, I—" she started to say, but Mason was already running as fast as he could across the grass toward the cows. She ran after him. She wasn't ready for how fast he was. That was new. By the time she caught up to him and pulled him to a stop, they were only about fifty feet from the herd. The cows and the two men were watching them.

"Mason!" Mason 106 said.

He ran toward the boy.

"Mason!" Sandy White Face called. "Get back here!"

"Mason!" Farmer yelled. He ran toward the woman and little boy.

Mason 4½ was wriggling, trying to get away from his mother.

"106!" he called.

Mason 106, who got to Mason 4½ and his mother before Farmer did, stopped abruptly, just when Farmer and Sandy White Face and Mason 4 ½'s mother all thought he would crash into them.

"Mason?" Mason 4 ½'s mother said, reading his ear tag.

Farmer, somewhat out of breath, came up next to Mason 106. Sandy White Face got there too.

"Mason," she said. "You do not take off like that."

Mason 4 ½'s mother told *her* Mason the same thing.

"You scared me," Sandy White Face said.

Farmer said, "Your son's name is Mason."

"We met him yesterday," Mason 106 said.

"I'm Farmer," Farmer said.

"Hi. Lisa," Mason's mom said. "Your cows talk. No wonder they made such an impression on my son."

"I think my calf Mason named himself after your son."

"Your name is Mason?" Mason 4½ said. "I thought you were 106."

"I thought you were 4½."

SIXTY-SEVEN

BY THE TIME SANDY got to Sutter Park, barricades blocked its entrance. A uniformed policeman was standing in front of the barricades. Sandy pulled her Subaru off the road and rolled her window down.

"Officer?" she said.

He came over to her.

"I can't get in the park?"

"It's full."

"I'm Mrs. Farmer," she told him. "My husband's the farmer whose cows they are. I need to get in there to help him."

"Nice try."

"I'm serious."

"People are parking across the street and walking in," he said. "Over there."

He gestured toward what looked like a vacant lot next to an apartment complex. A dozen or so cars were parked there. A family with several young kids was walking toward her from that direction.

She waited till there wasn't any traffic on Cherry Bottom Road, then pulled forward and turned into the vacant lot. As she approached the parked cars, she saw a huge man sitting on a golf cart. He was pointing for her to park next to a green minivan. She parked.

When she got out of her car, he'd driven the golf cart up close behind her.

"Ten dollars," he said.

"It's not free?"

"No, it's ten dollars."

"There's no sign."

"We keeping costs down."

"How about five dollars?"

"Those cows talk. For all I know they over there singin' and dancin.'"

Sandy still hesitated.

"Come on now. You know you want to see them cows."

"Oh, all right." She gave him a ten-dollar bill.

"We appreciate your business."

She walked toward the park. She crossed Cherry Bottom, then walked along the shoulder of the road to the park entrance.

"He's charging ten dollars," she told the policeman.

She walked around a wooden barricade and headed down the park's small road on foot. Within a hundred feet she saw the first parked car. It was half off the road, facing the entrance she'd just come in. From that point on it was an uninterrupted line of parked vehicles all the way in to the back of the park where the duck pond was. Even the parking areas of the several picnic shelters were jammed full of cars.

She picked up her pace a little. The situation was clearly out of hand.

When she came out of the woods, she was astonished by what she saw. A swarming crowd of people filled the parking lot. Overall the mood seemed positive and fun. Kids were running around, people were taking pictures (so many selfies), there was a lineup of food vendors, more barricades, and police. Off by themselves in the open grassy area she could see Farmer and the cows. A young couple and a child were with Farmer.

A Channel Four News van was parked nearby. A cameraman was taping a young woman in a red dress standing in front of the crowd. Behind her some people were clowning—making faces, waving to the camera. Sandy could hear the reporter saying, "This growing lively crowd of Channel Four viewers here to witness the sanctuary these gentle cows have found..."

Just then, Sandy heard—or felt, in her stomach—a powerful rumbling. Turning to look at the noise, she saw a diesel pickup truck coming slowly down the park road. It was pulling a livestock trailer.

The truck stopped before it reached the parking lot. A policeman walked up to the driver's window and talked with whoever was behind the wheel. Then—with the policeman out in front making sure people were not in the way—the truck slowly turned, heading toward Farmer and the cows. It was a big trailer. Watching it turn, Sandy could see on its side the words Columbus Polo Club.

She hurried to follow the trailer.

A policeman tried to stop her but she rushed ahead rather than bothering to explain herself.

SIXTY-EIGHT

MONROE HAD DONE PRETTY WELL. He had parked thirty cars, with room for maybe twenty more. *That's five hundred dollars! Those cows turned out to be good luck,* he thought.

He was on the golf cart, in the shade of a big oak tree, when another vehicle pulled in: a black Jeep Commando. He gestured for the driver to pull up into the next spot. When the Jeep was parked, he rode over to collect his fee.

The driver—a man—got out of the Jeep wearing camo fatigues and army boots. Green and black greasepaint was smeared on his face.

"That'll be ten dollars, my man," Monroe told him.

"I don't have any money."

"Well then get your raggedy Rambo ass on outta here."

The man didn't seem to notice what Monroe was saying. He went around to the back of the Jeep and opened its hatch. He pulled out a 30.06 rifle. It had a scope on it for long-distance shooting. He checked its bolt action, then slung the rifle over his shoulder. He grabbed a knapsack that was in the Jeep and shut the hatch.

"You part of some kind of reenactment or something?"

The man in camo said, "It's C-Day." His left eye was twitching fiercely. "Operation Charlie Oscar Whiskey."

"You know, I'm gonna give you a discount. You go on ahead." Monroe had the cart in reverse and was slowly backing away. "You have yourself a nice day."

Jackson was already walking toward Cherry Bottom. He crossed the road. Avoiding the park entrance and the bike path, he plunged into the thick underbrush of the woods and disappeared.

That can't be good, Monroe thought. He rode over behind the Jeep Commander and got his phone out, took a picture of its license plate.

SIXTY-NINE

FARMER, LISA, AND DANNY WATCHED as Martha Guildersnap's truck, pulling a big aluminum trailer, came slowly toward them. The cows watched too. They were bunched close together, too distracted to graze.

Masons 106 and 4½ were off by themselves, one sitting cross-legged, the other one lying down, back legs splayed out, front legs tucked under his chest. They were talking excitedly about who knows what.

The truck was coming so slowly that Sandy could keep up, trotting alongside the trailer.

The truck stopped near the cows and Thomas got out, still wearing his dark suit. He nodded to Farmer and the cows, then went around to help Martha Guildersnap out.

Sandy came up to Farmer.

"You're right on time," he told her.

She said, "I can't believe all these people. I had to park across the street."

"Pretty wild." He introduced her to Danny and Lisa. "That's her boy Mason over there."

Thomas escorted Martha Guildersnap to where they were standing.

"Well, here we are at last," Martha said. "I'm sorry it took so long."

Farmer made more introductions. Then he told everyone, "I'm going to go look at the trailer."

Walking alongside the trailer, Farmer was impressed. It was beautiful—sleek and silver—and over eight feet tall. The logo of the Columbus Polo Club was on it. It was a slant load trailer, with room for seven horses (or cows). Inside, it was gorgeous. It had black non-slip flooring; padded slant dividers; little webbed bags full of fresh hay hanging in each space. It was a bit awkward that it had individual stalls instead of an open interior. The cows would prefer being all together. But Farmer could work with this. It helped that the cows would be able to see each other over the low dividers.

When he came back around to join everyone, Sally Martinez was there too.

He could hear Martha Guildersnap telling her, "I am retiring from public life, Sally."

Danny was telling Lisa, "I work at this bookstore over on Lane Avenue…"

Sandy saw Farmer coming and met him a little apart from the others. She handed him a Snickers bar which he immediately opened and took a bite of. He was so hungry. She said, "The trailer's OK?"

"It's awesome."

"Well, let's load them up and get home."

Farmer said to Thomas, who was standing by himself, "So, I'm going to start putting them in the trailer. Is that OK?"

"Certainly. May I assist?"

"Maybe if you open the back door."

He seemed hesitant.

"I'll show you," Sandy said.

She and Thomas walked toward the back of the trailer.

Farmer went to the cows.

"You guys ready?"

"We're ready," Helen said. "It looks like a nice trailer."

"It is. There's even a little hay inside. Probably that same alfalfa Martha brought you earlier."

"Nice."

"OK, well, come on then. Let's go." He walked toward the back of the trailer. The cows fell in behind him.

He saw the two Masons were up on their feet. He called in their direction, "Mason! We're going!"

Lisa called too. "Come on, Mason!"

Her son said, "But Mason's going to take me for a ride."

"No," she said. "Come here."

Farmer kept on. At the back of the trailer he found the rear door lowered as a ramp. Sandy was in the trailer standing to the left, ready to shut divider bars between the cows. Thomas was gone; he must have gone back to Martha Guildersnap.

"OK, we need to go in one at a time," Farmer told the cows. "Sandy will have to swing a divider shut after each of you gets in. OK? Who's first?"

Helen came forward. She stepped onto the ramp, bringing the whole back end of the trailer down a little. She walked in and to the front of the trailer. Sandy swung the divider bar shut till it clicked into place. It made a nice stall for Helen, just a little wider than she was and plenty long. She noticed the mesh bag of hay hanging in front of her and started nosing it.

"Next," Farmer said, and Sandy Short Tail walked into the trailer.

"Hi, Sandy," she said.

"Hi," Sandy Wife said, shutting her in beside Helen. These names were going to take some getting used to.

Then 42 came in.

When Sandy had 42 secured, it was Joe Martin's turn. She said to Farmer, "I want Martha to be with me."

"I know," Farmer said, "but there's not room. I was going to put Martha and Mason together at the end. It's a little wider there. I think that's best."

"OK." She walked inside the trailer.

"Joe Martin?" Sandy Wife said.

"He's an old man I met. A Former Farmer."

OK, Sandy thought. She shut the divider till it clicked.

Farmer saw Lisa had not been able to get Mason 4½ to come to her. He and Mason 106 were still off by themselves, in a world of their own.

"Oh, for God's sake," he said. He told Martha and Sandy White Face, who had yet to be loaded, "I'll be right back. I've got to get Mason."

"Hold on," he told Sandy Wife.

"I'll come with you," Sandy White Face said.

Danny was trying to help Lisa, who was getting frustrated, telling Mason 106, "Come on, little dude. It's time to go."

"Mason…Mason," Lisa kept saying.

Farmer could see that one of the uniformed policemen had left the barricades and was coming over. He was staring at the Masons.

Suddenly, Mason 106 knelt down and Mason 4½ swung a leg over him and got on top. Then, with Mason 4½ hanging on, Mason 106 started running. He wasn't going anywhere. He was just running in circles. They were having fun.

But this upset just about everyone. Lisa was afraid her Mason would fall and get hurt. Sandy White Face was mad her calf was not listening. Farmer was not happy; there's no place for excitement of any kind when loading cattle. But more upset than any of them, somehow, was the approaching policeman. He kept glancing back and forth, between a piece of paper he was holding and Mason 106.

He said to Farmer, "That's a bull!"

"No," Farmer said. "He's just a calf."

"No!" the policeman said. "A bull! He's got that kid!"

He pulled his pistol from its holster.

Lisa said, "That's my son! Don't shoot!"

Farmer said, "They're playing!"

"Halt!" the policeman yelled at Mason 106, who was so busy having fun he hadn't noticed anything.

"Farmer!" Sandy White Face said.

The policeman had his gun up in two hands, prepared to shoot.

Finally, Mason 106 noticed the commotion. He stopped running. He knelt and Mason 4½ got off. The two Masons were standing together, about twenty yards away from the adults.

"Ma'am," the policeman said. "What is your son's name?"

"Mason," she said.

"Mason?" the policeman yelled. "Listen very carefully." He still had the gun up in two hands. "I want you to do exactly as I say. I'm going to count to three. On three, I want you to run to me just as fast as you can."

"One… Two…"

"But—" Farmer said.

"Officer—" Lisa said.

"THREE!"

Both Masons came running toward the policeman as fast as they could. Of course, Mason 106 was much faster.

"NO!" Farmer yelled.

The policeman fired four times.

He would have fired a fifth time, or completely emptied his pistol, had he not, without knowing why, found himself flying through the air.

Sandy White Face had charged him and, head lowered, rammed him squarely in the butt, raising her head as she made contact so that he was flung, like a rag doll. When he landed, he no longer had his pistol. His first attempt to move caused him excruciating pain. He had a broken leg.

Lisa was already with her boy, on her knees, inspecting him to make sure he was OK. Sandy White Face was with her calf, licking him, telling him to be calm.

Another policeman—Officer Perkins, the one Farmer had met with Vincent—came along. He picked up the policeman's pistol. "Is everyone OK?" he asked Farmer.

"I think so." He looked around and saw Sandy Wife staring from the back corner of the trailer. The trailer was moving around a little, the cattle inside upset by the ruckus.

Danny was near Farmer. Sally Martinez was there too. Closer to the truck, Thomas was just getting up. He'd grabbed Martha Guildersnap and got her on the ground, then dropped to cover her, protecting her with his body when the shooting started.

Sandy called to Farmer, "The other calf is loose." 102. Farmer couldn't see her. She must have gone behind the trailer.

Thomas was offering to help Martha Guildersnap up but she waved him off. She'd had the wind knocked out of her and needed to just sit there a while.

Sandy White Face came leading Mason 106 toward Farmer. "I think he's OK," she said. "You look."

Farmer ran his hands along Mason's back, up and down his legs. Mason was trembling but was not injured. "He's fine," Farmer told Sandy White Face. "Go on and get in the trailer." She and Mason 106 went back toward Sandy Wife.

As she entered the trailer, Sandy White Face told the nervous herd, "Everything's OK. It's over."

Sandy Wife shut her in.

Mason walked in too. Sandy Wife shut the end gate. The ramp was still down. They still needed to load Martha.

Officer Perkins was down on one knee talking with the policeman who did the shooting. Farmer and Sally Martinez came over.

"What the hell, McCarthy?" Perkins said.

"He was charging! He was coming right at me."

"You called him!" Farmer said.

"No, I told the boy to come. Mason."

"They're both named Mason," Farmer said.

McCarthy looked stunned.

"You know, you really screwed up," Perkins said.

"That bull was going to gore me," McCarthy said. "I had to defend myself."

"Gore you?!" Farmer said. "He doesn't even have horns."

"He has horns," McCarthy said. "I saw horns."

"Shut up, McCarthy," Perkins said. "Don't say anything."

"My leg is broken," McCarthy said. "That other cow attacked me. She assaulted an officer."

"She was just a mother trying to protect her child," Sally Martinez said.

"What's it to you, lady?" McCarthy said. "Mind your own business."

"Well, as I am from the mayor's office, this *is* my business."

"The mayor's office?"

"I am mayor Jenkins's chief of staff," she said. "And you need to start thinking about some other line of work."

Martha 102 had been hiding behind the trailer. She was so careful and timid, nobody saw her come around the front of the truck. She walked to Martha Guildersnap, still sitting in the grass. She lowered her head and touched Martha gently on her left shoulder with her nose. Martha looked up and smiled.

"Are you OK?" Martha 102 said.

"Yes, honey. Aren't you the sweetest thing. I'm just resting." Then she saw Martha's name tag.

"You're named Martha?" she said.

"Yes."

"After me?" She'd had so many things named after her—each time for a price. None of them meant anything to her now.

"Yes. I picked Martha. Because you are magnificent."

"Oh, honey," Martha said. She was crying. She reached up and stroked Martha 102's head.

Danny said, "What's that noise? It's coming from the woods. Does anyone else hear that?"

Thomas said, "Something is beeping."

"Right on!" Danny said. "Like when a delivery truck is backing up."

"Oh no," Farmer said. He told Sally Martinez, "Vincent said something about needing to be careful if Mr. Jackson starts beeping."

"Oh my God." Sally told Perkins, "Officer, we may be in danger. A disgruntled employee, a former marine, may be in those woods. It's reasonable to assume he's armed and dangerous."

When Perkins looked toward the woods where she'd pointed, he saw Thomas already rushing up the hill in that direction. He'd never seen anyone move so quickly or smoothly, particularly wearing a suit like that.

Thomas disappeared into the woods.

He soon found the source of the beeping: Ron Jackson, in camo, his face smeared with greasepaint, and wearing a little crown of ferns he'd fashioned. He was lying on the ground, in agony due to a bullet wound in his left hand. Not a serious wound as it turned out, but one that hurt a lot just the same.

Later, in the same interrogation room Lernovski had been in that afternoon, Jackson would tell detectives how he'd found most of the cows already loaded into a trailer before he could get into position to shoot. He was hurrying to get a shot off, aiming at a full-grown cow that had a white face, but was distracted by a lot of shouting. He turned and saw a policeman draw his pistol and aim it at a different cow—one of the little ones. When the pistol went off, firing multiple times, Jackson heard one bullet zip through the leafy treetops well above his head. Then he was shot in the hand. His rifle was knocked away and he collapsed to the ground in pain.

He started beeping. He was backing up, trying to do a reset. To before he'd been shot. Or had lost his job. Or had first laid eyes on those cows. It wasn't working very well, maybe because he was also whimpering.

At some point he looked up and saw Thomas standing over him. A slender man dressed in an elegant suit watching him closely.

"Keep back," he told the man. "I may be wounded, but I'm a marine. I can kill you with my bare hands."

The man said, "I too have served."

"Oh yeah? In what branch?" Jackson sneered.

"I am not at liberty to say. If you will permit me…"

He reached out, so quickly Jackson never even flinched, and touched him lightly behind his left ear, causing instant and complete paralysis. Jackson was conscious; he could feel the pain from his wound; he just couldn't move. He remained that way as they loaded him onto a gurney and took him away in an ambulance.

Poor Jackson, who had not managed to keep it in the cage. His paralysis lasted only a few hours, it turned out; but his troubles were just beginning.

And lucky Chris McCarthy, whose bold action in defense of the cows was witnessed by mayor Jenkins's chief of staff Sally Martinez, who then gave numerous interviews lauding his bravery and incredible skill. She herself had been in the sniper's line of fire and owed her life to McCarthy—a true hero.

It turned out to be a much bigger story than Angela Lind or even Bob Jones could have imagined.

With the cows all loaded, the trailer's rear ramp raised and shut, it was time to go back to the farm.

Thomas was behind the wheel of Martha Guildersnap's truck. In the back seat were Sandy and Martha Guildersnap. Farmer was walking to his truck, still in the parking lot. He would follow the trailer home. Danny Young had decided to tag along and was going to ride with Farmer.

Lisa, having exchanged phone numbers with Farmer, promised Mason they would go visit the cows the next day. Mason had been brave, and later, when home, would capture the event in a series of drawings that would be on the fridge for a very long time. Lisa also gave her number to Danny.

Sutter Park was never that busy again, and that was fine with Vincent and Betty.

Martha Guildersnap did give Sally Martinez that check the mayor's campaign was counting on—one of her last acts before retiring from public life. The money came in handy, but it turned out the mayor didn't need it. His performance in the debate, just hours after Chris McCarthy saved the day, proved decisive and secured his reelection.

It was Farmer who suggested Sandy ride to the farm with Martha Guildersnap that day. What was he thinking? Left alone together for nearly an hour like that, they talked about and solved many problems, some of them his. They made arrangements that would change the farm and all their lives forever. Farmer should have known something like that could happen.

Or maybe he did.

Maybe it was like he'd left a gate open for them.

ACKNOWLEDGMENTS

Many thanks to my beta readers. Marie most of all. Marla Hattabaugh and Binaebi Akah Calkins provided line edits! I am grateful to Kathy Harrison; Sylvie Cercelet; Lorene Nash; Tracey Nesbitt; Mark Maxwell; Chris Heuing; Tory Herron; Celia Ruckel; Leonard Volk; Eric et Michele Wiley; Big Page; Jane Byrd Terlizzi; Jaime Moore; Leslie Dybiec; emmajean15. RJ didn't get to read it, and I'm sorry about that.

I got over the hump with the help of the Writers' Group at Wild Goose Creative in Columbus; thanks, Andy et al. A couple seminars I took at the Thurber House helped too.

It has been an education and a pleasure working with Brad Pauquette and Boyle & Dalton. Brad's developmental edit improved my manuscript considerably, in deft and insightful ways. As did Emily Hitchcock's copy edit.

I owe so much to Half Price Books, a wonderful company, and my many longtime colleagues there.

Long live the Worthington Farmers' Market!

There are farmers who taught me as much as I could learn, mainly Lonnie and Kelly and Otto, all now gone. I miss them.

And finally, I couldn't have done this without Marie. I admit it. She's been a role model, partner, and friend throughout, and I love her for much more than that.

ABOUT THE AUTHOR

JOHN WILEY is a central Ohio farmer and writer. He grazes cattle on one hundred acres of lush pasture and—with his wife Marie—sells grass-fed beef at the Worthington Farmers' Market. John was an English major once, and he has always been a storyteller who feels that facts deserve to be polished up a little and embellished, for their own sake as well as to benefit the audience. *An Inconvenient Herd* is his first novel.

John Wiley can be reached at upthelane@hotmail.com. Send him feedback about the book! He is available for readings and interviews and is always up for a good conversation about grass farming.

Follow book news on Facebook @AnInconvenientHerd and at: www.AnInconvenientHerd.com.